C000161321

MAU MAU CHILD EXPERIENCE

BORN AND RAISED IN THE KENYAN MAU MAU UPRISING ERA

The Autobiography of
Alice Wanjikũ Mangat

Copyright © 2018 Diverse Cultures Publishing, All Rights Reserved

For details of consultancy and training services from Alice Wanjikũ Mangat and for information about how to apply for permission to reuse the copyright material in this book or any other of our publications, please contact the Author Alice Wanjikũ Mangat.

No part of this book may be reproduced or transmitted in any form whatsoever, electronic or mechanical, including photocopying, recording, or by any informational storage or retrieval system without the express written, dated and signed permission from the author and copyright holder. The right of the author to be identified as the author of this work has been asserted in accordance with the United Kingdom Copyright, Designs and Patents Act 1988, copyright, Designs and Patents Act 1988.

Disclaimer

This publication and its contents are provided for informational purposes only. All information and ideas are provided in good faith or in opinion of the author, and the author's research findings. To the best of the author's knowledge and experience the information is true and honest. The author, reserve the right to vary or change any such opinions subsequently.

The names of people in this book have been changed to protect their privacy.

Editing and Layout: Amina Chitembo & the Diverse Cultures squad.

Cover Designed: Ahsan Chuhadry, Graphics Designer

Main photo of Alice Wanjikũ Mangat: Guenter Flores

Mt Kenya Background: Royalty-free Image purchased from iStockphoto.com

Published by Diverse Cultures Publishing, UK.

Website: www.diverse-cultures.co.uk

Email address: publishing@diverse-cultures.co.uk

Postal Address: 28 – 29 Maxwell Road, Peterborough, PE2 7JE.

Paperback ISBN: 978-0-9957396-6-6.

DEDICATION

I dedicate this book to my dearest late parents Gacoki Njŭgŭna and Sunder Singh Mangat who taught me the values of life journey, healthy morals, honesty, faith in God and truthfulness. They both came from cultures where they were taught to worship in diverse ways than that of Christianity, nonetheless they both knew the existence of Almighty God respectively. May our Creator give them a good place in Eternity.

I would like also to dedicate this book to all our freedom fighters especially those who died during the struggle of Mau Mau. May our Good and Merciful God grant them eternal rest!

CONTENTS

CONTENTS

ACKNOWLEDGEMENT

In great humility and due respect, I thank God my Heavenly Father, for the life that He chose for me and all storms and happiness He allowed me to go through. All have been EXPERIENCES THAT TAUGHT ME A LOT OF VALUABLE LESSONS and gave me strength to continue without giving up. For all those who caused me pains as well as those who caused happiness of any kind to me, I pray that my God whom I love and worship, may bless you all! I also forgive those who did or wished me evil. May God bless them too.

For the talents and WISDOM, I have to master all, glory and honor is to you, my Creator.

Thank YOU, MY GOD!

Nĩ ngatho Ngai wakwa!

Asante Mungu wangu!

Danke Mein Gott!

INTRODUCTION

Born at the time of Emergency declaration in Kenya, I came into the world right in the middle of the most dangerous time of Kenya's independence struggle between the British colonialists and the Mau Mau rebellion. Of course, Mau Mau were struggling together with those who were trying desperately to negotiate diplomatically with the Colonialist for freedom.

Mau Mau, the freedom fighter group were tired of those non-effective negotiations and decided to use force by fighting the colonialists and operate from the forests. The name is initials of *"Mzungu Aende/Arudi Ulaya, Mwafrica Apate Uhuru,"* The European should go back to Europe, the African should achieve/get his freedom.

That is exactly what they were fighting for.

Between 1952 and 1960 was the pick of the struggle before we achieved Independence and later in 1963 the self-Government. My childhood was an experience of its own kind and that of many children born at that time, who survived because many died of hunger through poverty and oppression. The most exceptional aspect regarding me, was being born from parents of two very different cultures and origins particularly, at that time.

A man from a small village in District Ludhiana, Punjabi India coming all the way to meet my mother in Kenya, also in a small village, in the middle of colonial struggle and bear me, was truly an exception. During this period, such a relationship was absolutely rear. I believe that, God must have had a very special purpose for my life to have enabled this DNA and I believe God has still a perfect plan for me and in regard to the generation of those two-lovely people (bless their souls). I pray that the Living God will fulfil His purpose for us and help us do our part by earnestly seeking Him daily through prayer and His word. Glory be to His most Holy Name!

The main reason which inspired me to write these series of books about my life, which I started writing in 1986, was to show people in Africa that Europe is not the paradise and the green pasture we all believe it offers. The discrimination, racism, the fight for acceptance both in Kenya and in Germany made me want to give these experiences further. In my opinion, though discrimination and racism were extreme in Germany than I ever imagined, I experienced a good share of the same in Kenya too, even in my own family.

However, the immigration politics in Germany is such that it has no favors for the immigrants but strictly to favor their own country's interest. Of course, they get cheated a lot by those who are clever and use illegal methods to survive, but the honest immigrants suffer extremely.

To achieve my stay-permit genuinely and a decent job was pure grace of God, and I would not want to give an impression that this is an easy task. Many go through much more suffering or are forced to do immoral things to get it. In these kinds of wrong choices, many turn to criminality, alcohol, drugs, prostitution, etc. through desperation. They get completely stranded in the end and lost that they cannot even go back home. Unless one comes through a government scholarship, or good business connection, I would advise our youth against the marriage arrangements especially, which are most common and the only remaining loophole to get a stay permit. They are indeed very dangerous. The fruits of these mistakes are harvested by the poor children who are born on these mix marriages which almost 95% are without love. Luckily, I did not have these experiences myself, but I witnessed many such ugly cases.

It is my sincere hope that my book will encourage our youth in Africa to try to make it in their own countries than wonder all over the world where many of us suffer a lot in a hope of improving our life.

Thank you all who are interest to read about my life story, promoting and encouraging me at the same time. May God bless you all!

The second volume of my book will be published soon.

Alice Wanjikū Mangat

CHAPTER ONE

It was warm Tuesday evening in the hilly countryside of Rūngǐri, and the red-soiled ground was giving its smile to a very windy brown August weather. The clouds moved here and there as if to surround the sun just about to arrest it in the evening hours. I was sitting outside in front of our hut when my mother came from her *shamba* carrying a bunch of firewood, tied up with a rope on her back. On top of the firewood, was a *kǐondo* full of sweet potatoes.

This was usually all that my mother ever seemed to bring home from the *shamba*. In my opinion and belief, this should have come to an end, because I was fed up of eating those damn boiled sweet potatoes three times a day: for breakfast, lunch, and supper. All I thought was that she did not want to cook other things and I did not want to understand the words she often used in Kikuyu *"Nǐ kwa ng'aragu mwana wakwa!"* (It is hunger period my child). I did not dare complain anymore because every time I complained, my mother would break into tears repeating those same words.

Sighing heavily from the weight of the heavy load of firewood and a kiondo (African basket) on top she was

1

carrying, she put down the kĩondo and then let the bunch of firewood fall from her back with a thud. Looking in my direction, she saw me sitting near the door of our hut, digging a hole on the ground with a piece of stick.

"What are you doing there alone Cikũ?" She asked me in a very tired voice.

"Why aren't you playing with the other children?" I kept on digging avoiding looking at her and did not give her an answer.

"Have you swallowed your tongue, or have you become deaf?" As if waiting for such words to be said, I suddenly started crying endlessly. My mother came quickly and lifted me up from where I was sitting.

"What is wrong with you my little girl? Did anybody beat you while I was away?" She asked worriedly. Lovingly, she wiped my eyes and removed the long black hair from my face and tied them behind with the long-plaited ones hanging on my back. She always loved to comb my hair and tie it all at the back looking neat until she came back in the evening and find them flying all over my face. Looking at her rather questioningly, I said promptly.

"Why does everybody call me *Kamũthũngũ* (small white)? I do not like that name, and I don't like anybody calling me so! I hate the name! After all, I am not a *Mũthũngũ* (white). I will not play with them again. Moreover, they also pull my hair, and it hurts *mama* (mammy)," I said sobbing.

Marirũ was a slim rather tall, and fair complexioned woman, who was the third daughter in a family of five children, three daughters and two sons from her mother, though her father had other wives who also had several other children. She spent her early years in the village during the tough time of colonialism in Kenya. Due to her beauty and her fair complexion, her real name Gacoki, was never mentioned. Instead, people gave her the names "*Marirũ*" (which means beauty or decorative), from the time she was a small girl, or they simply called her *watũitho* (daughter of *Tũitho*, also a nickname of my grandfather).

Marirũ was a favourite daughter of her father, who was very proud of her. She told me once how her father would share with her the *"rũkũri"* which is a special mixture of milk, blood and fat fried meat called in Kikuyu *"ngarango."* She said that if a father gave you a sip of that from his calabash, it meant that you were his favourite.

"I would have chosen not to be his favourite. Yak! What a horrible stuff!"

I said, and my mother laughed.

When she was a grown-up woman (teenage 14-16), she got married to quite a wealthy man near her village, who paid her dowry according to the wishes of Marirũ's father and she was blessed with two sons. This made her father even more proud of her. The marriage did not last, however, and Marirũ had to take care of her children alone, and her husband took another wife after trying to bring Marirū back without success.

She never talked about it herself; I came to know the reason later. Marirū started her new life without him, hard and challenging as it was at that time. From the time he took on another wife, he did not turn his thoughts to his children because the new wife he had taken was barren and out of sheer jealousy and envy, she poisoned the thoughts of her husband never to care for his children again.

Marirū was therefore left with the responsibility of providing the means of existence for her children on one side, and the fight against female acceptance since she was living alone in those days of traditional patriarchal beliefs on the other. She worked for European houses as a house girl or nanny. One of these families took her to Mombasa, and she was forced to leave her two boys under the care of their aunt the younger sister of her husband. The whole family opposed her decision to move to Mombasa, but none could convince her to stay, and it hurt her parents making them very angry with her. After a while, the British family decided to go back to England, but my mother decided to stay in Mombasa where she had met a man whom she had two more boys with, but both died as babies. When she got a daughter, she decided to go back to her home village. Marirū took the death of her babies to be a curse since the whole family were against her new lifestyle and leaving her little boys behind, therefore she went back to Kikuyu Station. She took over her duty to bring up her now three children up. This continued for quite some time, and then one day, she met yet another man, whom she liked and who helped her during her struggle to feed her children, and whom she later married (lived together not formal marriage). Providence had that in the third marriage; the man was very different and contrary to the previous ones, in that he was kind, serious and more responsible and loved her very much.

She met her third husband, an Indian businessman in the nearest town of her birthplace. The man was much older than Marirũ, and was not married, nor did he have any family in Kenya at all. All his relatives were in India, if ever there were any alive since he had left India as a young man and never went back. This was another most courageous and unusual step Marirũ ever took without caring what the village people would say. The man seemed to love her sincerely, and she cared for him as well, and that was all that mattered. Many women envied her secretly, and other despised her. After knowing each other, the Indian man who lived near Nairobi the big city where his business was located, Marirũ was forced to move to Nairobi as well, but her elder sons were left with her relatives in the village although they were no longer small children. She only took her youngest daughter with her. The Indian husband took the responsibility of feeding the children of her previous marriages and gave her security and even that of her children. Her life was divided into two because she had to go now and then to visit her two boys and take food to them and at the same time look after her husband.

In this third marriage, she was first blessed with a son. The Indian man was very happy to have a son in his old age. Unfortunately, the boy died when he was one and a half years old. The loss and the sadness of this death lingered for a long time, and she had lost all hope of giving her third husband another child due to her advanced age. She kept on praying, and after some time, God fulfilled her wishes, and she could give her husband another child. This time it was a daughter, who came out plump, beautiful and healthy. This was a joyful moment for Marirũ, and her lost hopes of getting another child was proved otherwise. She gloated over her new blessing, and soon she was the talk of the village. The only disadvantage was that the small girl chose a wrong moment to be born.

Weak and pregnant, Marirũ was separated from her third husband, not out of their own will, but in accordance with the emergency declaration and restrictions. The political situation became unbearable especially for the Kikuyus, the tribe which was mainly fighting against the colonialism. It was almost impossible for a Kikuyu to get permission to live in a big city especially Nairobi. Marirũ as a Kikuyu woman, people who were highly suspected to be Mau Mau members, had to suffer the pain of leaving her husband during the pregnancy, to go back to her native village. She could not abandon her two boys again without knowing whether she would get a permit for her travelling back and forth or not.

Mau Mau as my mother told me and what I came to learn later, was a revolutionary movement fighting against the British Government in order to claim back their land which the colonialists had stolen. Although no European knew the meaning of the word Mau Mau, all Kikuyus and freedom fighters knew what it meant. My mother told us that is was a Swahili sentence initial of what they were fighting for, that is *Mzungu Aende/Arudi Ulaya, Mwafrika Apate Uhuru,* meaning "The European should go/return back to Europe, the African should get freedom."

Most of Kikuyus were under oath, and they took it very seriously, that they would rather die than give out any secret. So, I was not surprised later when I found out that in many books the meaning of Mau Mau was not known by the European writers. Some of the Europeans who declare themselves as Africa experts did not believe me later when I told them the meaning of Mau Mau, claiming that if the letters were initials, then it should have been in Kikuyu language. What they forgot is that, the freedom fighters were from all the tribes, obviously majority coming from Kikuyus. The guerrillas fighting in the forest were all Kikuyus, but many other tribes were fighting and helping the movement from the towns and villages all over Kenya.

Marirũ's two lives, between her husband and her children, were no longer possible. After the emergency was declared Marirũ chose to be near her children in fear of colonial brutality which deteriorated. Soon after her return to her place of birth, the colonialists went a step further and burned all the huts in the private farms, to move all the people into planned reserved villages for control purposes. Many people were forced to leave their *shambas* where they cultivated their food and the place of their birth and heaped up in a place where they had not chosen. The living conditions were hard. There was little or no place to cultivate. Most of the men were detained, and their health was endangered, their human rights tampered with, and their means of existence reduced to a bare minimum.

In this terrible infrastructure, Marirũ was supposed to prepare the birthplace of her child. Marirũ's husband remained in Nairobi, and despite his adequate wealth to enable him to take care of his wife and the coming child, found it hard to keep in touch with her. He lost contact with her completely when she was moved into a reserved village. The permit for Marirū to visit her husband was impossible to get at that time. The Indian businessman gave up the search because it was also not safe for her if he kept on enquiring about Marirū. During this struggle, he also met another younger woman whom he had a hope of getting more children with, and who diverted his attention from his wife in the village and the unborn child completely.

One afternoon in April, Marirū had pains in her womb. Knowing what was soon coming, she talked to one of her neighbours about it. The woman kindly gave her some encouragement and told her to keep on hoping for the best. The pains grew stronger and stronger, but the child did not come that day, nor that night. The next morning Marirū had to report to the communal labour, which was compulsory community work for installation and building of roads, home guard stations, etc. On this April morning, the pains finally turned into severe stomach muscle oscillation. Marirū was suffering and could not hold it any longer. She whined and groaned, and eventually, she fell, and one of the home guards was called to consider her matter. When he saw her, he could read from her face that she surely was in severe labour pains, so he asked two women to accompany her home. It was only through God's grace that she did not give birth on the way. In her hut, the two women who were permitted to accompany her home laid her on her bed. The beds were built in the hut, composed of four poles dug into the earth, connected to each other with twigs and wood, built into a rectangle. On top of this, was a stuffed mash sack of dry grass as mattress, now and then one would place on top of it either an animal skin, or some bed sheets if one could afford them. For the top cover, a thin blanket was used.

It was on this type of bed in her hut, on that April day that Marirũ, with the help of the two women, was blessed with her fair complexioned daughter. Everyone in the village came to see the new blessing of God to a woman banned from her own birthplace to this cruel and merciless new homestead. Despite the hard-living conditions, the small girl grew up quick and healthy. She acquired straight long black hair, coupled with this very fair complexion almost like that of her father. The little village guest was very different in outlook in comparison to her mother, the half-sister and brothers, and people of the village. At first, she did not notice the difference herself, but later, she began to have small incidents, for example, the nickname "Kamũthũngũ" given to her by her playmates.

It was not only children who called me "Kamũthũngũ," but also the grown-up people although they had no ill feelings against me. I started noticing the difference between other people and me, and together with these nicknames, the whole thing started affecting me seriously. It troubled my mind that one day I ventured to ask my mother, although such an opportunity was rare. Despite my age of four years or five, I could still notice how life had changed since my two brothers were put in detention and after my sister Njeri was admitted in hospital with a severe tetanus infection. My sister Njeri was the fifth child of my mother and was also born during that period of struggle of Mau Mau soon after me, from the same first husband who was still trying to win my mother back to him despite the misunderstandings they had because he claimed to love her still. My mother on the other hand in desperation of trying to survive agreed to accept his help but found it hard to live with him. The result of this backsliding was my sister Njeri, her last born. I could not see Njeri after she was admitted in hospital, and although I learned later that she was in hospital for four months, I thought it was a very long time. My mother talked and cried over her every night saying that probably when she gets to the hospital the next day, she would find her dead. Njeri was in a critical condition in coma, in an intensive unit for three months. She kept on praying and hoping to find her alive the next day, although the doctors had given up hope on her. This wonderful, courageous woman who loved her children so dearly did not give up hope, and she kept on praying to (Ngai wa Kīrīnyaga) the

God of Mount Kenya to give her strength and further courage.

Marirũ was not a Christian, and she did not want to associate herself with those new religions which were spreading all over the country, and which in her opinion brought a lot of hatred between the families and discriminations which was not normal in Kikuyu culture. In any case, she believed in God, and she prayed the way her parents showed her, and she believed strongly in the "Ngai wa *Kĩrĩnyaga*" (God of Mt. Kenya) whom they believed was everywhere and heard every word which was said and every prayer. The God of those *Wazungus,* who came to rob them off their *shambas* and their country, and who were evil and cruel, she did not want to have anything to do with him. She believed that the *Wazungu's* god could not be possibly the true Living God. Today after I know all that I know, how could I blame her for believing so? Separating missionaries and colonialist was difficult.

"How could the Creator of Heaven and Earth (*Mũmbi wa igũrũ na thĩ*) allow such surely?" I heard her ask many times. Who could blame these people who lived under such conditions? The Christianity was brought to them along with brutality of the colonialism.

The days were empty, lonely and long for me, after my sister was admitted in hospital. Apart from that, I was more afraid of children since they were taking advantage of teasing me more, now that my sister was not there. We were always left home together, and I took care of her or rather we took care of each other, while our eldest sister helped my mother to look for food, firewood and draw water from the river. My mother could cultivate in a small piece of land where she planted a lot of sweet potatoes. This crop normally survives all kinds of weather, and that is why we had sweet potatoes throughout the year. That evening being so fed up of eating them, when I got my share I burst into tears, but regretted the action immediately after I saw the pain on my mother's face.

"Now what is the matter Cikũ?" My mother asked me.

"Don't mind her, mother. She is always crying for nothing these days," said my sister Mũmbi. I did not want to hurt my mother, so I turned to my sister.

"You are always giving me those fat sweet potatoes, and you know that I don't like them. I don't want to be as fat as these potatoes," I said in tears. My sister laughed loud, and my mother smiled and lifted me in her arms.

"It would not be bad if you became a bit fat Cikũ. You are far too thin, that the wind might blow you away one of these days," my mother said with a weak smile. True I was very thin.

I suppose my mother knew that one day I would question her about this difference between the people in the village and me, because when I cried, she looked very worried and a bit shocked, especially after I told her the reason. Probably the question came earlier than she had expected. So on that day when I asked, she took me and held me lovingly in her arms.

"Cikũ my little girl, the children are just envious of your beautiful hair. They all like you and like to play with you," she said.

"But I know that I am different from them, and I want to know why! Mummy, you don't have hair like mine, nor my sisters and brothers. Why do I have different hair from everybody? Why does Kiarie call me *"maguanyĩrĩ?* Please tell me, Mummy!" I begged sobbing.

"Oh Cikũ, you are too young to ask me such questions. I will tell you when time permits. Your brother just teases you by calling you *"maguanyiri,"* and I will tell him to stop calling you names when he returns. Now I must make fire and prepare food for you, or aren't you hungry?" She reacted to my question tactfully, but I knew the nicknames irritated her as much as me, because I heard her forbidding my brother to call me that name always. However, she could not stop the villagers.

"Now be a good girl and help me to bring firewood in the house, so that I can make fire and warm the hut as well," she added. She then put me down and untied the rope from the bundle of firewood, and I started taking some of it little by little inside the hut. I was not satisfied with her answer, but I was afraid to annoy her and at the same time unhappy, not only because of this unanswered question, but I missed my sister Njeri very much and felt very lonely without her. I did not understand what kind of sickness she had that made her stay in hospital for so long. I could also not understand where my brothers had gone to and why it took them so long to come back. If only they could all come back home together, my mother and all of us would be happy again.

Later that night after my mother had put me in bed, she started talking to my elder sister Mūmbi about the problems we were going through. She did this almost every evening.

"Maybe I should try to get a pass to go to Nairobi and ask Cikū's father to help us. It is possible that he has been trying to look for us without success. And with all the restrictions maybe he has given up", she said weakly.

"But he knows at least which area we are living, and it would be easier for him to keep on looking for us than you going to Nairobi. I am so afraid of you going there. If anything happens to you, I do not know how I can manage alone with Cikū, Njeri in hospital and all the problems. Please, mother, don't go there," begged Mūmbi. My mother kept quiet for a while and then gave a sigh and said. "I found Cikũ crying today and she said that the children were teasing her again. I think it is not nice to leave her alone here at home even though Wanduta keeps an eye on her and I also think it is time that she sees her father and knows why she is outwardly different from the other children. But how should I do that?" She sobbed." Oh God our Creator, what sins have we committed? My two sons are suffering in detention, the other is lying in a death bed, and there's practically no food in the *shambas*, no rain, nothing. God forgive us if we have sinned against you and deliver us from the hands of Nyakerũ (white)", she mumbled her usual prayer.

I had heard those kinds of prayers almost every night when I was already in bed since sleep would not come quickly due to hunger, fear and sometimes cold especially in the months of July and August. My sister Mũmbi who was by then fourteen years old was an immense help and comfort to my mother. My mother would talk to her every night about the problems we were facing, and I would listen to every word. Most of the discussions I could not follow, but I knew a little of what was going on. Njeri in hospital was the major worry for my mother. She also worried a lot about my brothers too, but this was a normal situation for every family in the village. Almost all men especially young ones were arrested and put in detention as Mau Mau suspects. In the villages, only women, children and sick or old men were left. Therefore poverty, sorrow, fear, and bitterness against colonialists were common in the whole neighbourhood.

My mother hardly ever slept. She would wake up very early in the morning to go to the hospital and see her child before she reported to the communal work at eight in the morning. In the afternoon, she would go and draw water from the well for those who were well off in exchange for very little money or food. Those were normally people who were serving the colonial government and indeed loyal to them. The water well was about three kilometres from the village. By so doing, she would earn some money to buy oil, sugar, tea leaves and sometimes milk to take to Njeri in hospital. One water container of five gallons would earn her twenty cents, and she carried two on top of the other, to earn more money. Afterwards she would draw water for our own use and then she would go looking for food. Despite Mũmbi's help in most of the activities, it was still too much for her. Every morning when I got up, my mother was long gone, and I would see her again in the evening, just for a few hours. When I grew up, she would show me the markings which were left on her head while making her hair. It was a hollow line across her head caused by carrying the heavy water containers.

One day my mother woke up at two o'clock in the morning without knowing because the moon shone very brightly, and she thought it was around six in the morning. She didn't notice when she went out of the hut that it was full moon. Her mind was fixed on her sick child in a hospital bed surrounded by red curtains in coma, fed with tubes through her nose and whom she could not help, except pray for her and wait for a miracle to happen. She went to the hospital which was more than eight kilometres from the village. The village traitors (home guards as they were called) saw her leave and reported immediately. Leaving the village at such an odd time, she was obviously suspected of being a Mau Mau informer, weapon and food supplier. When she arrived at the hospital, she met one of the African doctors on duty and who was treating Njeri. He happened to like my mother a lot or sympathize with her because of her love and devotion to her sick child and probably because he was a devoted Christian. He noted with interest that she did not miss even one day to come and see her child. The doctor was aware of the hardship most of the mothers were going through, with their children sick and hungry and their husbands in detentions. He admired the courage all those women had and thought how strong they really must be to cope up with all those difficulties they were going through. He often talked to my mother about these problems, trying his best to give her encouragement and telling her about Jesus whom she did not know and did not want to know. Marirũ's mind was fixed to her sick child, to be able to pay attention to what the doctor was telling her. She liked him due to his kind and humility, but Jesus was a foreign topic for her, and a God of the white as far as she was concerned. The doctor was surprised though to see her at such an odd hour.

"Did you sleep here today Mama Njeri?" The doctor asked her.

"No, I have just come from our village," she said. The doctor looked at his watch puzzled as if it had stopped, and when he saw that his watch was running well and what time it was, he was shocked.

"Mama Njeri, do you know what time it is?" He asked.

"No, but it must be nearly six-thirty," she replied.

"No Mama Njeri. It is nearly four in the morning," the doctor said. Now it was my mother's turn to be shocked.

"Oh God, the moonlight cheated me, and I thought it was nearly morning," she said weakly.

"Oh Mama Njeri, your worry, love, and devotion will definitely heal your child. I will also pray for her. Wild animals could have killed you on the way," he said worriedly.

"Come to my office, and I will make you a cup of tea, and then we will go and see Njeri together."

My mother was shocked to discover what danger she just went through without the slightest idea.

It was fortunate that this doctor happened to be on night duty because he knew my mother and therefore could save her later. As soon as my mother reported to the communal work, she was picked up by the home guards and brought to the station to be interrogated about Mau Mau. She tried to explain to them that she had no connection to Mau Mau and neither could she have time for such things even if she might have wanted, with a sick child in hospital. She told them what happened and no one believed her. Therefore, she was beaten almost to death before she remembered the meeting with the doctor earlier in the morning. She told the Mzungu station master about it, and they enquired in the hospital, and the doctor confirmed her statement. This saved my mother from going to detention or being beaten to death.

I remember this incident very well because it was one of my most scary days of my life. While my mother was being interrogated, about five home guards and two white men, armed with guns came to our home. I was sitting outside alone as I got used, to avoid children teasing me, playing alone and listening to an old woman who lived across our hut and who usually kept an eye on us as my mother asked her. We called her „ *Cũcũ wa Nduta*" (the grandmother, daughter of Nduta or Wanduta)). She was always sitting outside her hut talking to herself while searching for lice in her clothes and killing them by pressing them between her two thumbnails. I feared those lice coming into my hair, so I kept quite a distance from her. My mother made sure that my hair was free from lice by washing me with paraffin every now and then and combing my hair through very thoroughly looking for any sign of lice. So, I hated them and the way they made me scratch my head.

Sometimes the old lady would address me if I was near her, but I only understood a little of what she said since I did not pay full attention and the fact that most of what she said was in proverbs or cursing the white man's evil behaviours. I wish now I was old enough to listen and understand what she said. It would have helped me a lot in my life.

The home guards kicked the door of our hut and stormed inside turning everything upside down. I did not know what they were looking for and I was so scared to see them so angry and holding guns. I thought that was the end of my life. The white man approached me when he did not find what he was looking for.

"*Iko wopi Mama*? (Where is your mother?)" He asked me in broken Swahili, as if he did not know.

"She has gone to communal work and to see my sister in hospital," I answered with fear and in fluent Swahili. He looked at me probably wondering where I learned Swahili.

"Who else lives in this hut?" He shouted. I could not answer any more questions. I just stared at him my mouth open in fear, though I understood fully what he asked. *Cūcū wa Nduta* came to my rescue and answered for me.

"It is only poor Marirū and the remaining two children who are living in that hut. Leave the child alone white man, you are scaring her, whatever you have against Marirū she has definitely not broken any law," said *Cūcū wa Nduta* in Kikuyu language, which one of the home guards translated to the *Mzungu*. I wanted so desperately to run away, and I think the white man predicted this because he held my hand to keep me from running away. I started sobbing loudly. "Shut up" he shouted at me. I kept my mouth shut, but the sobs came out accompanied by tears. He let my hand go when he saw how scared I was, and I ran to the old woman who was begging them to leave me alone, forgetting about her lice and clinging to her leg. They left after they were convinced that they could not find what they were looking for in our hut but after a thorough search.

My mother came home later with a bleeding and swollen face. The old woman told her what happened. I was too scared now again to see my mother's condition to say anything. The garbage which my mother collected from the house waste to bring to our small *shamba* as manure was scattered all over our hut and it was stinking. The little clothing, we possessed was thrown down on the floor with the garbage. Everything in the hut was turned upside down. All our beds were demolished, and the fireplace was dug up like there was something hidden there. All they found there was a calabash full of *Mūratina* (Kikuyu beer) which my mother made and sold it to people in the village secretly at night. This is an alcohol brew which is made of honey, sugar cane juice and a special plant (*Mūratina*) which helps intoxicating. It was not allowed, and therefore they smashed it into pieces which made the smell unbearable. If they were not busy with that other serious Mau Mau suspect matters, my mother would have gone to jail again for a while for that, but luckily, they just ignored it. She was caught several times with it and locked in for several weeks, but she would simply not stop brewing it, claiming it was the only income that she had.

Many women of the village had seen when my mother was picked up from communal work, and they were very worried about her. Normally if anybody was picked up, that was the last time people saw of him/her again. He or she would be beaten to death or put into detention, and many of them died there. So, they all came to our hut after communal work to enquire why my mother was arrested. They were all happy to find her home, though beaten up. But that was nothing compared to what might have happened to her, if the doctor had not saved her. They helped my mother to clear, to build up our beds again, and to make a new fireplace. The grass mattresses which were also destroyed had to be meshed up again. Her wounds were treated with herbal, which my mother was indeed an expert. Within a few days, she was as good as new.

Many would ask now the question: What was Mau Mau? This how I heard the story.

Mũgo wa Kĩbiru was a Kikuyu prophet, a future teller, and a wise man. He prophesied many years before the Wazungus (Europeans) came to Kenya that sometime in the future, strangers would come to Kenya. These strangers would be light colored skin like the stomach of a frog. They would wear clothes which made them look like a butterfly, and they would bring with them a huge iron snake (train), which would have as many legs as a caterpillar. He also warned that those strangers would be carrying sticks which would spit out fire which killed; therefore, people should not fight those strangers, and should not be allowed to come near their homes. He prophesied further that, those strangers would take their land. However, these strangers would bring a lot of wealth.

The British truly came wearing funny clothes like butterflies, they were light colored like a stomach of a frog, carrying guns, and they began to build railway where the huge iron snake ran through. The British announced that all the land in Kenya would belong to Britain. Kenya families, who had lived on their lands for generations had to give up their land, so all Mugo wa Kabiru's prophesy had come true except that the wealth was from our own land which was taken out of our land.

This oppression went on for more than 70 years. Kenyans were fed up of the colonial government, and they wanted their land back. Many people were killed who tried to oppose the colonial government. All negotiations were not working, and so a group of Kenyan men who were sent to fight in foreign countries came back after the First World War. They had seen worse and were angry with the colonial oppression and discrimination which they had experience also in other countries like India. They had learned and had experienced the war and all that is involved like using guns and all that involving fighting a battle. When they came back, they started organizing their fight against the Kenyan colonial government. They called themselves "The forty Group." They had all come to an age group of 40 years when they started fighting in secret and later they were known as Mau Mau.

The meaning and the idea behind Mau Mau rebellion as I wrote before was: "**M**uzungu **A**rudi/ **A**ende **U**laya, **M**wafrika **A**pate **U**huru" (The Eropean should go/return (back) to Europe, the African should get freedom). The Mau Mau started their rebellion openly at the beginning of 1950 though it existed secretly before. The Colonial government felt threatened and declared the state of emergency soon after that in 1952-3.

The settlers held most of land, i.e., from 300 to 500 acres each, which were bought next to nothing if at all bought. Many held big farms as early as 1900-14 such as Dalamere, and Grogan who became very rich by selling land to other settlers. Almost all the settlers benefited the cheap labor in their farms. Kikuyus are by culture farmers, and they believe very strongly in the soil. It was painful to see their farms in the hands of the white settlers where they were made to work for practically nothing. The struggle for freedom went on for many years until Kenyans lost their faith in political negotiation which favored only the whites. Mau Mau took it up to free their beloved soil.

Not all Kenyans were behind the Mau Mau, (though majority were secret supporters) reason being their method were too brutal not only to the whites but to their own people who refused to join hands with them in the struggle of independence. Their brutality scared the colonialist, so they took great measures to fight back. They were of course more advanced in fighting battles with modern weapon, where Kenyans had only few guns, bows and arrows. Although Kenya's first president Jomo Kenyatta together with other freedom fighters were put in detention for over 7 years, accused of being the leader of the Mau Mau, Kenyatta was totally against brutality method and wanted to negotiate instead.

Mau Mau thought the negotiation was taking them nowhere and the colonialists were still oppressing the Kenyans, and nothing was moving. Therefore, they took up the only way they thought would scare the Colonialist away from their land. They ignored the leaders like Kenyatta and went right on with their operation of terror claiming that over seventy years of colonialism was enough for them. Both Mau Mau and the freedom fighting leaders were fighting for the same thing but using different methods. Many of them, however, supported Mau Mau though secretly.

Since Mau Mau were not only killing the Colonialist but their own people too who refused to join them and instead joined the colonial powers, to get favors, became a great confusion to many people. Most of the home guards (as the colonial royals were called), were really harassing their fellow Kenyans, but Mau Mau dealt with them and their families accordingly. This irritated most of the people and scared them from joining it. The colonial government publicized all that Mau Mau had done (with a lot of exaggerations to scare people from joining the movement), and they were indeed very brutal to the Mau Mau than they cared to admit. There was confusion all over the land as to whom they should believe. However, Mr. Davidson quoted in his book *"Histories of the Hanged"* as follows: *"Contrary to public perception, only 32 European settlers died in the rebellion and there were fewer than 200 casualties among the British regiments and Police who served in Kenya over these years. Yet more than 1,800 African civilians are known to have been murdered by the Mau Mau, and many hundreds more to have disappeared, their bodies never found. Rebel losses were greater than those suffered by the British security forces. The official figures set the total number of Mau Mau rebels killed in combat at 12,000, but the real figure is likely to have been more than 20,000.*

The brutality in dealing with Mau Mau was such a great one in comparison to other African countries who had similar rebels. As Mr. Anderson writes; *"The war against Mau Mau was fought not just by the military or by the Police, but by the civil administration in pervasive campaign that sought to strip the rebels and their sympathizers of every possible human right, which at the same time maintaining the appearance of accountability, transparency, and justice. Nowhere was this more apparent than the Mau Mau trials. In Kenya during the 1950s the white highlands wanted to use the most brutal method, clamoring for the public execution for convicted Mau Mau fighters, preferably immediately following the trial and without the right to appeal, so that Africans could witness for themselves the dreadful final rituals of British justice. Mau Mau war has until recently being strangely anonymous. The names of the Mau Mau generals have been known, and some of them have even been acclaimed as heroes – Dedan Kimathi, Stanley Mathenge, and Waruhiu Itote, are the most widely known. However, the subalterns of the movement, the food carriers the couriers, the recruiting sergeants and oath administrators, the treasurers and fundraisers, the assassins and enforcers and of course, the ordinary foot soldiers in the forest, have remained shadowy, and nameless,"* writes Anderson.

"Many settlers took it as their responsibility to take the law into their hands. Settlers punished their laborers and domestic staff with a whip (kiboko) made of rhinoceros hide. Floggings on the farms were part and parcel of the African workers experience. By the early 1920s, the deaths of several African servants from beatings at the hands of their European masters earned Kenya's white settlers an unenviable reputation for brutality. Flogging was far commoner punishment for Africans in Kenya than in neighboring Uganda or Tanganyika, where settler influence was absent. It is difficult to avoid the conclusion that Kenyans were flogged more because Europeans believed they needed to be flogged. Physical violence was an integral and characteristic part of European domination in Kenya from the very beginning of colonial rule, and by the 1920s it was already ingrained as part of Kenya's peculiar pattern of "race relations," wrote Mr. Anderson.

Reading all the history of Independence struggle and experiencing some of the brutality personally in middle 1950s as a child, it is my opinion and that of many that the Mau Mau should have been recognized as heroes of the struggle to Independence and compensated well by the new Kenya Government. *"However, whatever is said and written, it is true Mau Mau history is about the loss of British Empire and the making of a new free Kenyan Nation!"* I fully agree with Mr. Anderson.

I personally salute all those involved in Mau Mau, those dead and some still alive and their families, because without them, the colonialists were obviously in Kenya to stay and they may never have moved out of Kenya. They loved Kenya and were very comfortable in all they were benefiting, without shame of oppressing Kenyans. Typical of colonialists.

A Kikuyu leader who died in British custody before the end of the nineteenth century, Mr. Waiyaki was popularly believed to have been buried alive by the British. For this reason, a Kikuyu female prophet instructed that an European should be sacrificed in the same manner. The victim they chose was Gray

Leakey, a Kikuyu speaker and a relative of Louis Leakey, who had acted as a translator on the trial of Jomo Kenyatta.

A General of Mau Mau at that time named as Tanganyika appointed General Kaleba to carry out that ritual. Leakey's house at Nyeri was broken in, and they strangled Mrs. Leakey and their Kikuyu cook hanged, and Leakey captured. They took him into the forests of Mt. Kenya, high up in the mountain where he was buried alive and upside down. The body was found through Mr. Leakey's cook's son who followed them and later showed the British where his body was. Such brutality was known all over.

In this chaos, I spend my early childhood.

CHAPTER TWO

Marirū decided to take a risk and look for her Indian husband for help. She could not go on like that, so she had to try. The first husband who lived in the same village was wealthy enough to support his children, but he did not care, neither materially or morally, and he refused completely to help Marirū or even care about his sons in concentration camp, not even the sick one in hospital. Marirū begged him several times for help, but all she got were harsh words thrown at her.

"I am not able to help a prostitute. Go and tell your Indian men to help you. You have brought me nothing except disgrace and shame in our society by giving birth with an Indian! Get out of my sight! I was ready to help you, but you know my conditions. You must come back and live as my wife, and I will try to forgive you for all you have done." I heard her repeating these things to other relatives or friends in tears at night when she had put me in bed and thought that I was asleep. "He wants me to go back and make me a slave I was before, to help my children and me! Let them starve to death, if that is what he wants. I

33

made clear to him many years ago that I cannot bow to the oppression women are put through by their husbands in our society. Some of these men treat us like animals."

She, therefore, tried several times again to apply for a permit to enter Nairobi, but was not granted. Eventually, she decided to take the risk and go without a permit. Her elder daughter Mũmbi and friends tried to discourage her from taking such a significant risk, but she had made up her mind, come what may. Marirũ did not make it to her husband but was arrested on the way. Being her first offense to move around without a permit, she was sentenced to three months imprisonment. Marirũ left her two daughters Cikũ and Mũmbi at home alone, Njeri still in hospital and her two elder sons in a detention camp. Mũmbi got the news about her mother's arrest and immediately took over all the activities to support herself and her younger sister. She also took over the duty of visiting her youngest sister Njeri in hospital every day. It was almost impossible for her to fulfil all the duties her mother did, together with her own, but she tried, and the neighbors and family helped her. After a few weeks, she got used to the routine.

One month went by, and Njeri woke up from coma and improved a lot in hospital. She was moved out of the intensive care unit, and Mũmbi could feed her with a baby bottle. Njeri who was a strong and healthy child before she fell sick, had become very weak caused by the brain damage she encored in her coma condition. The doctors told Mūmbi that, Njeri could go home after a few weeks, but that she needed to be given a lot of attention. She could not walk, speak or even feed herself anymore. She was a baby all over again. This was going to be even more difficult for Mūmbi being alone at home without her mother, but the massive surprise to be written on Marirū's face when she came back and found her daughter at home from hospital was worth the pain. Mūmbi asked her relatives for help, and they were all ready to help her, in every way they could, except our stepfather who refused to give her any help. There was nobody who did not have sympathies with this young girl who was loaded with such a heavy responsibility at such a tender age although there were many similar cases like that to be seen all over in the villages.

One day before Njeri came out of hospital, she went to her step-father's house and asked him for some milk to take to her sister in hospital. The man refused to give her the milk and Mūmbi was so angry that she burst into tears and insulted our step-father.

"You must be a very cruel man. No wonder my mother left you. If your daughter dies in hospital, I will bring her to you so that you can eat her flesh. I hate you," and she threw the bottle she had carried in case she got help on his face and ran out of the house. Mũmbi was a very brave person and was not afraid of anybody. In African culture though, and at least at that time, such an action against one's father, stepfather or even an elder person was unheard of.

Mũmbi tried all her best to fulfill all the duties which were heaped upon her shoulders, and she almost managed, except that she didn't earn enough money. It was not easy for her to carry two water containers, one on top of the other like our mother did, but since she was not obliged to attend to communal work due to her tender age, she was able to go to the river several times in a day. Njeri finally came home, and I was overjoyed to see her again but sad to see her condition and to discover that she could no longer speak, walk or even feed herself. All this time she was in hospital, I did not visit her since children were not allowed in intensive care unit where they could be infected as well. I had begged my mother and my sister several times to take me with them, but they refused. Mũmbi took me with her sometimes only to accompany her on the way, but I was not allowed to enter the hospital ward, therefore I waited outside. My sister, who was strong, intelligent and knew many things, needed to learn all a new from me since we were most of the time left alone. I felt very big and proud to do it. Most of the children in the village had no time to enjoy their childhood. Each had a responsibility of younger siblings or such kind.

While Mũmbi went to look for food or draw water, I was left with my sister at home, and I helped her learn how to talk and walk again. I was also forced to take over some responsibilities at home like washing the dishes, sweeping the hut every day, which I hated and refused or ignored to fulfil most of the time. Mũmbi would, therefore, beat me up thoroughly, but this did not stop me from neglecting my duties, although I gave all my attention to my sister Njeri, the duty I enjoyed most. Mũmbi had never liked me and was very unkind to me in many situations i.e. beating me, refusing to give me food was one of her punishment and worse still making me stay outside in the cold until very late at night. This was due to the fact that when my mother was not around, all her friends including my cousins who were her age would come to spend the evening in our hut, talking about boyfriends and other teenage stories which I was not supposed to hear. I knew that she exaggerated her anger as far as I was concerned, though there was nobody else to take her frustrations out with. In time, I got used to her punishments and took it as routine.

God was really with us, because time passed by and friends and relatives helped and gave us a lot of encouragement and confidence, and within no time, my mother was back home. I will never forget the happiness on my mother's face, which I had never seen before, when she saw us sitting outside our hut. First, she did not believe her own eyes, and when she came nearer, she was convinced that it was her two small daughters sitting and playing together like before. She ran and took Njeri in her arms although Njeri did not react and was still very weak. Njeri looked at me surprised with a lot of questions on her face since I was the only person she knew and trusted best. She seemed to have not known who that was. She had forgotten all of us and always stared at us probably asking herself, "Who are these people?"

"That is mummy!" I said to Njeri, but she did not react.

"Oh, thank God of Kirinyaga, our Father Almighty!!! You have answered my prayers! You have given me back my child", she said half in tears and with laughter. She turned and saw me holding my sister's feeding bottle, looking very dirty with a running nose and my hair which was not combed and full of lice was almost covering my whole face. Mũmbi never bothered to care for my hair at all in my mother's absence. She hated it and many times she'd wanted to cut it off but was afraid of my mother because she'd warned the whole family never to cut my hair under any circumstances. I came to learn later that she was very jealous of me.

"Oh, come here my baby. You, poor little girl," she said holding me against her right thigh with the other hand. I had also started crying probably because of the sudden appearance of my mother, and the fact that she was also crying. I think the joy of seeing her also overcame me, and to realize that the severe daily punishments from Mũmbi had come to an end. Although I took her punishments as routine, I grew afraid of her and hoped every day for a moment like this, where my mother would appear from nowhere. She put my sister down and started working on my hair. She immediately noticed it was full of lice and she took the paraffin from our hut and applied it to my hair. After a few hours, she washed my hair applying some coconut oil, spend almost the evening combing it while cooking at the same time and talking to friends who came to see her. She combed all the dead lice out, and I felt so relieved from the itching. She repeated this often to make sure that, the lice and the eggs had no chance to come back again. My hair looked very neat when my mother was around.

Marirũ was to be seen smiling with her daughters, but the thought of her two sons in detention camps continued hounding her mind. One day she received a letter from her eldest son, Kiarie that her second son Mũkiri was very ill and would probably be dead by the time she received the letter. Marirũ did not know what to do because there was nothing one could do in such a situation. Many families received such letters and even sometimes worse letters, stating the death of two or three members of a family. The only thing she could do was to pray for yet another miracle to happen.

In 1955-58 most of Kikuyu men were in prison. These people were held in detentions without trial, and most of them were not convicted of any crimes, but just as suspects of being Mau Mau members. Jomo Kenyatta was one of the most feared politicians by the colonialists and freedom fighter in Kenya, and he was also detained for seven years. He was among those detainees who were suffering in the detentions. A few years later things changed politically, and many people were released from the detention. Rumors were going on that Jomo Kenyatta, would be released soon and that Kenya would get its independence.

Marirũ did not get any other letter from her son, neither from the authorities stating the death of her second son which was a normal procedure. But still, this did not comfort her at all knowing that the colonialists were capable of anything. All that was in her mind were the words which were written by the eldest son in the letter that his brother would probably be dead by the time she received that last letter. Therefore, she was expecting her elder son to appear alone and deliver the message that his brother had died and buried by the colonialists. But God had heard her prayers again, and the miracle happened again to this most courageous woman who believed and trusted her Almighty God of Kirinyaga (Mt. Kenya). Both her sons returned home, and the family was re-united again.

Kiarie told us the whole story in tears how our brother Mūkiri survived very severe pneumonia after he had sent the letter to us. Kiarie told us that they had all given up hope on him because he had been ill for almost a week without any medical attention. They tried to hide him because sometimes the colonialists shot the sick people who were not able to work instead of taking them to hospital. Luckily there were about five men from our family who were put in one camp by coincidence, and therefore they managed to hide him from the guards. But one day, one of the guards discovered Mūkiri, and it happened that this guard was a kind man who sometimes helped the prisoners in any possible way he could. He found Mūkiri in a critical condition and called the prison doctor immediately. Luckily, on this day, there was an inspection from the press, and the doctor took the necessary action to impress the press committee. Mūkiri was taken to hospital. A few weeks later, he left the hospital fully recovered. The authority did not write to us, and my elder brother did not manage to send any other letter to us after that and we did not hear from them again until they were released.

Due to the change in the political situation, the colonialists loosened their restrictions and let people look for work outside the villages. There was no more communal work, this was done by prisoners. People could move from one place to the other without special permits, but not in Nairobi city.

My mother got a housemaid job in one of the European families because of her Swahili knowledge and previous experiences. But the work was even more difficult, because there were no free days for her even on Sundays, and the salary was almost nothing. She left home very early in the morning and came back very late every night looking very tired. Mũmbi got a part-time job at a nearby dairy, and my brothers worked in different European farms. Mũmbi was also responsible for the housework since my mother had no free time.

Life became a bit bearable as far as the financial situation was concerned. We could drink tea with a bit of milk and eat other things than just sweet potatoes. Signs of independence were quite visible. The colonialists were really pressed, and it looked like they were almost giving up. Mau Mau fought desperately with the colonial government. The villagers started campaigning by singing the freedom songs without fear, and many families were re-united again, so there was joy and hope written all over their faces. There is nothing important to a Kikuyu person than his own piece of land. They were fighting desperately and courageously to get the land back from the colonialists.

One Sunday morning while having our breakfast, consisting of maize porridge cooked in water with little sugar and which was prepared by our mother before she left the house, Njeri and I were surprised to see our mother back again, and our surprise was turned into a great horror when we saw what had happened to her. She was covering her mouth with her headscarf which was full of blood. When she removed the headscarf from her mouth, we saw with horror that all her upper teeth were outside. A dog had bitten her upper lip off.

Marirū had gone to work that morning, and because it was on a Sunday, her masters had slept longer than usual and forgot to lock their two shepherd dogs which were very dangerous. As soon as she entered the compound, the dogs attacked her suddenly, and one of them tore her upper lip off. She had other injuries on her body, but that was the worst. Her masters were woken up by the barking of the dogs and my mother's screams for help. The master got up and called his dogs, but it was too late. The white man saw what damage his dogs had done to Marirū, but he did not even bother to give her a first aid let alone taking her to hospital. Instead, he sent her home and replaced her immediately.

The village people contributed money to take her to hospital, and in the hospital, they had to cut a piece of her flesh from her thigh to be able to join her lip together again. It was not done very well, but at least her teeth were covered even though her mouth was deformed and she did not look as beautiful as before anymore. Although I was still very young, I could hear and understand the bitterness in everybody towards those white people who had no mercy. I asked myself again and again why those dogs were not locked up and why they chose to bite my mother. Several nights I had nightmares about those dogs though I never saw them. I wondered why those white people were so cruel to their workers who worked so hard for them. Our mother was taking care of those white people's children other than being with her own children the whole day and half of the evening. I was also afraid that I was one of those evil white people since everybody called me "Kamuthungu," though when my mother talked about my father she usually referred to him as an Indian. Both these terms made no sense to me. I only hoped that my father whom I had never seen was not a Mzungu, and the thought that he could, be made me feel very uncomfortable.

I could hear a lot of discussions among the people who came to see my mother. The colonialists were ruthless and evil people who did not recognize an African to be of any value. They treated their dogs better than Africans. How could this be possible that a human being despises a fellow human being so much? How can a stranger come in your house, take all what belongs to you and make you a slave on top of that? Would these people allow that in their own country wherever they came from, that a stranger takes over their land, rules them as he wants and mistreats them so much on their own soil? All these things were said again and again that one had to think about them no matter how young and dumb one could be. All freedom songs were composed about these things and we children sang along. I started to pray and wish that my father was not a Mzungu, those cruel and shameless people, as the grown-ups called them.

Jomo Kenyatta was almost being released from detention, and everybody hoped that as soon as he was free, Kenya would achieve her independence.

Marirū like many other parents regretted very much that she could not be able to educate her older children due to all that had happened with her life and the political situation in Kenya at that time. My brothers had managed to go to school before the emergency declaration but had to stop before finishing the primary grade. Education seemed to be very important for the future, to deal with those white people. Her only hope of having educated children in the family was her last-born children Njeri and me. Mumbi was too old to begin with the school. Njeri's health improved a lot, and she could speak and walk again with the help of walking sticks. Marirū had no money to fulfil her wishes. She wanted desperately to send us to school, but the little money they all came up with at the end of the week, was only enough to buy a few necessary things. The school needed school fees, uniform books, etc. How was she going to manage all that? Where would she get all that money? It was not much, but for two children it was a hell lot of money for her. She made up her mind to try again and contact my father to seek help from him.

She got information that there was somebody in the next village who was working in Nairobi and might be able to deliver a message to her husband. It was still not completely safe to travel from one village to the other, although the government regulations were becoming a little bit flexible. She managed to deliver a letter to be taken to her husband, but on the way back she was again arrested on curfew and was put in prison. The letter reached her husband, and he applied for a permit immediately to visit his wife and the child.

A few days later, we were sitting outside our hut where Mũmbi left us with my sister Njeri, before going to draw water from the river, when my aunt (the elder sister to my mother) came running to us and took my sister Njeri tying her on her back, me by the hand and dragged me half running. She was out of breath and murmuring things I did not understand. I did not know what was wrong, but she kept on saying something like "Your father, your father has come to see you." Our cousin, her daughter met us on the way, and she ordered her to take my sister Njeri and return home and wait for us. She dragged me along now very fast.

We went to the main road where I saw a packed car and two most scary men came out of the car when they saw us coming. They were wearing white turbans on their heads and had long black and white beards to the chest and looking almost like Wazungus. I thought my aunt had gone mad to imagine that one of those men could be my father. I was horrified when one of the men started coming towards us his eyes fixed on me, and I wanted to run away. My Aunt tightened her grip on me as she felt me trying to free my hand from her. I hid myself behind my aunt shaking with fear.

The man tried to talk to me in Swahili, but I kept on hiding my face and refused to even look at him.

"Aunt please let us go! This is not my father. You do not know my father," I begged my Aunt. Incidentally, the man understood all that I said though I spoke in Kikuyu language.

"Of course, I am your father, now stop being afraid and come to me, I will not hurt you." He said in Swahili and very lovingly his voice shacking like he wanted to cry. He stretched his hand towards me, but I refused even to touch him. I was crying hysterically now that the man thought it better not to try any further. He talked to my aunt for a while, and all the time his eyes were fixed on me. My father spoke in Swahili which my aunt understood part of it, and she answered in Kikuyu. That is how they communicated, but the conversation went on somehow. As usual, without my mother's care, I always looked very dirty because my sister Mũmbi was simply not bothered about me. My hair was always uncombed and very dirty. My only dress which I possessed was dirty and torn, and of course, I was barefoot. This is how my father found me on his first blink to his only daughter. He told my aunt to wait for some time at the main road, that he would come back soon. He went back to the car wiping his eyes with a white handkerchief, and drove to the nearest shopping Centre, which is Kikuyu Station, the place they had met with my mother.

We sat on the roadside and waited. I did not know what or why we were waiting because I did not pay attention to their conversation, but my aunt seemed to know what she was doing. I tried to beg her to let us go home before those horrible men came back, but she only smiled at me.

"If we stay here, those men will find us here Tata (Aunt)!" I said to her.

"They are surely going to find us here because we are waiting for them and don't call them "the men" that is your father! "She shouted at me.

"No, no I told you, you do not know my father. That scaring, terrible looking man cannot be my father."

"Keep quiet Cikũ, if I tell you that is your father, then you better believe me. You will see that I am telling you the truth. Just be patient my child. Your father is not scaring terrible-looking man. I don't want to hear you say such horrible words about your father."

I gave up urging with her and had to wait on because she was holding me firmly on her lap that I could not even run away. We seemed to have waited for ages, but eventually, they came back. The man gave me a big parcel which I refused to receive, but my aunt received it for me and opened to show me what was inside. My eyes started to shine when I saw a nice dress, a pair of rubber shoes which were two sizes bigger than me, sweets of different kinds and biscuits. I had never tasted such things in my life before. My aunt received a basket full of delicious foodstuff which she was supposed to give to my sister Mũmbi. I was so happy about those things, that I forgot my fear of the man. He lifted me up and tried to talk to me, and I could see tears rolling down his hairy face, but I did not know why he was crying. He stole a few kisses on my face now and then, trying to hold me tight on his chest, but I pushed him away. After they left, my aunt came back with me to our hut and waited for my sister Mũmbi.

My aunt was so excited herself that she told about this incident again and again to whoever she came across and even the years that followed. In the evening, the man came back with my mother. He had gone straight to the authorities and had paid my mother's fine which was about thirty shillings and therefore she was released. It was surely a joyful day for all of us.

This man whom everybody apart from me seemed convinced that he was my father, brought a lot of changes into our lives. We were supposed to move from the village I had known all my life to a big city, Nairobi, so that we, Njeri and I could start school. For the first time in my life, I ate things I had never tasted in my life and what I had the appetite for instead of sweet potatoes day in day out. I would drink sodas, juices of all kinds or milk when thirsty instead of dirty river water. I slept in a soft bed with warm blankets and clean bed sheets instead of the hard-straw mattress which in most cases had nothing on top and full of bugs. My hair which was shabby when my mother was away and most of the times full of lice was well combed and tied up with lovely silk laces. My mother kept on fighting those lice with paraffin in the village, but they kept on coming back. This time, I was taken to a doctor in Nairobi who gave my mother some medicine to get rid of them once and for all. I wore lovely dresses which I could change every day and not a shabby torn up dress which had to be washed at night when I went to sleep and dried in front of the fire, so that I could wear it the next day.

In other words, my life changed drastically, and I felt like another person all together. The only thing that I could not understand was why this so-called father did not look for us earlier. Where was he all the time while we were suffering? When I came to our new home for the first time, I found out that the man was very wealthy. He had three lorries which were used for his business and a Volvo car for his private use. It was the same car he came to the village with the first time. I somehow did not accept the man at all in spite of his efforts to win me. He bought me all kinds of toys, dresses, and sweets, but he soon noticed that I was not impressed by those bribes. I could not even accept to have any conversation with him. Whenever he tried to talk to me, I would respond in Kikuyu language which I knew he could not master though he understood quite a lot. Sometimes he would pretend not to understand in the hope that I may speak Swahili to him, but I would just look at him. My mother was so furious with me and could not understand my behavior. She taught me how to speak Swahili since I was a baby and I could speak the language very fluently, and I even spoke to my father's workers who were not Kikuyus in Swahili. Whenever I stood in front of my father, no Swahili word came out of my mouth, and if I was forced to say something to him by my mother which she often did, then only in Kikuyu language or I would break into tears.

One thing that I was relieved and happy about was that my so-called father was not Mzungu after all. I came to know the difference when I met our Mzungu neighbor who was a business partner to my father. My father also referred to him as Mzungu and also complained about his cruelty to the Africans. The workers also referred to both as "Mzungu" European and "Mhindi" the Indian.

The difference between the two men was quite big both in appearance and in behavior. The Mzungu did not associate himself with the Africans, neither with my father except on strict business. The Mzungu lived alone with his wife and two huge shepherd dogs, which were trained to tear anybody apart who came near his house. They had no children. Those dogs reminded me of the ones which tore my mother's lip off. They horrified me, and I made sure not to go near the Mzungu's house. The only people from our neighborhood who went to the Mzungu's house were his cook and the shamba boy (Gardner). My father also went there when he had something to discuss with him, and the dogs knew him. My father lived with the Africans, sharing their sorrow and hatred of white colonialists. Everybody could come to our house, even the workers of the Mzungu usually came to my father for help or any kind of favor and not to their master the Mzungu.

The nickname "Kamuthungu" seemed to disappear since it was only the children in the village who called me that, so there was nothing to worry about being Mzungu anymore. The matter was cleared out as far as I was concerned. My father was actually darker than my mother, if only he could not wrap that long white cloth on his head which made him look so ridiculous and the long white beard, he could have passed for an African.

Many people were working for my father and from many tribes, e.g., Luos, Luhyias, Kambas, Kikuyus, etc.

So, Swahili was the mode of communication among the workers and the employers. Whenever I spoke to the workers, or with their children while playing, I spoke in fluent Swahili better than all of them, and I caught my father several times watching me playing. He always tried to approach me and say something hoping that I could respond to him in Swahili, but I automatically changed to Kikuyu language.

My mother almost beat me up one day for the first time in her life. Kikuyu women usually discipline their children by spanking them on the buttocks or pinching them hard on the thighs, which is very painful. My mother somehow could never beat up her children although my sister Mũmbi was fulfilling those duties for her, especially where I was concerned. There was not a day in the village I know of which passed when my mother was not around where Mũmbi did not hit me. She always found a reason for it, no matter how small. Fortunately for me, Mũmbi refused to come with us to Nairobi because all her friends were in the village. We only met at the weekends, and most of the time, my mother was always with me, and so the beatings came to an end.

"Cikũ, could you go and call your father outside and tell him the food is ready," my mother said to me.

This is one of the duties I hated most. I went to where my father was working on one of his lorry which was out of order. He was working under the lorry, and I did not know what to do. Usually, when I got such a message for him, I would go to him and touch his hand to draw his attention, and then deliver the massage. This time I could not reach his hand, and there were no workers around because they had all gone for lunch. I stood there trying to find out what to do, but the name "father" could not come out of my lips, and I could not think of any other name to call him.

"He cannot hear, he is working under the lorry."

"Did you call him? He surely would hear you." My parents had already discussed my behavior, and my mother knew that I did not want to mention the name "father."

"What has gone into your silly little head Cikũ? You do not want to talk to your father in a language he can understand, but you are able to speak with everybody else in Swahili! And why, if I may ask, can't you call your father's name?"

She was holding me by the shoulders looking at me like she would hit me. I have never seen her so angry with me before. She pushed me hard on the children chair that the chair fell backwards with me on top. She did not even bother to help me up but went out to call my father herself.

The next day my father called me and said that he was going to town to buy some spare parts for the lorry which was out of order, and he wanted me to accompany him.

"No, I do not want to go with you to town. I want to stay here and play with the other children!" I said almost in tears.

"Oh yes Cikū, you will go with your father to town!" my mother said. She looked at me with anger, and I knew I had to obey or she might hit me and still I would end up in that car. I realized I had provoked her to the extent of beating me.

My father's car was a left-hand-drive. I sat for the first time in front of the car next to him alone. Those days the Volvo cars were built in a way that the front and back sits were like two big sofas built in the car and not a separate seat for the driver and the passenger like they are made today. The front passenger's door was not locking properly, and my father warned me to sit near him and not near the door, and I should not lean on it. I was still scared of sitting next to him, that I kept on moving little by little away when he was not aware until I find myself on the other side of the seat. He pulled me near him several times with anger, but I still kept on doing the same. We came to a corner where my father had to take a sharp turn to the left, and there I took my chance to move far from him. The door opened suddenly, and because the window was open, I tried to hold on the door, but the turning of the car overpowered me, and I flew with the door hanging on the window. The door hit the front of the car, and

I was thrown right in the middle of the road. Luckily, there was no car coming from the other side at that moment. I got up quickly, and before my father could bring the car to a standstill, I was sitting next to him shaking, sobbing and scared to death.

The whole thing happened so quickly. My father was so shocked at first that he could not do anything but hold the steering wheel so tight gaping at me. Shakily he took me in his arms and started touching me all over as if to check whether all parts of my body were still together. He spoke in Punjabi saying things I could not understand but it sounded like the prayers he said every morning, saying similar things to what he said in the mornings when he took his bath. I always wondered why he had to say his prayers aloud and disturb all of us even wake us up and we could not understand a word of what he said.

He asked me if I was hurt, and I shook my head, showing him the only place, which was hurting and that was my hand. I had a small scratch on my hand which had started bleeding. My father could not drive anymore, so his driver who had come with us took over, and we drove to the doctor. The doctor examined me thoroughly to make sure that I had no injuries. After that, we drove to a temple where my father went in to pray for a very long time while we waited outside. I must have reduced his life by ten years that day because he came out looking so old, weak and scared. The shock remained for many days, and he was telling everybody the whole story of how he would have killed the only child he had in this world, sometimes in tears, and I noticed him drinking hard liquor more often. When he was drunk, he took advantage of telling me how much he loved me and that he would have died if anything had happened to me, and that I was the only important thing in his life.

That car accident made my father never demand to take me with him against my will, unless my mother came with us. The fear of my father somehow also seemed to have reduced, and I would agree to go near him, even sit on his lap for some time. The only thing I could still not bring myself to do was to speak to him in Swahili language.

Sunder Singh Mangat, son of Dhasonder Singh, was born in District Ludhiana in Bunjab India around end of 18th Century. He ran away from India during the First World War and came to Kenya like many Indians who came about building of the railway lines in Kenya. He was not married in India, and his sisters and brothers were much older than him when he left them. His whole family died, and the only person he had still contact with was one of his nephews. He started his business sometimes during the Second World War, as a General Contractor. He operated near our village in a town called Kikuyu Station, until the time he moved to Karura Forest area near Nairobi.

He got contracts from the Ministry of Forests and Wild Life to cut down the old forests which were planted for firewood purpose and building materials. He was the major firewood supplier of Mr. Smith (our Mzungu neighbor) who had a brick and clay work factory. My father, therefore, supplied him with the firewood which was used to burn the bricks. This was the reason of his moving into that forest area. During his stay in Kenya, he never married though he might have had many affairs, until he met my mother. I was, therefore, his only child as far as I know.

We lived on the outskirts of Nairobi city, in the middle of Karura forests. The place was named after the brick "Matofali (brick)" factory. I liked the place very much compared to the crowded village where I grew up. We had enough place to play, and I could play the entire day because I did not have to do any housework or even look after Njeri who was now strong but not completely recovered, and we had house girls. I was sent to do a few things at home, like collect the milk which was done by our housemaid, but we were asked to accompany her by my mother, wash dishes sometimes, cook some easy dished, etc.

"You must learn how to do housework Cikũ. Don't ever expect the housemaids to do all your housework, the maids get sick also sometimes, or they are not available all the time. Apart from that, they are also human beings, and they get tired as well," my mother would say if I complained that the maid should attend to all duties. My mother treated the housemaids like one of her daughters. Most of the times they were our relatives i,e, my cousins who were from very low-income families, and my mother took them in order to help the family financially. Most of them did not go to school, or rather their fathers did not believe in educating girls. They only did some duties like cleaning, washing, collecting milk, etc. My mother did all the cooking.

I came to miss the place the moment I moved out later, and in fact, I know this was the best of my life time, living with both my parents who loved me dearly.

Therefore when I was growing up, my mother showed me how to cook, both Kikuyu food, Swahili and the Indian dishes which she cooked very well. I also learned to combine these cooking methods to make delicious meals. I really enjoyed cooking, and I benefited a lot from her talent. We were not allowed to eat beef at home because of my father's religion, but this did not disturb us much, since Kikuyus normally eat a lot of mutton and my father usually bought mutton, chicken or pork. The Singh's dishes are mainly vegetables and chapatis or *rotis* made of full grain flour. They eat very healthy food, and I learned from my mother and father a lot about eating healthy food. I never saw my mother lying in bed sick, neither my father, except later when he got blood sugar problems. He refused to take tablets and cured himself by eating the right things and reducing his weight. They were both very healthy people. We had a small shamba at the back of our house which was about half an acre, and my father had planted all sorts of fruits, i.e., mangoes, oranges, guavas, all sorts of berries and vegetables. He was also very good at planting herbs of all kinds. We needed very few items from the shops. I loved our garden very much, and I spend most of the time eating fruits on the trees. My mother warned me many times that I might find a snake up there also looking for something to eat. I thought she was scared that I would fall down, but soon I discovered that she was right. I saw a few harmless snakes sometimes, and truly I was scared of them, so I stayed clear of them. My mother killed every snake she came across no matter how big or small it was.

My sister Njeri and I started school soon after we moved to Matofali in Karura forest. Many parents sent their children to school, and we were all put in the same class though some of the beginners were quite old. Some of my classmates were almost grown up men and women. Most of the girls dropped out soon after we started in the first class to get married or due to pregnancies.

The school was about ten kilometres from our house, and we had to go through a thick forest to reach school. We were a group of children from our area that went to the same school, since it was the only nearest one. My father drove us sometimes in his lorry and insisted that we should all walk together back home. Therefore, we had to wait for each other to walk home together.

Although Njeri had fully recovered outwardly, her brain was somehow more damaged, and she was not able to learn anything. Children in school were expected to work hard and be disciplined but the teachers those days were exaggerating. We were beaten up so much for little mistakes, or punished by hard labor, or sometimes both. Njeri suffered the most, and the teachers did not want to understand that it was not her fault. I was so sad for her sometimes, and I did not know how to help my poor sister. I tried to help her at home by showing her how to write, but eventually, I gave up because she simply could not learn. She was kept in standard one for over three years before my mother decided to stop her from going to school, and in those three years, she never learned even to write her name, any alphabet or any number. The smaller children came and left her in class one, and the humiliations were too much for her. She was always crying in the morning when we had to go to school. She had to go through a lot in school, and the children called her dumb and stupid. I was somehow relieved when my mother decided to stop her going to school.

My mother gave up hope on her ever being educated and looked forward to my progress in school. She urged me every day to work hard in school, but sometimes I was so fed up with the teacher's cruelty in school, that I wished she would stop me from going to school as well. She would be so excited at any good result I brought home but did not seem to realise what we were going through. My mother believed in discipline, and she said she was happy that the teachers were so serious with us.

"Just do what the teachers ask you Cikũ, and they will not beat you up, but if you do not follow their instructions which you are supposed to, then you will surely get punished, one way or the other. It is good that they are teaching you to be responsible. "*Mtaka cha mvunguni sharti ainame mwanangu*". This was her favourite proverb which says; "If you want something underneath, you must bend to reach it." Just like Cũcũ wa Nduta, my mother could never speak about anything without finding a proper proverb to fit her statement. In fact, this was all very common from the women of her age at that time. Today you may hear many women of advanced age doing the same or quoting Bible verses to their children including myself.

CHAPTER THREE

I changed school when I was in class four and went to a Catholic missionary day school which my brother recommended back in the village. He said that the Catholic missionary schools were better and the children were much more disciplined. He also had an argument about the big forest we had to pass through to get to school. I did not know then their hidden agenda; I came to know later. In the meantime, both my brothers were married now and had built their new houses in a village plot they managed to buy, with the financial help of my father. We had no land anymore, and their father refused to give them a place to put up their houses. The school which my brother Kiarie recommended was near the village where they had built their houses, almost the same distance as the previous school. The new village was not far from where we lived during the emergency time. I was supposed to stay with them during the week and go to my parents in Nairobi at the weekends and on school holidays. I came to know later that this was just another way of bringing my mother back to the village other than living with an Indian.

My parents were not very happy about the idea especially my father, but they thought my brother knew better as far as education was concerned and therefore agreed. All the children were supposed to be Catholics in that school including the parents. I was not born in Christianity, and neither did my parents know about it since my mother refused to join the new religions brought by Wazungu. She refused even to see the inside of a church. She was a strong believer of God's existence but did not want to have anything to do with those new white men's religions. The colonialist and religions were hard to differentiate for the Africans at that time.

"The god of a white man is definitely a cruel one. How can their god let them do the things they do to other human beings? The God of Kirinyaga expects us to love one another, help one another, fear and respect Him! Their god must expect them to hate, enslave and eliminate other human races. Worse still they do not even respect or fear their god. I do not want to have anything to do with that god!" She would say. Who would blame her attitude in her situation and through experience of colonial brutality? My father was from a totally different culture and religion namely a Punjabi Sikh.

Many people were converted into Christianity either Catholic or Protestant, and they tried very hard to get my mother to join them, but she refused completely to go near any church except on funerals or weddings of a relative where she would sit on the grass outside the church until the whole service was over. It was like she was afraid of the inside of a church. She would murmur almost to herself about our culture being destroyed by the new religions, all the time.

"Marirũ, you should accept Jesus the Saviour of all humanity. Come to church and be born again by the spirit of the Living God! You need a Christian name," one of our converted Protestant neighbors told her one day. She had no idea who Jesus was.

"Accept who? What are you talking about? Now you do not even talk of God but always about accepting Jesus! I accept the Living God of Kirinyaga, and He is enough for me. I do not need another name either. I am very much satisfied with my names which my parents and my friends gave me. Your new language of the Wazungu is very strange to us. If you want to follow them do it but leave me alone".

"You will end up in a big fire of hell Marirũ if you do not listen to what I am telling you," the neighbor insisted. Most of these "new born-again people," as they called themselves, followed Christianity as my mother said to achieve the favors of the Colonial Government. True enough many were, not because they understood the true work of Calvary for our salvation, mostly also due to language communication.

"Ach, leave me alone with your hellfire. What sins have I done more than those Wazungu for God to take me to that hell? If there is hell, and their God is a real one, then there is no more space for me in hell. After all, I have never killed. How many of our people have they killed? How many of the people who fight for our Mashamba have they put in concentration camps? That hell of yours is surely full of Wazungu, or God must be preserving it for them," my mother said.

"I can help you to understand their God as you call Him, that He is also your God, the same one you believe in. Marirū you are a good person at heart, and I do not know a stronger woman than you in the village. I know that you are a living God's believer but there is much to learn about God and you need to join the church. The missionaries have taken your daughter into their school; surely you should be grateful," the neighbour continued.

"These white people tried to rob us our land and our existence but failed. Now that we have almost achieved our independence, they have thought of a new weapon to get us trapped again. These missionary schools are spreading like hot fire. Do you think that they are building these schools for a good reason? I do not believe it. I am sure they want to brain wash our children to be against us one day," my mother said and today I fully agree with her.

A Catholic mission owned our school, but the Africans ran it. We had, therefore, African teachers who were also devoted Christians Catholics, and not the white sisters like the boarding schools which I came to learn later that they were even worse in brainwashing. Many children who were attending these boarding schools started looking down on their parent's African culture when they came back on holidays and started speaking their mother tongues with a funny accent. Two of my cousins were in such schools, and my mother observed their behaviour and commented a lot about it.

One of our teachers came to talk to my mother about attending the Holy Mass, but the answer was the same.

"The children come to church every Sunday, why must I come?" She asked the teacher.

"Your daughter could be sent away from school if you do not join our church," the teacher said.

"Why should you throw my child out of school because of my failure to attend the church? If this is a sin in your eyes, then it is my sin and not my child's sin,"

"But those are church regulations that we must get the parents of our children in school to become Catholics, so that they can help the children to grow up as good Christians."

"Oh, I see, the colonial regulations are dead, now you call them church regulations. These Wazungu are very clever indeed. Well, I told you I would not come to your church, and I do not want to follow those churches. Just leave me alone! If you want to punish my child because of my sins, and if that is what your God orders you, go ahead," she said finally.

The teacher did not know what to do neither did I know how to convince her. He did not want to see me out of school, but he advised me to devote myself to Christianity, even if my mother was not. I went to church every Sunday and became very devoted. I loved to serve in church, and I had a very satisfying feeling in doing such. I prayed rosary as often as I could and memorized the morning prayers in school where I usually led. I joined the Region Maria and became very serious of the Catholic faith. I believe till today that the spirit of God was manifested in my soul at that time due to my devotion to Catholic religion and to our Blessed Mother. I had a good foundation which guided me all throughout my life. I loved the miracle stories of Jesus and found them to be so exciting. In fact, I dreamed very often about Jesus and seeing him doing those miracles personally as if I was there. I loved the story of Mary, and I loved her dearly and the Angel Gabriel and Michael too who were fighting the evil attacking us. I believe till today sincerely that as the Angel Gabriel called her "full of grace" that she is able to share with us some of those graces. Though the priests were Irish and their Kikuyu language was very broken, I could still understand the readings and homilies paying so much attention to every word or read the story later in books if I could find one. In Catholic churches, there were hardly any bibles to read except the Liturgy Mass order books. My mother was not against it at all if we left her alone with this issue. My father was also not against it, since he could not teach me anything about his religion, due to our communication problems and the fact that I could not speak Punjabi language. He was very devoted to his religion himself, though we did not understand anything about his way of worship. He often attended the Singh temple and took me with him especially when they celebrated Guru Nanak their prophet's birthdays or so, where we ate all sorts of delicious Punjabi dishes. I thoroughly enjoyed those celebrations to eat all those Punjabi delicacies and see all those Singh women dressed in those strange but very colourful clothes. My mother never came with us. I did not agree to wear Panjabi clothes, so my mother dressed me well with long dresses than usual, combing my Indian hairstyle with nice silk ribbons but still they all stared at my father and me whispering to one another, and I could imagine why my mother never attended those gatherings. She would be odd one even than me since she also refused to wear Panjabi clothes.

Everybody in school had to be baptized, and so I started working very hard on learning catechism. I continue to recite the Holy Rosary which gave me a lot of peace, and I became the school morning prayer leader and joined the church choir. I loved Christianity very much, so much that I found myself sometimes trying to convince my mother to come to church with me. I had no success. I loved to worship Jesus, pray rosary and do the duties of charity like helping anyone in need which brought me a lot of joy. This is what was demanded to the members of Region Maria, and I continued with this act all throughout my lifetime. My mother watched me with interest but never said a word to stop me. She listened to us in the evening when she came to visit us singing with my elder sister, and she said that we sang very well. She even sat there quietly when we prayed rosary with my sister and said "Amen" sometimes with us.

"Mama, Father Kelly says that those people who do not go to church are sinners. Come with me this Sunday. I am sure you will like it," I would say.

"When are you all going to leave me alone with this church business? I have said a thousand times that I do not want to become a Christian and I mean just that. You go to church and get baptized. Why do you all bother me so much?"

"At least you should give it a try mama. Come this Sunday and hear us singing! Most of the parents will be there," I insisted.

"My dear child, showing your face in the church does not mean that you are not a sinner. I have seen how those hypocrites are, who call themselves devoted Christians and walk with a book they call the Bible in their hands. They have the poorest hearts. Most of them do it to impress those Wazungu to get favours from them, and not because they are good people. I can pray my God if indeed He is the same God we worship anywhere and He would hear me if I am sincere, and not necessarily show my face in those Wazungu churches". Somehow what she said made sense that I could not afford to be angry with her, though I sometimes felt helpless. I knew deep inside that she was right not being able to pinpoint where that wrong was. Most of those devoted Christians were traitors, and everybody knew that, therefore I stopped pressing her further to come with me to church. What surprised me was that she was not against us neither following the teaching of Christianity nor attending our Sunday Mass. She was ready to help anyone in trouble, and all villagers came to her for favours. My mother had a godly heart, and she was very wise in her cultural decisions. She was also a traditional midwife, and she helped many mothers to bring their children into this world. If there were family problems, she was usually invited to give her opinion and solutions. People honored her opinions.

In any case, I worked very devotedly to the Catholic Church. I passed the catechism test which was not easy at that time, but Father Kelly (our Parish priest from Riruta Precious Blood) and who was in charge of our school wanted to know more about me. He was also the head of the boarding school where my cousins were.

"Who is your father?" He interviewed me once he came to visit the school.

"His name is Sunder Singh Mangat."

"So, he is a Singh he is not a Christian, and neither is your mother, isn't it? What a strange combination!"

"Yes, father."

"What religion is your mother?"

"She belongs to the Kikuyu tradition religion. She believes in God too father Kelly, but she does not believe in Christianity."

"Doesn't your father want you to join his religion?"

"That would not be possible because I do not speak Punjabi language."

"Isn't he against you being a Catholic?"

"No father Kelly, he is not against it, and neither is my mother."

"You have done very well in catechism, and you have been participating very well in our church, but I will have to think about your baptism. Have you chosen a godmother?"

"Yes, father, my cousin Mary Wanjikū Kuria who is in your boarding school in Riruta."

"Oh! I see, I know Mary and I will let her know my decision before the end of the week."

After a week, my cousin Mary came home for a weekend and informed us that Father Kelly had rejected my wish to be baptized claiming that since my father was an Indian, I would change my religion later when I grow up to join my father's. I was so sad and miserable that I could not even eat. My mother got so worried and could not understand why it was so important for me to be baptized. I cried day and night. My mother had bought me a nice white dress for the occasion and had even agreed to come with me to church for my baptism which she noticed meant a lot to me. She brought the dress to me in the village at my brother's house. My father back in Karura Forest was not aware of what was going on because my mother decided that we should not tell him about the baptism at all.

"I have been telling you all the time that these are funny religions. The other day the teacher said they would throw you out of school if I do not go to church, now they want to punish you because your father is an Indian, huh?" My mother said with anger.

A week later, my cousin came back on Saturday evening a day before the baptism and advised me to dress as I had planned and go to church like other baptism candidates, that she would try again to convince father Kelly. My mother was so furious about this news and decided after all not to come with me to church.

I avoided any discussion with her about religion, because I always ended up feeling totally confused. I loved my faith in Catholic religion, and I wanted to be part of it, but on the other hand, my mother's words had a lot of truth in them as well. Why should they punish me because of my parents' sins, if at all they were sins? Both did not choose to be born in a different culture of non-Christians. Did it not matter what I wanted? Would Jesus reject me because I was born of two non-Christian parents of different cultures? Those were the questions running in my mind all the time. Deep in my heart, I knew that my mother had a remarkable natural intelligence and I loved her very much, on the other hand, there was another voice in me which pushed me to persist on the baptism.

The baptism day came, and I woke up very early. Actually, I had not slept much, and when I tried to, I only ended up having nightmares about father Kelly's rejection. My most horrible dream that night was that Father Kelly threw me in a big pit and I kept on falling and falling without coming to the bottom. Suddenly some force pushed me up again. I woke up screaming and sweating. My mother tried to calm me down, but I did not tell her what my nightmare was all about.

Today after knowing how the devil works his intrigues to block us from getting near to God, I know that Father Kelly had nothing to do with it but the evil one was behind it all to stop me receiving my baptism and my salvation. After that dream, I was afraid of falling asleep again and decided to stay awake till morning. It was one of the longest nights in my life. I dressed myself, and when the rest of my family woke up, I was ready.

"Cikū, forget about this baptism and come back home to Karura with me. You will only be more disappointed," my mother told me. Obviously, the devil was not only using father Kelly but also my mother to try to stop my baptism. My elder sister Mūmbi seemed to be sorry for me too, and she wanted me to go to church as my cousin had advised.

"No, mama let us go, we might be lucky. Mary said that Father Kelly might change his mind, especially if Cikū appears in church ready for baptism with the others," she said. The name "Father Kelly" send horror all over my body.

"Ok! It's your problem if you want to be humiliated in front of your schoolmates," my mother said. The three of us, therefore, left for church, my cousin Mary, my sister Mūmbi and me. We were the first to arrive in the church. We waited outside, and after a while, the other baptism participants started arriving accompanied by their family members. Father Kelly arrived, and my cousin took me to him immediately. They spoke in English which I could only understand a little, though

Father Kelly could speak quite understandable Kikuyu but with a strong British accent, which I had got used to.

"Please Father Kelly, you must re-consider your decision. This child wants desperately to become a good Catholic. You must give her a chance. See she is all dressed up and excited for baptism. You cannot send her home without baptizing her," my cousin begged.

Father Kelly looked at my face which was swollen from crying, and I think this made him change his mind. He knelt in front of me looking straight into my eyes which made my heart almost come out of my chest and asked,

"Will you promise me in the name of God that you will not change your religion later?"

"Yes father, I promise you and swear in the name of the living God that I will not change my religion ever. I will always be a good Catholic". He stood up, and I knelled myself pleading to Jesus to help me facing the cross in the church in tears, which made him smile as my cousin told me later and she also smiled and cried at the same time. I could have promised him my own life if he wanted just to agree to baptize me on that day.

I said those words holding a Catholic Prayer book, a rosary and a candle, not from father Kelly's wish, but because I came holding them as expected from all the baptism participants. Due to my faith in God and in the

Catholic religion at that time, I felt very responsible for that vow, and I devoted myself even more after this occasion. Father Kelly baptized me and gave me the names Alice Mary. I had to change my name from Cikũ (Wanjikũ) to Alice, a foreign name which my school teacher gave me and which I did not know its origin. I was happy to get the second name after the Blessed Mother of Jesus. Later on, I received the sacrament of Confirmation, and I remember I traveled alone to Riruta Convent where the ceremony was to take place with the Bishop. My cousin was waiting for me at the bus stop. I received yet another name "Magdalena." So, my full Christian names became Alice Mary Magdalena.

I knew my name Cikũ was the short form of "Wanjikũ," and I was named after my grandmother. This grandmother I was named after was not my real grandmother because she was the mother of my mother's first husband and even though my mother was separated from him, she was still recognized as his 1st wife. My mother had to follow the Kikuyu tradition since she was not living with my father at the time of my birth. According to my mother, she did not want to give me that name though, but the women who helped her during my birth were from the same family as her first husband, and when they saw that it was a baby girl they all shouted "It is Wanjikũ" before my mother could say anything. Changing the first pronounced name of a child is taboo. There was nothing else she could do, therefore the name had to stay although my mother was not very happy about it. Mũmbi was named after my grandmother (mother's side), and Njeri was given the name of the elder sister of her 1st husband who looked after my brothers when they were young and the fact that she was indeed the biological child of my step father.

Everybody in school had to call me Alice and not Cikũ or Wanjikũ anymore. The name was so strange to my ears that sometimes I did not respond to it if somebody called me. At home, everybody continued to call me Cikũ, but in school, we were all forced to call each other by those Christian names, or we were punished if we used our original names in the school compound. I was also very surprised when my mother started calling me Alice as well, though most of the time it depended on her moods. It sounded so different when she said my name since she could not pronounce the letter "l," which does not exist in Kikuyu language. It sounded like "Aresi" or "Arethi" She said the name did not sound bad after all, but I suppose she wanted to get rid of Wanjikũ which was given to me without her wish. I remember my father making a lot of fuss that she named me after her first husband's mother. She tried to explain the reason, but my father did not want to hear or understand it. They urged until my father gave me a Punjabi name

"Nanki" which my mother was forced to call me instead of Wanjiku. He brought a small book full of girl names written in Punjabi and I was to choose any from the names by just pointing at any name in any page. I pointed the name "Nanki." They tried to call me the name for a few days and then they fell back to the old routine. However, I hardly reacted on the name at all, so slowly it faded away. My father could not pronounce "Cikũ" either, so he called me "Jiikũ." A total confusion! But I got used to Alice!

In our village school, things were not much different from the first one in Karura Forest. We were beaten up so much, that sometimes we were afraid to go to school. On top of that, we would be punished by making us draw water from the river which was about two-kilometer uphill and wet the class floor which was not cemented and therefore very dusty. We also had school gardens where we planted a lot of vegetables. However, I did not know what happened to them when harvest time came. We were supposed to water them too, if there was not enough rain and of course look after the plants ourselves. In short, the learning conditions were very hard, and we did not enjoy our lessons at all.

Many children repeated classes or dropped out due to poor results at the end of the year. I was lucky to continue till class seven without repeating. This was the last year of the primary school, and we had to do a national examination to enter the secondary schools. It was the hardest examination, and I think they did it purposely because there were not enough secondary schools for all the children to continue with higher education. The Government secondary schools were very few, and only the best from different schools were admitted there. The rest of the children would either repeat, drop out or those with better passes would go to the private secondary schools (which were increasing rapidly) if the parents were rich enough to afford them.

Therefore, it was clear to all of us that it was going to be a very hard year and we had to work hard. We got a new teacher who was even stricter than all the others I had come across. Life in school became almost unbearable. Few parents were against this brutality, but most of them were for it saying that we needed discipline and we had to be pushed to work hard. My mother although she wished for discipline, had come to realize how brutal the teachers were and she became against that opinion especially after her experience with Njeri. She had come to believe that if the teachers were kind and patient enough with Njeri, she might have had a chance to learn like other children. She realized that Njeri feared the teacher's brutality and this made things worse for her. She was therefore for the discipline but not brutality.

One day during the first term of the final year of primary education, one of the eldest boys in our class wrote something nasty on the blackboard about our teacher. He came in that morning very serious as usual and looked like he was already mad at us. My God! When he saw what was on the blackboard, he blew off.

"Who the hell wrote this on the blackboard?" No one answered.

"Am I going to get the answer or not?" We all kept quiet.

"All right I presume you all have an idea who did this and of course support him or her! I am not going to teach a bunch of thugs who have no respect for me. You are all going to work in the garden today instead of cramming for your exams if this is what you want."

So, we were all sent out of the classroom to the school garden where we had planted maize, beans, and potatoes. He knew that this was a very severe punishment for us with a national examination facing us, but sometimes I thought that those teachers simply did not care. We were also not supposed to urge with the teachers, and none of us was ready to tell the teacher who the person was. I was the youngest in our class, and whenever we got such punishments, they told me to sit somewhere and keep a watch on the teacher in case he would come to inspect what we were doing. I took my book "Tom Sawyer" which we were reading in English literature and hid myself where I could see the staff room door, to read. The others were also working in turns while the others studied.

Because of the anger against the teacher, they uprooted all the young maize plants and re-replanted them on purpose. I did not know what was going on, but I came to find out the next day. The whole maize garden was dead the next day, and we all knew what would happen to us. Our teacher, together with the headmaster went to the nearest bush and cut sticks to beat us up with. Each was to receive twenty whips either on the palm of the hand or on the backside. After the first one was beaten, and I saw the pain he went through, I decided that was the end of my studies. I stood up, collected my books to go home.

"What the hell do you think you are doing Alice?" The teacher asked me with the headmaster looking on, who came to witness and question us as well.

"I am going home, sir. I do not want to be beaten for things I did not do. I come to school to learn and not to be beaten and punished every day for nothing. I have had enough of this."

"Excuse me sir," said John the eldest boy in our class who was almost twenty years old, and who had caused the whole trouble," It is true she had nothing to do with all this, and I feel bad that she has to go through all this when it is not her fault. I will agree to receive my beatings and hers as well sir," he said in guiltily.

"No John, I have had enough of this school anyway and enough of education if this is what it means. I am going home, and no one will stop me," I said bravely.

I left the classroom, and neither the teacher nor the headmaster who was watching the whole incident said anything. I heard the teacher turn on to John asking him to mention who did it but I did not care about his reply, I was already out of the classroom. I closed the door behind me and went home. My brother was at work, and my sister in laws tried to send me back to school, but I refused and went to Nairobi to my parents instead. When my mother saw me, she first thought that something terrible had happened in the village and that I had been sent to deliver the message.

"What is the matter Cikū? Why are you here today? Why aren't you in school?"

I started crying and could not tell her what happened for a while. She calmed me down convinced that somebody had died in the village. Eventually, I took hold of myself and told her what happened.

"I am through with the school mama. I am not going back to that school no matter what you tell me. That is real hell. I am sure we shall fail the examinations anyway. We do not learn anything, it's only beatings and punishments like we are slaves," I finished tears rolling down my face.

"OK. You know I am also against those punishments, but you have only a few months remaining to do your examination, try and bear with them a little longer my child," she begged.

"Never! In any case, if I go back, he will simply kill me for what I did. Nobody walks out of that monster's class like that and goes back again. I will not be able to put anything in my head because of fear of him. He is simply brutal, and I am not going to waste my time again."

I don't think that my mother had ever seen me so serious. She seemed to understand me because she kept quiet for a while and then shook her head.

"Then we must look for another school immediately so that you do not miss your examinations. I will talk to your father about it this evening." I was so relieved to hear this and to know that my mother was on my side.

My father was sort of relieved that I was coming back home. As an Indian, he did not want me to be far away from him now that I was a teenager.

"We can get her a school in Nairobi city. There are many schools there, and she can travel by bus alone, if she can come from your village till here alone. I think a daughter should always stay with her parents, especially at her age," my father said.

The next day we started to hunt for a place in standard seven. It was next to impossible because no school would take me in the middle of the year where all the C.P.E. (Certificate of Primary Education) candidates had already been registered. The only possibility was to go back to my school or repeat in standard six and do my C.P.E. the following year. I chose to repeat. I got a place in many schools, but I chose a private school where I heard that children were not beaten. Muslim community owned it, and it was a girl's school. The school impressed me the moment we entered the compound. It was so clean, and the pupils were so tidy and smart in their uniforms, which was a combination of a green skirt, green jacket, white blouse and a green tie, black shoes and white socks. Young Muslim girls wore white trousers under their skirts and a white scarf (chuney) on their heads or hanged it on the shoulders. To me, they all looked decent and gorgeous at the same time.

The school was completely different from the ones I had attended before. It was a modern two storey building, with modern equipped classrooms. The desks were like a small table for each pupil, where one could open from the top and keep books in a boxlike area. Some had locks where we could lock our books inside. I had never seen such desks in my life before. In other schools, we had long banks and long tables which we were all squeezed on. There were more Indian Moslem children than Africans, especially in the primary school. In fact, when I joined the school, we were only two non-Moslem African children. In the secondary school, however, there were more Africans. Most of the other Africans in the school were either Somali children or those from the Kenyan coast, and they were all Moslems. It was a very big school with each class having three or four streams according to merits, which were named alphabetically. The class "As" always had the best pupils followed by the "Bs"; and Cs.

I was placed in 6A after doing a test in English and Mathematics well. Our class teacher who was also our Mathematics, sports, and domestic science teacher liked me a lot because I was one of her best pupils in all her subjects. The English and General Subjects (Geography, History, and Biology) teacher, however, did not like me at all. I was good in English grammar, but my spoken English was not good at all. I was not the worst in the class though, but still, I noticed immediately that she had something against me. My class teacher was a young Pakistan lady, and the English teacher was an elderly lady from Goa in India.

She was the class teacher of 7A, which I was supposed to join the following year. As I came to learn later, I was going to be the first African child to be in her class. This knowledge did not please her at all, and she did not hide her feelings about it. Her class was the most famous in the whole school, because all her students usually passed the C.P.E. with As and Bs.

This Goan lady whose name was Mrs. De Souza did not believe that an African child was able to achieve those grades. I was obviously classified as an African child. The fact that my father was an Indian did not play any role here. Somehow, I was puzzled because when I was in the African school, I was called Kamuthungu (small white), and when I came to the Indians, they called me African. Mrs. De Souza was a racist (a vocabulary I came to learn the meaning later from another schoolmate), and she became so cruel to me that I started to experience racism being practiced on me personally. I noticed her dislike of me immediately she came to our class for the first time and this slowly turned to hatred day by day. I could not speak English fluently, or rather I did not trust my spoken English at all. In the previous schools, we were speaking only Kikuyu or Swahili with each other. English was really spoken only when we were learning it as a subject. In the new school, all the children, even in the lower classes spoke fluent English which was the only language allowed in the school compound. All subjects were performed in English language. They all spoke it though with a very strong Indian accent, but at least they all had confidence in speaking which I did not have. This was not strange considering that they learned it from the nursery school which I never attended, and their parents were not illiterate like mine were.

Mrs. De Souza noticed that I lacked confidence in speaking English and made use of it to embarrass me all the time if I made any pronunciation mistake in speaking. The Indian children would tease me the whole day by repeating the mistake, and she just smiled to the children who were doing that as if to tell them "Go on!". Our class teacher, on the other hand, was always on my side, and she tried her best to help me. She scolded the girls if they made any remark about my Kikuyu accent English. Mrs. De Souza could not throw me out of the class because it was not her class, but she was trying her best to make sure that I did not go to her class the following year (as I came to learn later). It was difficult for her because I was also a good pupil, except for a few mistakes which other pupils made as well.

My worst weakness was forgetting my homework or some of my books at home. The Indian children all had some notebooks where they wrote their homework, and Mrs. De Souza always said it so fast and in that funny Indian accent which I was still not used to, that I would not understand and was afraid to ask her. So, I would end up not doing my homework for such reasons. None of the girls tried to become my friend, though I tried so hard. They did not even want to sit with me, so I volunteered to sit right at the back on my own. I came to learn later that as a Christian I was considered an infidel and dirty for them. If I forgot my homework, Mrs de Souza would make me kneel in front of the class the whole lesson while the other children knelt only for a few minutes. If I was the only one kneeling, she would pretend to have forgotten me completely.

I tried to speak English fluently, and by the time I caught up with them which did not take long, I had really suffered a lot. I tried to read as many novels as I could. At first, it was difficult to understand everything, but in time I learned to read novels. My most favorite novels were from James Hardly Chase. I was always holding a novel in hand in the bus, back home that sometimes I neglected my homework also because of those novels. My mother did not know what kind of books I was reading, and she thought I loved school and books very much to be cramming for school work all the time. In any case, I came out with a better accent than them, but I could imitate their Indian accent very well, and I paid them back for all the teasing they did to me. The whole class seemed to support Mrs. De Souza in her campaign to get rid of me, and I hated them all for being so cruel.

I made friends with another African pupil whose name was Nelly, and she was in standard 7B waiting to do her C.P.E. We also lived in the same direction, but she had to go much further than me, so we took the same bus to go home, or sometimes her brother took us with him in his car.

"How do you get along with your classmates Nelly?" I asked her one day. She was also the only African pupil in her class.

"Oh, don't ask me about those crazy Indians. I hate them all, including some of the teachers like De Souza," she said.

"You mean you have problems with her like me?" I asked getting excited.

"I am sure you have it worse than me, because she must be trying to get rid of you before you get to her class next year."

"Oh my God! But why?" It is like my eyes were open suddenly.

"Because you are an African and she does not want any African child in her class. Only super intelligent Indian children are supposed to go to her class, and she does not believe that an African can be that intelligent," she said in sarcasm and twisting her mouth. "I went through all that with her last year. She is a stupid racist," she continued. Nelly was one of the best pupils in her class. She always took either the first position in any test or second and never beyond that. She fought desperately not to be defeated by those Indians, and she taught me and helped me a lot to be good in my class as well.

"What is a racist?" I asked her. I never heard of such word in my life before.

"Oh, those are people who believe in colour bar (this was similar to the word "karambaa" I often heard my mother use in regard to whites). They hate us Africans and believe we should not go to school. They are people who still believe in colonialism and not realize that we got independence and that, this is our country," Nelly said, and I could hear the bitterness in her voice, almost like that of my mother when she spoke of white people. Although Nelly was one class ahead of me, she was almost four years older than me and seemed to have an answer to almost everything.

"I chose to come to class 7B although I was supposed to go to her class because she terrorized me just like she is doing to you. I hate her so much," Nelly said.

"What should I do Nelly?" I asked

"Talk to your class teacher Mrs. Ismail about it and let her put you in another class next year and not in 7A which will be hell for you. She is a very nice lady, and she might listen to you," Nelly suggested. I made up my mind to talk to Mrs. Ismail about it the next day. I did not wish to go to Mrs. De Souza's class either, after what I heard and experienced. She had won her dirty game.

"Mrs. Ismail, is it possible to change my class and go to class 6B? Mrs. De Souza does not like me and does not want me to go to her class next year," I told her without fear. As usual, I did not want to beat about the bush. I had also learned in a brief time how to converse freely with the teachers, something which was very new to me. In previous schools this was not possible, no matter how polite one could be, we were not allowed to urge with a teacher. She looked down for a while like she was aware of the tension between me and Mrs. De Souza herself and said slowly.

"Class 6B is full, and there is no chance of you going there. You are doing quite well in my class, and Mrs. De Souza complains that you forget your homework much too often, or do not do it as she wants, but this is not a reason to want to change your class. Your class tests look very good."

"But she dislikes me a lot, and no matter how hard I try, she only scolds me. What should I do? My classmates do not like me either, and I do not know why. I simply do not want to stay in that class because I am very unhappy there," I insisted.

"You cannot ruin your chances because of your classmates. Think about the C.P.E. You stand a better chance if you stay where you are Alice!" Mrs. Ismail said.

"I don't think I will have a chance at all if I stay in that class, Mrs Ismail. I am even ready to go to 6C."

"You can't be serious Alice. That class is full of lazy children, and you definitely do not belong there. Ignore your classmates and do what Mrs. De Souza wants you to do and you will not have any problem with her." Huh! Talking like my mother!

I was not satisfied with her answer, but I took her advice and ignored those silly Indian children. I also tried not to forget my homework, but still, Mrs. de Souza always found something wrong with me. She would complain about almost everything; my school bag was untidy, my uniform was not ironed properly, my handwriting, etc. Some of the Indian children were so filthy and stinking in our class, but she never complained about them. I did not argue with her though I sometimes felt like screaming at her just like I felt like hitting those nasty class mates. I always told Nelly what was happening and she also got fed up of hearing those things every day.

"Why do you let those Indians frustrate you? Beat them up! Don't you see how my classmates fear me? No one dares come my way because I always hit them hard. They are so stupid and big cowards. If anyone of them is nasty to you in the class, especially when the teacher is not around just hit her hard," Nelly said laughing.

So, I began to fight them all. I became very aggressive towards them with all the anger which had built up in me. If anyone of them was rude to me, or said a nasty thing, I would hit her hard. Oh my God! I have never seen such cowards in my life. No one hit back, and I only needed to beat a few of them. They all became very scared of me and stopped that silly behavior. It was as simple as that! I could not believe it!

"You should have told me this earlier. My God, they have such big mouths, but when it comes to fighting, Oh! Oh!", I told Nelly laughing. The attitude in the class changed as far as the classmates were concerned, but the situation with the teacher remained the same. They reported me several times, but I always had good reasons for hitting them, and some of the girls even decided to be on my side to avoid me hitting them.

One day, I poured ink on my desk accidentally, and Mrs. De Souza became so furious that she slapped me hard on my face. I started nose bleeding immediately, and when I saw the blood, I forgot that she was a teacher. I took my school bag with anger and threw it on her. All the books flew all over, and I ran out of the classroom heading towards the headmistress office. The teacher came after me, and I ran down the steps two at a time. I reached the office long before her, and at that time, my white blouse was full of blood. When the headmistress saw me, she was horrified. This is exactly what I wanted. I wanted to put my message through that this teacher hated me and this was my best opportunity. I always nose bled easily even if anybody just touched my nose. In fact. She had not hit me that hard, but I was determined to put up a nice show.

"Oh my God! What has happened?" The headmistress asked in her strong Indian accent.

"Mrs. De Souza beat me up," I said screaming. At that time, she also came in, and when she saw so much blood on my clothes, I think she also got a shock and scared.

"What? Beat you up? That is impossible. Mrs. De Souza tell me this is not true! You know that we cannot afford this kind of a scandal."

The headmistress was a small woman with a voice like that of a small girl. She looked so shocked that I knew I had that evil teacher where I wanted.

"These African children are so terrible, I only slapped her lightly on the face, and she hit me back with her school bag. The whole class witnessed it." Mrs. De Souza defended herself, but I could see that the blood which was flowing from my nose irritated her. They laid me on my back on the floor and started to apply first aid to stop the bleeding. I am the only one who knew how to stop it, and I made them sweat for a while. I kept on spitting clots of blood from my mouth which was flowing from my nose to my throat, due to lying on my back. When I was satisfied that I had scared them enough and before I over-bleed, and the headmistress in real panic and wanting to call a doctor, I got up and went to the bathroom with all of them following me. I poured water on my head which was the only way to stop my nose bleeding. Lying on my back made matters worse. I lost a lot of blood though that I got scared myself.

After this incident, where the headmistress asked me kindly not to tell my parents, Mrs. De Souza hated me even more. I did not care because I had learned to fight for my rights. They helped me to wash my blouse to eliminate evidence, so nobody at home came to know about this incident. English was one of the most important subjects, and I realized that she was doing her best to hit me with the tests every time she got a chance. She gave me very little points especially in a composition, claiming it was not good enough. After some time, I realized that I was the one who would lose in the game if we went on the way we were going. I could not afford to risk anything again as far as my C.P.E. was concerned. Therefore, I had to change the class somehow and avoid Mrs. De Souza's class the following year.

One day we had mathematics in the first two lessons which was followed by English subject after the break. I had forgotten my homework again, and I knew what was coming. She had warned me that if I forgot my homework again, I would have to bring my parents to school. My parents, Oh my God! I was ashamed of presenting my father in school with his white turban and long white beard. I did not want my schoolmates to see him. He could not even speak English. My mother could not speak one word of English either. I decided to change my class without their help, even though there were only a few weeks left to close the school for Christmas holidays. I went straight to class 6C, the only parallel class which had fewer pupils. However, there were more Somali children than Pakistani. My class teacher had a mathematics lesson in class 6C after break. She did not notice me immediately, and after a while, she asked a question, and I was the only one who raised a hand. She looked around puzzled like she thought she was in a wrong class.

"Yes, Alice . . . Eh . . . what the hell are you doing here?" She asked very surprised realizing that she was in the right class, but I was not. I stood up looking down to avoid her eyes and did not answer.

"I am talking to you!" She came to my desk and lifted my face up forcing me to look at her. I started crying.

"Please Miss Ismail, I do not want to go to 7A next year. If I stay there until we close the school, then I will definitely end up there" I said sobbing.

"You cannot stay here. I will not let you leave my class no matter what problem you have with Mrs. De-souza," she said changing her voice.

"And how can you dare change classes without permission. Are you really interested in school at all? Are you interested in passing your C.P.E.? I do not believe this Alice."

"Yes Madam, I am, and you know how hard I am working, but Mrs. De Souza makes life very difficult for me. She is too hard on me in every way. I cannot stand her anymore just like she cannot stand me. Please, Mrs Ismail, help me! Don't let me go to her class next year,"

She looked at me sympathetically and said,

"Come with me; we have to talk to the principal about this." I followed her to the headmistress's office. The headmistress was also furious with me at first.

"What? Did she change her class without telling you? This is unheard of. Do you think this is your father's school to do what you feel like?" I did not answer.

"What are we going to do?" asked Mrs. Ismail. "She is quite a good pupil, and I cannot let her stay in class 6C. This will automatically put her in class 7C next year."

"Is there no chance of putting her in 7B?" The headmistress asked.

"No! There are even more children in 6B now."

"But definitely the best pupil in 6B might be willing to change places with Alice next year?" The headmistress suggested.

"But, we cannot do that without talking to her parents first."

Oh! I did not want it to go so far, I thought with panic.

"Then arrange to see Alice's parents before the school closes and see which child you can put in 7A next year, and talk to the other student's parents as well," the headmistress said.

"Yes, I think that can be arranged." It was decided that I bring my parents, or at least one of them to discuss the issue with the headmistress. In the meantime, I had to go back to my class. Mrs. De Souza was only too glad to hear my rebellious story and the result.

I did not know how I would explain this to my mother. She had no idea that I was being discriminated in school. I was afraid of telling them knowing that I had left the other school on my own. I was ready to go through this fight alone. I told Nelly about my feelings and as usual, she had a brilliant idea.

"You just bring one of the women who sell vegetables here outside our school and present her as your mother. I have done that often even bringing different ones, and they never noticed. Those women are very co-operative knowing how demanding the schools can be."

"How can she agree to represent my mother on such an issue?" I asked,

"You do not have to tell her the truth, just say you have made some mistakes and they want to throw you out of school unless your mother talks to them. They do not speak English at all, and you will have to translate everything yourself," Nelly said laughing as if it was a big joke.

"I do not know how you can take everything so easy? This is not a game!" I said angrily.

"Neither do I take it as a joke. You will do the same with your mother, so why bother her to come all the way here to listen to their bullshit? It is decided anyway, and this is the best solution for you, and you know it. Anyway, I only suggested it. You do not have to follow my advice if you don't want," Nelly said lifting her shoulders.

"OK it makes sense anyway but where will I find such a co-operative woman to do it?" I asked her

"Don't worry. I will help you get one."

We managed to get an old Kikuyu woman who sold vegetables from door to door near our school, and she agreed immediately.

"Yes, my child, I will come with you. These people do not know how hard we must work every day to pay the school fees and food for our children. It is their job to look after you in school. Why do they bother us so much? They can punish you if you make a mistake."

We had told her a story about my mother having a market stand in Limuru about eighty kilometers from Nairobi City.

"How can your mother close her market stand for a day to come here? Come I will talk to them," she said bravely. I was shaking already with fear. I translated the conversation between the headmistress, Mrs. Ismail and the old lady. She played her part so well like a professional actress. I love our Africans, Jacks of all trade! She even scolded me so genuinely that Mrs. Ismail was fully satisfied. I was so scared that they would notice our trick and then I would be in more trouble, but none of them noticed. They shook hands later, and that was it. I was placed in standard 7B the following year, and Mrs. Ismail like a miracle became my class teacher again which made me very happy.

All these were things I could not discuss with my parents. I believed they would not understand anything about what was going on, and my father might have suggested changing my school as he had suggested before to a Singh Community School especially if he knew about the discrimination, which I did not want. He seemed to have something against "Muslimanas" as he called them, though he did not say why. I came to understand the hatred between Pakistan and India later. I do not think that he was afraid of me being converted to Islam because he knew how devoted I was with my Catholic faith, but still, it was disturbing him that I was indeed in that school right from the beginning.

I missed our community and the activities we used to participate in our school regarding the worship, and I missed going to a lively church like the one in the village. The only church in our near was in Nairobi town in a small area called Parklands, and the only place I could attend Mass was a small convent chapel in Muthaiga where they held a mass very early in the morning at 7 a.m. for the nuns, and my father had to take me there leaving home at 6.30 a.m. and wait for me in the car until the mass was over. Fortunately, it was not as long as the village mass. It took longest 45 minutes. We were very few people from outside attending the mass, but the nuns allowed us. I just discovered it by chance. I insisted on going alone if my father did not want to take me, so he arranged that his driver could drive me there. Both he and my mother could not understand why I was so devoted, but they respected it. My mother woke me up early as I asked her and she noticed that I woke up very easily to go to church than to go to school.

However, this devotion in my faith started getting lukewarm because of many such problems. The mass attendance became fewer and fewer, and my father was just too glad when I said on Saturday evening that I would not go to church the next day. In the school assembly, we had a Muslim teacher who read their Koran which I also learned since all children were shouting in the assembly and there was also a Christian teacher who read us the Bible and said morning prayers together. The Muslim children also said some easy prayers with us, i.e., "The Lord's prayer." Religion classes were also separated for Muslims and Christians. I found this arrangement to be very fair since it was a Muslin Girls School. I presume these were the government conditions to start a Moslem school in Nairobi City.

Somehow, I felt very guilty of the way I was shutting my parents out of my life at such a tender age, and after the primary exams, I confessed everything to my mother who laughed so much to hear the story of the vegetable woman representing her. However, she felt so sorry for me for enduring all that discrimination, but always encouraged me that God was with me since I was so devoted to Him. All the time I felt that I had a spiritual mother, the Blessed Mother Mary who somehow helped me in all tricky situations.

CHAPTER FOUR

In standard 7b, Mrs. De Souza had about three subjects to teach therefore we still had to bear one another for yet one more year. I formed a habit of not forgetting my homework, which I discovered was very important for self-studies and which made my performance in the class tests improve tremendously. Mrs. De Souza changed her attitude a bit towards me, after all, she won her game that I did not go to her class, but I could see that she could never like me. Her change of attitude was because she saw I was not going to bow to her racism. I also guessed the headmistress had a long talk with her and she must have been warned about her attitude towards African children and that the government was very strict on any discrimination on African. The school could be closed if this kind of scandal would get to the authorities. I was still the only African in my class, and I wanted to pass my C.P.E., therefore, I worked hard. I was one of the best pupils in Mathematics, Swahili, English, domestic science and sports, and my spoken English had improved so much that I could speak even better than the Indian children and with a better accent, unless I wanted to imitate them which I managed perfectly. This made Mrs. De Souza sometimes very furious, though sometimes she was forced to laugh since I did it so perfectly.

I passed my C.P.E. with good grades which could have allowed me to enter any government school, but luck was not with me. I was not called in any school of my choice which were boarding schools. Our school was very concerned, and when we waited for a while without any response from the schools I had applied for, I was admitted in our secondary school. I was disappointed because I had passed well and should have got a place in a government secondary boarding school which I wanted so much. I was advised later to go to the ministry of education and ask them why my application had been rejected. My parents did not know anything of what was going on again. For them, a school was a school, and they were satisfied that I had been admitted in my old school. They were both totally against those boarding schools anyway. How right they were, I came to discover later!

I, therefore, went to the ministry of education on my own to enquire, but I had waited too long. I think most of African children were self-dependent since our parents did not know anything about the education system, and the fact that most of them were illiterate.

"Why didn't you come earlier?" A lady, who seemed very sympathetic when she heard about my case, asked me.

"I remember your case very well. We did not know that you were an African child due to your names. The schools which you had chosen were African schools. Usually, no Indians apply for such schools, and your surname made us believe that you were an Indian child. If you had come to us immediately, we would have got you a place, but now it is too late my dear child. All the schools are now full. As soon as your identity created this confusion, we took the next child. I am so sorry." What a silly excuse? Even if I was an Indian child and had applied for such a school, they should still have given me a chance. I did not understand the logic behind it all, so I went home feeling very bad. My identity surely seemed to bring me problems all over, but I decided not to let any of these stupid discriminator individuals bring me down. I did not tell my parents any of this not even that I had gone alone to the ministry to inquire.

My father talked daily of these kinds of discrimination towards him from all directions. His Indian people did not accept him because he lived with an African woman. The Africans could not accept him as one of their own either, not even my mother's children could accept him despite all the help he gave them while growing up, more than their biological father ever did for them. For them, he was only money provider and nothing else. So, I decided not to put oil in the fire already burning.

I decided to take care of my education quietly. I, therefore, stayed in my old school. It was not bad at all, and it had a good reputation. My father could afford to pay the school fees which were a lot for some parents. I continued to work hard in the secondary school, to pass my examination in four years' time which would allow me to do my final two years of higher school to get through to the university. That was not easy, because there were other thousands of children who had the same aim, and there was only one university in the country at that time. One had to be good in all subjects and throughout the six years, to get a place at the university or get a scholarship to study abroad. Anyway, I was determined to do my very best.

When I was in form two, I had shocking news that my father wanted to go back to India. My father seemed to have changed a lot, and he seemed to grow older every day. I think he was afraid like all other Indians who had made a lot of money in Kenya before independence, that they would lose everything. Most of the Indians in Kenya had taken Kenyan or British citizenship during colonial time. After independence, those who had British passports were given notice by the government to go to Britain, but those who had taken Kenyan citizenship could stay.

There were also many Indians who through the love of their country did not bother to take either one.

They maintained their Indian citizenship. My father was among this last group, and they were all asked to leave the country after independence. I came to learn that he had received a notice from the Government to leave the country. My sister and brothers except Njeri seemed very happy that my father was leaving and I came to discover much later that they organized all these chaos.

My mother took the matter to the Government claiming that he was her husband and that they had a child together. She tried to beg my brother to help her achieve a permanent stay permit for my father by escorting her to the government offices, but he refused. This is when I discovered that they were all happy about my father's decision to go back to India. My father became very aggressive to my mother as if she was the one who was deporting him. He gave me these suspicions of my brothers being probably behind all since they wanted my mother to go back to her first husband. They quarreled a lot, and I learned a lot about their life through these quarrels. I also learned from their quarrels about the other woman in my father's life after my mother left him when she was expecting me. He lived with that woman all the years we were suffering in the village.

That was probably the reason why he did not make big effort to look for us earlier. He had hoped that the new woman, who was also younger than my mother would give him a son. The son did not come, and in the end, he decided to come after the only child he had. He had received messages that my mother had given birth to a baby girl, and that was the reason why he had taken so long to look for us according to my mother's claims during their quarrel.

Had I been a boy he would have found a way and means to come earlier. He was looking for a son to carry his name forward. This made me feel unwanted, convincing myself that he did not love me because I was not a boy. I began to avoid him even more. He became so mean to my mother, that he could not even give her any money at all.

He was doing all the shopping himself to avoid giving my mother any money. She sometimes begged so much till I pitied her. He had a lot of money, and he was very generous to other people. So why would he not agree to give his wife money to buy what she needed? He was so generous before, why did he change his attitude towards her? As I came to learn later, it was all because of her elder children who were ripping her off every shilling she got from my father.

I sometimes thought I was the one to blame, due to my cold attitude towards him and refusing to accept him as my father. My mother had to work hard in her sugar plantation near our house, and she had to grow vegetables which she sold to my father's workers to earn some money. He did not even feel ashamed of it. My mother would not tell me anything to hurt me or make me hate my father whom she knew already I was not so close. She would always protect him, and this made me so angry with my father that I decided to do something about it.

My father could give me almost anything I needed, but I did not demand much. Sometimes because of my stubbornness, he would pretend to be difficult, but I always managed to get anything I wanted from him. I had never cheated him before, but now I started on the game for my mother's sake. I kept on demanding things and giving him two or three times the prices of the things I needed, and I would give my mother the balance. He never asked me for a receipt. I told him one day that the school fees had gone up and he never suspected anything. He just gave me the money, and I had to pay the school fees myself. My mother who knew all that I was doing looked at me fearfully.

"What if he finds out Cikũ? He would think that it is me who is teaching you to cheat on him," my mother said to me afterwards.

"I do not care if he finds out, then I will tell him the truth, that I give his wife the balance to buy her things because he cannot give her himself. He throws money around but never gives you any. Do you think that is fair?" I asked angrily.

"It is not fair, but still that is not a reason to cheat on your father, he could be right in his meanness since your elder brothers and sister keeps on begging me for money, and I do not have any of my own. I must beg him for their sake, and they are never appreciative. They do not even respect him for all the help he has given to them." She said almost in tears. He is very angry about my children.

"OK if you do not want the money, I will still steal from him and save it. He has not even bought you a piece of land anywhere, and yet he bought a plot in Nairobi for that woman he was staying with while we were suffering in the village. What do you have? Don't be so soft on him. You cook for him, wash for him, do everything like a slave, and he has no appreciation. He should give you some money, and you have the right to do what you want with it," I said. My conscience was warning me about my action, that it was not my business to poke my nose in their quarrel, but I ignored it and the fact that my elder sister especially was poisoning my mind anytime we met against my father.

"Be grateful that he educates you and he has done a lot for your brothers and sisters, who are supposed to be grateful to him and stop demanding more and more. I care more about your education now Cikũ than anything else," she said calmly looking down.

"Is that all? I am his child, and it is his responsibility to pay for my education," I shouted.

"Cikũ, be quiet now, don't argue with me about your father. It is a bad omen for a child to talk like that about her/his father. I have much to blame for his attitude!"

"You and your "bad omens," you can never see facts." I went out of the house in anger and left her holding her face with both hands like she always did when she was in sorrow. I loved her so much, bu she was so naive sometimes as my sister said. If sh begged my father for anything and he shouted at h that was the end of the matter. Other women w have insisted or shouted back until they got what wanted.

The trouble with my mother was that s not value money at all. She was not mat whatsoever. She always said that she was ric and that was enough. Many women who wer to Indians managed to get them buy a lot plots in the city for them after independen it was very cheap then as many settlers were leaving the country and selling th in a hurry. My mother did not even ge him, although there was not a single e did not raise the subject. My brothers really working on her to get someth pass it over to them later. My mo tricks. She knew they never car being but for their own greed of n

"If he does not see that I am his wife and he should give me what I need, then I cannot force him. The most important thing is that he educates my child," she would say comforting herself. My spinsters, however, were not interested in my education.

Before my father's case was considered, therefore, he had made up his mind to leave the country and go back to India. Probably this was another reason for being so stingy suddenly. He wanted to save his money to take to India.

"I am an old man now, and I would like to see my country before I die. At least I want to go for a few months, four to six and come back if necessary," my father said. By the time he broke the news of his final decision to my mother, he had already finalized all his business transactions in Kenya and booked his flight to India, which was to be in four weeks' time.

"But you cannot leave the country before your case has been considered! You must wait for a while," my mother begged in tears.

"Oh no, I have made up my mind," he said.

"What about Cikū, what should I tell her and what about her education if you do not come back?" My mother asked desperately.

"Well, I could take her with me if you allowed me and she wants." He knew very well that this was impossible, but for some reasons unknown to me he

"How can she break up her school for six months to come with you to India?"

"Why not, she can come back before me if she wants!"

"No, no, that cannot work."

They argued for days, but it was clear that my father had made up his mind to go and nothing could make him change it.

I was still too young to think seriously about my future without my father. For me, life would go on and maybe even better without my father's strictness. He was very strict with me like many Punjabi fathers are to their daughters. I was not allowed to show myself in our sitting room for example if there were men guests and he started quarrelling with my mother demandir that I should wear Punjabi clothes to cover mys since I was getting older.

I refused completely claiming that the childr school would laugh at me knowing that I had neve those funny looking trousers under the skirt b Chuneys (a thin cotton or silk material to c head). I was also not allowed to go anywh weekends without my mother or himself a started forbidding me my visits to my br village.

"She will end up like your elder daug say. My sister Mūmbi had become pre was eighteen, and that made my f

They were not in bad terms before, but after that, my father did not even want to see her again. Mũmbi did not marry the man who put her in that condition but married another man later whom she ran away with and left her baby under one year with my mother. The baby was still breastfeeding, and he gave us hell before he got used to bottle feeding. Both my mother and I spent many sleepless nights trying to calm the baby.

My father was so angry with my sister for doing such things like getting a baby on the rocks, leaving her baby behind and running away with another man. I traced her whereabouts which was very difficult since they were hiding themselves until I found them after almost a year. I would go to the village where I was told they stayed and asked from door to door if they knew them.

My mother did not know about this, and many times I got into trouble with my mother wanting to know where I got delayed for so long. I gave her all kinds of excuses, and because she really trusted me, she believed me. I eventually found somebody who knew them and told me that they had moved to other place near the city. She told me that they had moved to Ofafa Kunguni. I would go and wait at the stop near Ofafa until one day she just alighted a bus and found me waiting. That is when she her baby back unwillingly since her husband not want the baby. I confessed to my parents the of my coming late all that time, and they were shocked. Anything could have happened to me, and they wondered where I got such ideas because I was only about 11-13 years old at that time. These were the reasons why my father could not accept Mūmbi again, and in this case, I also could understand his anger. He never talked to her again till he left the country. --------. The whole family was very angry with my sister's behavior.

My mother told me later that when she met my father, Mūmbi was only a small girl and my father loved and spoiled her by buying her all kinds of things. After I was born my sister being a small girl of ten, became very jealous of me knowing that my father would probably love me more being his child. She never got over that jealousness all the years. I came to find that out later and knew why she was so bad to me all those years in the village.

I loved her a lot and wanted to be near her and to learn more from my elder sister, but she never wanted me near her. I remember when I got my first period, I had gone to visit her and I wanted to ask her for an advice. I just could not bring myself to do it. I wa afraid of her knowing for sure she would scold me asked her. She scolded me all the time and critir me for almost everything I did and never taug anything. Njeri was like a small girl becaus sickness, so I could not discuss anything either.

My elder sister, therefore, was the reasons why my father was so protective to me especially now that I was a teenager. He did not want to me to end up like her.

When Kiarie and Mũmbi heard about my father's departure, they came immediately to Nairobi to see my mother.

"How can you let him take all his money with him to India?" I suppose it must have been too late already. In fact, as soon as he got the notice to leave the country which was a year or two earlier, he began his arrangements quietly.

"It is his money! What do you mean? Do you mean I should tell him to leave his money with me?" My mother asked them.

"But Cikũ must finish her school? How will you manage to pay for her education especially if she wants to continue?" Kiarie asked her. My mother laughed sarcastically.

"You talk as if you care about Cikũ's education. God will provide! After all, he has left his business in my hands, and if you all help me to run the business well, we will not have any financial problem." The business had gone down drastically since the Mzungu left whereby his brick business was bringing my father ore profit. Although he wanted to leave everything th my mother, the business was not as good as it s before when the brick factory was running.

The next day both Mūmbi and Kiarie came to pick me up from school in the morning just after the first lesson, without my mother's knowledge. I did not know that my mother was not aware of it. They took me to the immigration office.

"This is our half-sister, and her father wants to leave the country in a few weeks' time and leave her behind without any money for her education. He claims he will return after six months, but we do not believe it because he is an old man." Kiarie explained to the officer in charge that my father had even sold the hotel he had built in Nairobi, therefore, it was obvious he had no plans to come back.

"Where is your mother?" He asked.

"She is at home," Kiarie answered.

"She is the one who should come here with the child's birth certificate to show that the man is indeed her father, and then we can arrange to demand some money from him to be deposited in a bank in his daughter's name. This money would be used to educate his child in case he does not return. If he comes back as he says, he could claim his money back," the officer explained further. My mother would not hear of it.

"How dare you do such a thing without asking r Have you all lost your minds? I will do nothing of th If he wants to leave money for his child's educa' will do it at his own free will. If not, then he will ta money with him. You are not going to do any' it either. Do you want to earn a curse through his anger with all of you and especially his own child because of money? Just forget about it all. Such things cannot bring you anything except trouble latter," she shouted.

"How can you be so foolish as to let him take all that money when you have a chance to stop him?" Mũmbi asked. She always had a sharp and loose tongue even to my mother.

Unlike young African girls having high respect for their parents, Mũmbi would insult my mother or any other person who annoyed her. I remember one day she called my mother "a dog." We were all shocked including herself after she spoke the word out. I think the word just slipped out of her mouth. I waited for an explosion from my mother or for her to break down with tears, but my mother just laughed at her and said; "How stupid can you really be! I have never seen anybody who abuses herself as you do. If I am a dog, what are you then? A dog bears a dog!" She also blessed her by spitting on her breasts, an action she always did when she was angry with us. I was really impressed at this answer that I had to smile, and I saw that my sister was ashamed of herself, but her nature never allowed her to apologize. Nobody could cope with her temper and even my brothers who seemed to be afraid of her outbreaks.

"Do you really want this money to be left behind for kũ, or for yourselves? I know you all and your greed for money. This man has done a lot for all of you. He fed you when your father abandoned you. You never respect him or accepted him to be my husband, and he knows that you all do not love or respect him. He is leaving the country mostly because of these kinds of rejection on your sides. He has been only a money maker for you. I am grateful that he did all he did for you, but are you? If I don't manage to pay for Cikũ's education later, you could all contribute and help. You need to appreciate that she is going to school and doing well and it is for our interest to see her finish her education."

"We have our own children to look after. If you let him take all the money with him, then you must see how you educate your child alone. I will have nothing to do with it," Kiarie said.

"It is alright. If all of you won't help me, God will provide for her. Forget about me going to sign papers against the father of my child to rob him off his wealth for your greed," my mother said finally.

"God helps those who help themselves. It is not fair what he is doing, and you know it. So, you should do something about it while you still can," Mũmbi said furiously. They gave up after they saw that she would not co-operate with their plan. My father did not know anything about these actions.

My father, therefore, left the country and took all his savings which must have been in millions. He sold his hotel which he had built just after independence in Nairobi and took all the money as well. It was a big hotel consisting of a restaurant and logins. We heard that he bought a big farm in Punjabi, District Ludhiana in India and bought tractors and necessary machines for farming. My father could only write in Punjabi language, therefore he always had to look for somebody to assist him in writing to us in English. We received his letters for a while, and after some time, the letters stopped coming.

Despite all other reasons for him to leave the country, I somehow believe that I was one of reasons also. I was very mean to him due to his negligence towards us before while we lived in the village and his behavior towards my mother. For example, one day he repeatedly said that I would end up like my sister Mũmbi because a Kikuyu mother bore me. As I said before, I could not speak Swahili to my father a language he understood better than Kikuyu.

When I was thirteen or fourteen years of age, I do not remember exactly, there were some political incident which had happened, and my father called me one day to listen to the English news in the radio and tell them what they were saying. I listened and translated to them, and suddenly, I was speaking in Swahili without my knowledge. I saw my father looking at me in a very strange way and realized the reason immediately. I was speaking in Swahili addressing him straight for the first time!

The language blockage was broken then, and the problem seemed to have solved itself that way. He was so happy to converse with me straight after that without having my mother tell him what I said. So, on this day I came in the room and angrily told him in perfect Swahili.

"I did not ask you to bear me with a Kikuyu woman! It is not my fault that my mother is a Kikuyu. If all Punjabi are like you, then I am glad that both my parents are not Punjabi!" I stormed out of the house in tears. My mother came after me, but I was faster than her. I went to our garden and climbed up on a mango tree. I did this often when I was angry with my parents. Luckily, I did not see more snakes which my mother reminded me often, though I thought sometimes she just wanted to scare me away from that habit because they could never make me come down till I was ready.

She said all the time that this was a habit for boys to climb trees. My mother followed me to the bottom of the tree, and she was crying. This is something I never wanted to see, my mother's tears caused by my stupidity. Kiarie and Mũmbi had caused her enough tears. I was determined not to make it worse. Still, I stayed up with my guilty feelings.

"Come down Cikũ immediately. How can you tell your father such things! What am I going to do now? I cannot face him for shame. Come down and go and apologise to him, please, I beg you, my child. I know you did not mean to say what you said," she begged.

"Of course, I meant it. He is so mean, and I hate him, and it is true. He does not love me either because I am not a boy. I have heard you discuss it many times." I refused to apologise completely and even refused to sit and eat with him from that day on wards. This surely would break any parent. I was his only child, and he had no more hopes of getting more children. When I grew up, and even today, I regretted those actions even though I committed them when I was a child and believed truly I had the right to remind him that since it was true. I hope and pray that before he died, he might have found a way to understand my stupid childish behavior and forgave me. I did not know what I was doing, and I did not know the details of his life either. The language communication barrier made it impossible for him to talk to me like a father would talk to his daughter. So, I knew very little of him and his family for example. My father, therefore, left for India for good. We all knew he would not come back, except my mother. She believed him that he would return after six months. He never did, and we never saw him again.

Life continued normally for me. I did not miss my father at all; in fact, I felt relieved because I got more freedom than before. I could visit my girlfriends, schoolmates and even spend a night with them something which was impossible before and they could visit me too. I started going to the English movies which I was not usually allowed. We only went to the Indian movies with my father before on Sundays, and I did not understand most of what was going on. I grew to like them, and until today I watch a lot of Indian Bollywood movies. However, it did not take long; I started missing my father when the realization came that my mother had a lot of financial problems, and no one was there to help her and when I realised that my father was truly not coming back.

I was very skinny with a flat chest at the age of sixteen. My hair was long and dark which my mother combed lovingly and tied it in a long tail behind or divided it into two long tails on either side, tied at the ends with silk laces. I hated that hairstyle and thought it was for small girls. I wanted to make nice hairstyles like the other grown-up girls in our school. Due to those regulations of the Singh religion of not cutting any hair in your body, I could not even dare ask my mother before. My father had warned my mother several times never to cut my hair. But now that he was gone, I dared ask her.

"Can I cut my hair short now mama? I hate this long hair!" I said one day.

"What? You seriously want to cut your beautiful hair? Oh my God! You children these days are so foolish. How can you even think of cutting your beautiful long healthy hair and think that you will look better without it? Can't you see how generous God has been to you? Many people envy your hair, and you want to cut it!" I knew that she loved my hair very much and was very proud of it. She combed it every night with coconut oil and morning before I went to school.

"Oh mama, it is so old-fashioned these days to keep long hair," I said

"What is fashion? I will never let you cut that hair. You do not even know how much I suffered with it before when I had no money, and I would draw water for people to get money and instead of buying us a pint of milk, I would buy coconut oil, or paraffin to fight with the lice in your hair. Don't even remind me of those days," she said sadly. I always avoided that kind of discussion, so I left it at that.

"After all your father might come back as he said. Why do you all behave like he is not coming back? What would he say if he finds you with short hair?" she added.

"Ah Mamie, you know that he will not come back. So, stop putting your hopes on that. If he was coming back, he would not have sold his hotel and take all his money." I said.

"Still you should not cut that hair I warn you." She said firmly.

I started cutting my hair though little by little on the forehead to form a pony. Whenever my mother saw any hair hanging out of the tail, she would pin it back to make it grow along with the others. She did not notice that I had gone through it with scissors because I was careful to cut little by little. I continued to cut it until I had enough pony in front. All these I learned from the older girls in our school. I also learned to shorten my school skirt as soon as I left home every morning to make it a mini.

My mother was not very strict, but I still respected her, and I was conscious of many things I was not allowed to do when my father was around and which she still tried to maintain. Soon after these ideas got into my head, my body also began to form another shape, my breasts started shooting out of my chest, and I started becoming shapely. I also noticed my interest in boys which I never had before etc.

Sex theme was taboo in African culture. Children were never explained about anything about sex at all. I learned these facts later that, according to Kikuyu tradition, these lessons were given to boys and girls during the circumcision ceremonies. Some special men and women were supposed to give these lessons to the group of the youth who were circumcised. They were taken to a special camp and stayed there for weeks learning all there was to it.

Since these traditions had almost disappeared and no circumcision ceremonies performed any longer, the sex education also seemed to disappear. The circumcision for the boys continue till today, but it is mostly done in hospitals, so no more traditional ceremonies are done. Therefore, like many girls of my age, I knew almost nothing about sex, marriage, childbirth, etc.

The government had just passed a law that sex education should be taught in schools. The teachers especially in such a school as I was in, which had a very strict Islam tradition, mentioned a few things about sex here and there but not clear. The school organised one day for us to see a movie which was called "Helga," a German movie about childbirth.

I have never been shocked as that day, to discover for the first time the fact where and how childbirth comes about. I felt the pain myself just watching it. I never imagined that a baby comes out of a woman that way. I could not imagine a baby's head coming out of a woman's virginals, leave alone the whole baby. When I went home, I could not help staring at my mother many times imagining how I could have come out of her body like that. That poor woman! And not only me but 8 children she had borne came out the same way. How did she survive all those pains? I felt so much pity and the fact that we were not very nice to her, especially my elder spinster.

My mother caught me several times staring at her in a deep thought.

"Why are you forming a habit of staring at me like that Cikū? What are you thinking about?" I could not bring the words into my mouth. I had thousands of questions to ask her, but I could not dare ask even one. I knew that this subject was taboo and she would never discuss with me such things, or so I thought.

Although my mother often helped to deliver babies in the village as a traditional midwife and she delivered all her grandchildren so far, I only heard the stories of the delivery by mistake as she told the neighbours, she never explained to us anything in details about it. In fact, she knew about traditional baby birth and all there was to it, and no baby died during her midwifery performances as she boasted proudly. But talking about what I saw in the film, never!

My sister Mũmbi lived in Nairobi city with her husband, and she had two more children, although her marriage was not working well at all. The drunkard husband was very irresponsible. He spent all his money in bars with other women and let my sister support the family with the little salary she got from the City Council where she was working as an office messenger. He still did not like Mũmbi's oldest child and mistreated him a lot. Therefore, I made a point of visiting them often because he was always afraid of mistreating the boy in front of me since he knew I would not let it.

The boy had also grown very much attached to me, and I always felt very close to him. I suppose this was because of the time I spent with him when his mother abandoned him. I made a point of being there on school holidays when he had night duties, where he would be alone with the housemaid and the children during the day. My mother knew what was going on, so she let me go there often. I had fought with him several times trying to stop him from beating the boy. He also had a habit of wanting to sleep with the housemaids, and most of them were afraid of him. He was somehow terrified of me and did not misbehave when I was there.

During those visits, I met Jennifer who was working as a housemaid near my sister's house. She was a very beautiful girl, full of life. She told me about her boyfriend and promised to take me out with her one weekend to meet him. She was much older than me, she cleared many of my questions since she liked to talk to me, and she taught me a lot of things I did not know. We, therefore, planned to go out one weekend together. My mother thought I was at my sister's place, and my sister thought I was at home. That was one of the advantages of not having telephones at home in those days.

This was my first outing at night in Nairobi city at the age of seventeen. It looked so different than the city I knew during the day, with all the colourful lights, neon lights shinning all over the tall buildings, etc. George Thĩnĩ, Jennifer's boyfriend, knew exactly where he was taking us. He had a car and drove us around the city before he stopped outside the Lobster Pot Restaurant. He was a big man, very handsome and charming, full of humour that made me laugh the whole night.

He loved Jim Reeves music, and he could sing almost all of them and so could I, so we sang a lot in the car together. He worked in a big Tobacco company in Nairobi as a sales manager, therefore he earned good money. I had only seen the Lobster Pot Restaurant from outside during the daytime and was shocked when I got inside.

There were Wazungu all over having dinner. We were directed to a table, and Thĩnĩ seemed to know the waiters there. They all greeted him warmly calling him by his name. After dinner, he took us for a drink at the Hilton Hotel and later to a nightclub "1900". I had never enjoyed my life so much before this evening.

"I cannot believe that people have been enjoying themselves so much in this city, while I just slept and had no idea about it," I exclaimed excitedly when I saw the nightclub.

"You are still young Cikũ, and you will even see more and better things than this," Thĩnĩ said, "Just don't be in a hurry."

I was naturally a good dancer. I only watched people dancing for a while, and I confidently tried out the same. We also held small parties in school often, and I noticed my flexibility when dancing. Thĩnĩ liked to dance, but Jenifer did not like dancing at all. So, I danced a lot with Thĩnĩ. I was so happy that I wished the evening would go on forever. I did not drink alcohol, but I was like a drunkard person.

The young man who was singing in the club took notice of me immediately and asked me later for a dance when he left the stage to somebody else. I thought I was dreaming and wished the dream would go on. We danced the whole break with him, and he just held me tight, whispering things like; "You dance very well; you are so pretty!" etc. It was my very first time to be in a man's arms like that, and it made me kind of scared. He went back to the stage to sing, and I went back to my friends.

"Hey, I did not bring you out to get involved with musicians. Those are completely wrong people to associate with, my dear girl," Thĩnĩ said.

"I think you are very old-fashioned. I just danced with the man! He did not ask me for marriage if that is what you are afraid of."

"I saw the way he "danced" with you."

"Leave Cikũ alone! Let her enjoy her evening without your silly comments," said Jenifer.

The man came and sat with us during his next break. He talked to Thĩnĩ, but he kept on looking at me and sometimes winking at me which made me very shy and had butterflies in my stomach.

"We have a music competition next Saturday at the university hall," he said looking at me. "Why don't you all come. It will be a lot of fun. All the bands in Nairobi will be taking part, and I count on every vote I could get", he gave us some advertisements' reflects.

I looked at Thĩnĩ and Jenifer excitedly. They were my only hope. I could not imagine going to such a place on my own.

"Please, please . . . Thĩnĩ . . . Jennifer?" I begged.

The boy smiled and looked at me.

"I can take you there if they don't want to come," he said.

"You could, that so? That sounds like a date," Thĩnĩ said sarcastically. We both looked down. Thĩnĩ was much older than all of us. In fact, he looked like the men who are called "sugar daddies" who normally are married but want to have fun with young girls. But fortunately for Jennifer, he was not married, and he called himself before he met her a "confirmed bachelor."

"OK. We will come if you promise to get us a wonderful place to sit and watch all of you in action," Thĩnĩ said.

"You only have to come early to get a good seat," the singer said.

When the man left Thĩnĩ started with his moral speech again. He had had quite a lot to drink by then.

"You know Cikũ, I met you today, and I like you a lot. You are quite a smart child, and I would not like to be guilty of showing you all these which could open the door to hell for you. These musicians are good for nothing. They are not for you. Promise me that you will not fall in love with him and we shall go on Saturday, otherwise count me out," he said.

"My God you sound like my elder brother," I said.

"I am representing him personally right now. If you don't listen to me, I will look for that "elder brother" of yours and hand you over. Listen, honey, I am not joking. You must finish your school first before you get mixed up with junks like these." I had a feeling he hated the man though he was very friendly to him.

"OK. I promise not to fall in love with him," I said raising my fingers up.

"Good girl!" he said sighing heavily from alcohol.

"Man, this guy is a bore sometimes. Don't listen to him. He is too old-fashioned," Jennifer whispered in my ear.

"Jennifer, I am right, and you know it. It has nothing to do with alcohol. I am not drunk!" He said guessing what Jennifer must have whispered to me.

"Did I say that?" Jennifer asked, and we both laughed.

"Ach, forget it," Thĩnĩ said waving his hand.

That week was one of the longest I had ever come across. I bought a new dress, bought some makeup and booked myself at a hairdressing salon for Saturday morning. I was determined to look my best. The hairdresser was a very friendly lady and knew her work perfectly. She helped me choose a hairstyle to suit my face without cutting my hair. She also liked my hair a lot and could not understand why I was complaining about it being so long.

She helped me put on makeup after my hair was done. Finally, I stood in front of a full mirror, and really, I could not recognise the person looking back at me in that mirror. I could not believe that I indeed, was the one looking back at myself. The person in the mirror was so beautiful and looked so different that it was impossible to believe that somebody can change her appearance so much. My mother would not have recognised me.

"Wow, you mean that is me," I said pointing at myself in the mirror.

"Yes darling, you must know that you are a young miss now, therefore you should know how to look after your beauty. I told you, you have beautiful hair if you know how to go about with it," said the hairdresser who seemed to be very satisfied with her creation.

I finished at the hairdressers at around three o'clock. I still had some hours before the evening came. I was supposed to meet Thĩnĩ and Jennifer at 6.30. I was afraid that the wind and dust would spoil my hairstyle. I could neither go home nor to my sister's place the way I looked. So, I decided to go and watch a movie. After the movie, I went to the meeting point and arrived right on time, and neither Thĩnĩ nor Jennifer recognised me at first. When I sat next to them, that is when they recognised me and both stared at me with their mouths wide open.

"Don't worry; I could not recognise myself either!" I said laughing. "Say something, Jennifer. Do I look good?" I asked Jennifer. They looked at each other.

"Jesus, you don't look good, you look gorgeous!" Jennifer said excitedly.

"Now I am really afraid to take you there. If that musician friend of yours sets his eyes on you, that will be the end of school," Thĩnĩ said shaking his head.

"Oh please, Thĩnĩ, give me a break. The man will be so busy with the competition for sure he will not pay attention to me. Most probably he has forgotten all about me," I said.

"I can see that you have gone through all the trouble to make that man crazy. Huh! Women, no matter what age, you are all the same. The poor guy's eyes will come out of their sockets today when he sees you," Thĩnĩ said laughing. We ignored him and went to the lady's powder room to chat more about my new look.

We had a quick dinner and left early to get a seat at a good place, and we managed just that. I did not see the man until he came to sing at the stage. There were about ten bands which were competing, and his band was one of the well-known, therefore came almost at the end with the other two of the best. We had received a list of ten competitor bands at the entrance, and his name was number eight. The number seven though was very good and he was cheered the most, and I liked him too. He did a James Brown number dancing exactly like him, which made the audience go wild myself included. So, I tipped the number seven. Thĩnĩ was very surprised, and they tipped the same as well. I had never seen the man in my life before, but we liked the way he performed his shows. He had the best voice too. He won the first price, and our friend became number three. I came to learn later that they were big rivals both in music and women! They both came from Mombasa as well.

Suddenly, I did not want to see the musician friend. After the announcements were made about the winners, we took off. Thĩnĩ was just too glad to leave. What Thĩnĩ did not know was that I had fallen in love with another musician. We went home to Thĩnĩ's house where we spent the night, and I just could not stop thinking about the young man who had performed so wonderfully. I started practicing the new dancing style which was soul music at that time. Every Saturday morning while I cleaned our house, there was a teenager program which brought all the top ten records on the music chart. I practiced in front of the mirror on a wet floor until I was satisfied that I could dance and slide on the floor like the man on the stage who had won the cup. I almost broke my legs many times trying the James Brown sliding styles, but in the end, I got it.

I heard about the afternoon "boogies" (afternoon dancing clubs for teenagers) in school, and we made a date with my classmate to go there. Josephine, my classmate, had just joined the school, and we became very good friends as well. Her sister Ann who was almost the same age attended a different school, and the three of us teamed up together at the weekends.

I started avoiding Thĩnĩ and Jennifer who were too busy planning their wedding. I was supposed to be Jennifer's best bridesmaid which I agreed. I had no idea that the man who had won the competition was to be the singer in that teenager's club where we had planned to go. I was shocked when I saw him standing on the stage singing a James Brown "Say it loud, I am black and proud" number. I had not told Josephine or Ann about him. My heart started beating so fast that I was afraid of going any further. I stood at the door watching him. I could not afford to go to the hairdresser that day, but I had let my hair loose at the back and formed a small beehive on top with a pony in front. I looked pretty good too.

The three of us went to the dance floor, and I noticed people looking at me including the singer himself! It seemed that I had practiced well. The band was singing soul music and blues, which the man who won sang and African music which was sang by somebody else. I could not trust myself to dance African music then in public because I was very shy. So, when the

African music started, I left the hall and went outside for fresh air. I stood outside the dancing hall looking through a window. The man came and touched my shoulder.

"You dance very well," he said.

"Oh, thank you! You sing very well too. I saw you at the university hall competition recently, and I voted for you!" I said

"You did!, Oh thanks a lot," he said smiling at me, the sweetest smile on a man I had ever seen so far. He was a very handsome young man. I was so nervous I did not know what to do with my hands. He noticed it and smiled.

"My name is Faruk. What is your name?" He asked.

"I am Alice" I answered quickly.

"Nice name. I am very glad to meet you, Alice. You are very beautiful, and you dance wonderfully."

"Thank you. Nice to meet you too," I said looking down.

"I have never seen you here before!"

"This is my first time to come here."

"Oh, I see, I hope to see you more often then," "*I bet you will!*", I said to myself, and he left to go to the gents.

The next weekend, when we arrived, we met him at the gate, and he ordered that we enter without paying. He was rushing to the stage to sing; therefore, I could not talk or even thank him. After he finished, he came straight where we were sitting and took my hand. I thought he wanted to dance, but he pulled me outside the hall. When we were alone, he just pulled me in his arms and kissed me!! I was so shocked; I wanted to slap him. I had never been kissed on my mouth before. He had put his tongue right through my mouth almost choking me. When he saw the fear in my eyes, he let me go. I ran to the lady's powder room, and he followed me right inside.

"Get out of here," I shouted at him

"Please forgive me. I am so sorry. I did not mean to upset you. I have just been thinking about you the whole week, and I almost went crazy."

"Get out!! Somebody will find you in here." He left but waited for me outside. Josephine came in then and just saw him come out of the lady's powder room.

"Hey what is going on?" I had started crying then, and my whole body was shaking.

"He . . . he . . . kissed me," I said sobbing

"Here in the toilet?" Josephine also shocked asked.

"Oh no, no, outside. He just followed me in here to apologise," I said tears running down my face and ruining my makeup.

"Then why are you crying? I wouldn't mind if he kissed me! All the girls are crazy about him. You should be celebrating you silly. He is the best musician in Kenya today! Wow!! Faruk Brown kissed you!" she said

"Give me a break," I said knowing that I was in hot soup.

After that weekend, I could not think of anything else except him and his rough kiss. What surprised me is that I wanted him to do it again if only more gently. He seemed to have been afraid of my reaction and avoided touching me again. He asked me to dance with him several times but did not say a word to me. When he was on the stage singing, his eyes were always fixed on me. I had no idea then that I had met with my fate even before my adult life had started!

CHAPTER FIVE

I took part in a teenager's dancing competition in those afternoon boogies, and I won the first price. I, therefore, got a chance to take part in a bigger competition which was to take place in a big club in Nairobi. The only problem was that the competition was taking place on the same day Thĩnĩ and Jennifer were getting married.

Before that I had never been to a dancing club except that first night I went with Thĩnĩ and Jennifer, despite Faruk's unsuccessful attempts to date me in the evenings several times. I knew that many girls were after him, some even from our school, and so I was a bit scared of meeting them all in the club where they were all running to try their luck with him. He called them his fans, but I knew that he had affairs with most of them. In any case, I agreed to go with him to the club that competition day, but I explained to him about the wedding and that I would join him in the club later that night. The competition was to take place after midnight.

We were busy with the wedding from Thursday till Saturday evening, and I was bone tired after the wedding and being the best maid. But I had to go to the competition. I had told Thĩnĩ and Jennifer about it, and they knew how involved I had become with dancing. So, they agreed to let me go during the wedding evening party. I just appeared at the wedding evening party and left immediately. Thĩnĩ got somebody to drive me with a motorbike to the club. I found Faruk in the club alright but sitting next to one of my schoolmates, who was in her final year, his hands on her shoulders. Before he could see me, I went to sit somewhere else where he could not see me and waited for the competition to begin.

When the competition started, my name was called out, and so I went in front, and that is when he saw me. I had a partner who had also won the first price on male's side. I danced my best despite my tiredness and won the first price again. He came in front and took me in his arms and kissed me in front of everybody. From then on, our relationship was confirmed.

He took me to his home after the dance, because I could not go to my sister's place neither to my mother's at such an hour of the night. Everybody thought that I was at the wedding. I told him that I had never been with a man before in a room alone and that I was not yet ready to sleep with him. He tried to convince me, but when I refused completely, he let me sleep in his bed while he slept on the sofa.

We had small dates after that, and we would go to the movies and of course, meeting every Saturday at the

Boogie clubs, but he was always very gentle with me. He never tried to kiss me again forcefully. At the end of the year, there was another even bigger competition than the one I had attended before and this time they wanted to choose "Mister" and "Miss" Soul. Of course, as a winner of the previous one, I took part and Faruk was the one singing for the competitors. I won the first price again with a lot of votes and both Faruk, and I were in the newspapers, Faruk being the best soul music singer and I, the best dancer in soul music.

The title red "Mister and Miss soul." That night I had my first experience in sex as I agreed to his pleading, breaking my virginity and that same night, I got pregnant. This is how unfair life could sometimes be. I had no idea about family planning, and I did not dream of getting pregnant on the first time.

After some weeks, I discovered about my situation, and even worse, Faruk was married before in Mombasa, and he had three children. All these came out because of the picture in the newspaper where we were together. I had appeared in several newspapers during that month, including a Swahili magazine cover page "Nyota." I had many schoolmates from Mombasa, and when they saw my picture with Faruk, they all came to me and told me about his true-life history.

You could see my picture all over in newspaper stands on the streets of Nairobi. I remember Josephine my girlfriend making a joke over this one day that I was competing with our president Mzee Jomo Kenyatta, who would come in the newspapers first the next day. I had a lot of problems in school and with my mother because of these newspaper publications. She knew nothing about my dancing or competitions, and how was I to explain this to an old mother in her 60s? However, one day she came in the evening and called me urgently.

"Look at this and explain to me all about it," she said throwing the magazine at me. I looked at the magazine as if it was my first time to see it. Since the magazine came out, I was afraid of her discovery and the questioning. I knew that even if she did not discover it herself, my sister Mũmbi would tell her and truly she was indeed the one who informed her and bought the magazine to show it to my mother. She was always trying her best to catch me on anything to report to my mother.

It looked to me like she did not want to remain the only black sheep of the family. She reported me on any small thing she knew or suspected about me. She had told my mother that I had a very old man as a boyfriend, because I met her several times in Nairobi city with Thĩnĩ alone going shopping for their wedding.

She thought Thĩnĩ was my boyfriend. I wished she could have come to me as a big sister and ask me first, but she aimed to spoil my relationship with my mother whom she thought and claimed loved me more than her. I explained to my mother who Thĩnĩ was and even invited them both to meet my mother. When she showed me the magazine cover, I obviously tried to dodge the question with my teenage foolishness.

"Oh! She is a nice-looking girl. Her hairstyle is just like mine." I had managed to cut my hair into a short Afro-style which suited me very well but which made my mother shed tears. Having had thick, strong Indian like hair, I achieved an equally strong afro-style exactly like that of Angela Davies, but my mother just hated it. I could not help sometimes laughing later in life, when I did the same thing with my children when they preferred crazy hairstyles, and it reminded me of my mother's anger about cutting my hair. I think her tears cursed my hair because since then, my hair does not grow longer than shoulder length anymore.

"She does not only have your hairstyle; she has your name too. Open the first page and see it for yourself," she said sarcastically. My mother could read Swahili and Kikuyu language though not very fluent. I have no idea who taught her how to read and write in Swahili. But I also knew that my mother was a tough person and very courageous. "Oh, you are right," I said still trying to fool her, she shook her head twisting her lips, and I knew the game had come to an end.

"Stop that Cikũ, I know it is you. All I want to know is what is "Miss Soul"? Have you got married secretly without telling me? I have always trusted you, how could you do such things behind my back?" She mistook it with Mrs.

"Of course, not mama, we just won a competition together. It is written Mr. and Miss soul. Miss is unmarried woman mama." I tried to explain.

"When do you do these things, and learn at the same time?" She was shouting now.

I had to tell her most of the truth except the deep relationship with Faruk. I told her that we were just the winners of the competition and that is why we were photographed together. She warned me to stop all those nonsense and concentrate on my school work, and if she heard any other thing about that damn "soul," she would call my elder brother to work on me. Her statement was so weakly spoken that I felt her desperation of not knowing what to do. I think she had to threaten me somehow and the only threat which came in her mind was my brother. She knew that I did not fear him at all and I would never listen to him anyway.

In fact, I felt that my elder brother and sister were happy to hear that I was on the wrong barn already and I was sure none of them would waste time to talk any morals to me. I apologised in tears and agreed with her knowing what shit I had already put myself into.

How could I tell her or even the man whom I slept with only once that I had become pregnant? He would never believe me. How could I let my mother down like this? It looked like I did not respect her at all but respected my father since I never did such things while he was still there. Why did I agree to go with Faruk on that night? And how could the nature be so cruel with me in a sense that, the first time I had my sex experience which was so painful, I become pregnant? I did not even enjoy it because of the pain. Thousands of questions were swirling round my head without an answer.

I stopped going to the boogies and one of my schoolmates who was in her final year helped me to have an abortion after I told her my problems. Nobody knew about it at home. Faruk came looking for me, but I told him that our relationship was over. I did not tell him about the pregnancy at all. He was surprised about my sudden reaction towards him and could not understand why. After the abortion, I concentrated fully on my school work and luckily all what I had gone through did not affect my school results.

I never stopped thinking about him, but I knew, like Thĩnĩ told me that I had fallen in love with the wrong person and I had to fight against that feeling. I could not believe that he was married. He looked so young, and according to him, he was under twenty. So how could he have three children unless he had cheated about his age which was all over in the newspapers?

Later, when we met again, he admitted being married but said that he was separated from her. He tried to explain himself that he started music business when he was very young, and his father forced him into an arranged marriage knowing that his carrier might take him away from them. His father thought he would tie him down with a wife and children. According to him, he could not deal with the situation, and after some years he left Mombasa and went to Uganda. He was not successful there, and he decided to come back to Kenya but try his luck in Nairobi where I met him. I did not believe his stories, but that did not stop me from loving him either.

My sister Mũmbi had separated from her husband and came to live with us. The second eldest brother Mũkiri also came with his wife and children to live with us. My mother let Mũkiri run my father's business, which he ruined completely. They all turned against me because my mother was still trying her best to give me all that I needed materially, trying to keep the standard I was used to before my father left. My second brother Mũkiri loved me, but my sister Mũmbi poisoned his mind completely against me, so he also worked on my mother against me.

"You do not have to give her so much pocket money. Other children take their lunch with them to school," Mũkiri said one day. She gave me 5 shillings for bus fare and lunch every day. When my father was there, I usually got 10 shillings which I demanded from him but gave my mother half of it every day. Mũkiri said one shilling was enough for bus fare which was about 50 cents one way. We stayed in school until 3-4 o'clock, and when I got home, it was well over 5 p.m. He said other children carried their lunch with them, so I should do the same. Usually, my lunch was only some scones and a small packet of milk and some fruits. I sometimes bought some mangoes which were sold by the Indians with pilipili to eat on the way home too. I then enjoyed my mother's Indian dishes in the evenings.

"Why should I do that, so that you can have the money yourself? This business was left by her father because of her so all of you must respect that," my mother shouted back. No matter what financial situation, my mother gave me my 5 shillings every day. They all hated me for this.

Mūmbi became most aggressive towards me even more than she had been in the village. My mother always came between us knowing that her jalousies towards me made her so mean to me and she would end up calling my mother names which made me very sad. My home became almost unbearable. There was a quarrel of some kind every day between my mother, Mūkiri, and Mūmbi and every time it was about money. I felt that my sister was also trying her best to distract me from my studies.

She kept on complaining that she did not go to school and blaming my mother for not educating her. My mother became very sad about all those quarrels, and it began to affect my school performance which was crucial because I was now doing my final year. There was no money to pay for my school fees anymore. All of them refused to help my mother to meet my school expenses, and the business went down completely. I was thrown out of school three months before my final examinations due to a long-pending unpaid school fees. I begged Kiarie my elder brother to pay for the school fees which was pending, but he refused completely.

The person I pitied most was my mother. She suffered the most with all these problems, and I simply did not know how to help her. If only she had not brought them to live with us, but they were her children, and she thought they might help her with the business which would have been a help to all of us. Instead, they ruined it completely through their material greed. My mother whom I have never seen sick began to complain about a few things like her eyes or tiredness. I would find her always holding her head between her hands in deep thoughts, a picture which made me so sad till today when I remember it. I could not bear to see her like that and knowing that I could not do anything to ease her pains. So, I made up my mind to go away and look for a job.

I could not stay with my family anymore. My poor mother was suffering so much, and I felt completely helpless. My brother Mūkiri became so money hungry that he was selling everything he could lay his hands on, especially the spare parts of the lorry which my father left for business. Luckily, I got a job in a hotel as a receptionist, and they offered to give me a room in the hotel, food, and six hundred shillings a month. I took the offer up immediately since it was the best there was so far hoping to look for greener pastures as time went on. I intended to do further studies in the evenings after work, or at least get secretarial training.

Faruk heard about me working in the hotel, and he visited me. He begged me so much to see him till I agreed to meet him in my room later after work. He told me he had divorced his wife in a Moslem way and that he would like to marry me. I refused and told him that I wanted to concentrate on my future, and I had no plans of getting married. He did not know anything about the trouble he had put me through, and I had no intention of telling him then.

What good would it have done? He begged me so much telling me that he loved me which put a heavy impact on me since I still loved him. So eventually I told him to give me time to think about it. Two weeks later, he came and told me that he got a job in Ethiopia for one year and he would like to marry me before he left to make sure that I would wait for him.

I refused to tell him that I could wait for him as he wanted. I told him he should go and when he comes back, then we would see if we still felt the same for each other. Although my mother also thought it was time for me to get married because she was afraid of me living alone in such a big city, I thought I was still too young to think of marriage. Deep down in me, I knew it was not right, so I ignored my mother's suggestion completely and refused Faruk's marriage proposal despite his begging and insisting. He made me promise to wait for him which I did in the end.

While he was gone, I went out with several boys, but there was nothing serious. I loved Faruk with all my heart, and no matter how I tried to get involved with other boys, it never worked. I believe strongly on the saying about the first love. It is not easy to get over it. Thĩnĩ, Jennifer, and all my friends were very sympathetic with me, knowing how much I was suffering, both in love life and at home. My head did not want Faruk, but my heart was dying for him.

I registered in a typing course after working in the hotel for three months. The job in the hotel was not the right thing for me. I needed something more creative, so I decided to start looking for a job during the day when I was free. I decided to enter every office and ask for a job. I first went to my knees and asked God to guide me to an excellent job. The first office I entered was motor vehicles Company, dealers for Mazda's, BMW and Tata trucks from India.

"I would like to see the personnel Manager," I told the receptionist.

"Do you have an appointment?" She asked me.

"No!"

"What do you want to see him about?" She asked.

"It is personal," I answered confidently.

"What is your name please?"

"My name is Alice Wanjiku." I never used my surname in Kenya. If anybody insisted on knowing it, then I gave my father's first name "Sunder" which sounded so nice to me than "Mangat" and the fact that my father had told me that his first name meant "beauty." She took the phone and spoke for a while.

"Please have a seat for a moment; he will see you now." I could not believe my luck.

The personnel manager turned out to be the ugliest Luo guy I had ever set my eyes on. Many Luo men are not particularly gorgeous looking at least not as far as my opinion is concerned, but this one was extraordinarily ugly and fat. He looked like a gorilla wearing clothes. He looked at me with hungry red eyes while shaking my hand, breathing heavily due to his fat belly. I knew what was coming. I had heard of the difficulties of looking for a job as a young girl in Nairobi. I hated those older men who always wanted to take advantage of desperate young girls. I had discussed this issue with many of my friends who had gone through such experiences.

"Please have a sit, what can I do for you?" He asked me. He sat down himself trying to hide his huge stomach under his jacket, and almost busting his shirt buttons. He had a very bad odour which filled the whole office.

"I am looking for a job sir," I said.

"What kind of job are you looking for?"

"Any job, I am not choosy," I said as if I could do all.

"Can you type?"

"Yes, I can," I lied. I had been in a secretarial school for almost a month and attending only twice a week. Therefore, at that time I could hardly type.

"We are looking for a copy typist right now, so if you can type, we might have a job for you."

"Sure, I can type."

"Please wait outside, and I will tell my secretary to give you a little test on typing to see how fast you can type." Oh God! Now I was in a fix.

The secretary was a Kikuyu lady, much older than me and when I sat in front of the typewriter, I just stared at it.

"You are supposed to type not admire my typewriter," she said.

"Listen my elder sister; I want this job, no, I need it desperately. Could you please help me?"

"How do you want me to help you?" She asked smiling, showing her beautiful set of teeth with a gap in the middle.

"Can you type for me and tell him that I did it? I have just started learning to type, and I really cannot type fast yet, but I promise you to learn day and night and do my work well." The lady burst out laughing. I began to cry.

"Hey, hey, that is not necessary. But how do you expect me to type for you and lie to my boss? If you get the job, who is going to type the work for you?" She asked seriously.

"Leave that to me. I promise you I will make it." I said wiping my tears.

"But we need a typist immediately."

"Oh, Miss please help me get this job. I will never forget you for this," I begged her. She pushed me out of the chair shaking her head and typed a paragraph from the letter I was supposed to type. I could only stand there watching with my mouth open to see the speed she was typing with. Will I ever be able to type so fast like that? I thought to myself. She pulled the paper proudly from the machine and gave it to me. I went with the paper to the manager. He spoke in the intercom machine and called her in.

"How do you find her typing?" He asked his secretary. We looked at each other.

"She is alright except she is not very fast. But I expect she will gain her speed soon." "God bless you," I said in my heart. "There are indeed kind people in this world. God directed me to this office today for sure". The Bible says; "*Ask, and it will be given to you*" I asked for help from the kind lady and she helped me though she did not know me. *"Knock, and the door will be opened to you."* I knocked at the office, and there I was sitting in front of the personnel manager. I started learning quickly that having faith in God makes everything possible, though I felt guilty of remembering this important fact only when I was in trouble. I hardly made it to church on Sundays.

"Thank you, Rachel, that is, all," he said to his secretary. After she had left the office, the man said to me.

"I think we could offer you the job, but there are a few things to be discussed. The General Manager has travelled, and he will be back within a week. He has the final word, but I am sure he will agree with my choice. Maybe we can meet this evening and discuss the rest of the details." I was waiting for that. This gorilla thought I could go out with him? It was true indeed this game was known to all the women in Nairobi looking for jobs. All men seemed to know the desperation of women in job search and obviously took advantage of it. I needed the job alright, but I was not yet so desperate. Well, I was well informed, and I was going to play his game to a certain extent. If he thought he was smarter than me, he had another thought coming. After all, he said he was not the decision maker.

"Why not, I would be delighted, but this evening it will not be possible. My boyfriend lives in Magadi, and he is coming today for some meeting or something. I have promised to meet him, so maybe we can make it another time if you do not mind." I said giving my most sincere smile and made it sound like I was looking forward to going out with him to get the job. It was true that I was dating someone working in Magadi and who stayed in our hotel every time he was in Nairobi, so he came into my mind. I was however not expecting him that weekend. It worked.

"When is your boyfriend going back?"

"I hope in a day or two. I will call you when he leaves."

"Ok my dear, I will wait for your call." The stress in "my dear" was clear to confirm to me that he had truly believed that I would go out with him. I knew the General Manager was due on the following Monday, and that was Wednesday. I called him on Monday morning.

"Oh! I am so sorry, but my boyfriend stayed on during the weekend, so I could not meet you," I lied. I had to make sure that he believed that I was committed to someone else. Not that it mattered to those kinds of men, but it was worth a try.

"OK. That is alright maybe we can meet another time. The General Manager is coming to the office today, so I would suggest you come over anytime today."

The General Manager turned out to be a very nice Indian man, and he hired me immediately. Of course,

I had made myself look like a top model in Nairobi. He asked me if I could do some modelling for their cars and I agreed. I started work the same week. I moved out of the hotel and stayed with Rachel, the secretary who helped me to get the job. She offered me to stay with her while I look for a place of my own and we became very close friends despite our age difference. Later when she saw that I was not a bad person, she offered to share the flat with me, and we could share the rent. It was the best opportunity since I was not earning much. Rachel became like my elder sister I always wished for. She gave me all kinds of advices I needed. She was the same age as my sister Mũmbi, but very different in character.

I made a lot of effort to learn everything in the office. I never went out for lunch but sat in front of the typewriting machine and practised. I learned how to operate a telephone switchboard, telex, and I gained my typing speed within no time. Rachel was surprised with my efforts and was glad to have helped me. Everybody in the office was happy with me, and they all liked and treated me like the baby of the company since I was the youngest, except the personnel manager. After I got the job, I refused to go out with him completely telling him that I could not go out with my boss. He was so mad at me after he realised my trick and started picking on me, writing me warning memos which were groundless. The general manager noticed it, and he called me in his office.

"How come you do not get along with the personnel manager? Everybody else is happy with your work including our customers, especially on the telephone except the Personnel Manager. Is there something I should know?"

I told him the whole story about how I tricked him. He laughed his head off. The General Manager also liked the way I worked hard to fit in everywhere. I could relieve all the girls in the office and do their jobs almost perfectly. I was the favourite of all our customers, at the reception and on the telephone switchboard.

"You are a smart girl Alice, and I feel you have a bright future. Don't worry he will not bother you anymore. I have heard the same complains from other girls in the office as well. This is not the first time." Rachel had told me how he harassed her too before.

He got a memo himself warning him not to date the girls in the office. He hated me from then on but knew he could not do anything about it. I had established myself in the office.

While I was working in the car company, I met a man who was much older than me. He was one of the best customers for our company. He had a very good post with the then E.A. Airways, and he was a good-looking man, always driving posh cars from our company. He was half Luo and half Luhya. He liked me a lot, and eventually, he told me that he loved me and if I could go out with him. I had a very special feeling for him, but after being with him for almost half a year, I came to discover that he was married, a fact he never told me. He made me believe all the time that he lived with his colleague who was a Tanzanian, and because the guy was a pilot, he was on the way all the time. I also travelled out of Nairobi a lot with him, like visiting his parents in Kakamega and he came to our place of work most of the time. We flew several times to Mombasa. I was very furious with him, and within no time I made another discovery. He was married to two wives who lived together with his eight children. We had a big quarrel about it, and I decided to stop the affair immediately. He had introduced me to his parents as his fiancée and told them that he wanted to marry me. They all kept his secret from me. How could I marry a man with already two wives? I thought he was crazy.

The man was not only good looking but very well known in Kenya because he drove in the most famous Kenya Safari Rally. At that time, it was called "East African Safari rally," later it changed to "Kenya Safari Rally. He even took me once with him to survey the roads before the rally. It was a crazy trip, and I swore never to go with him again. He drove fast and daring in our then very bad roads in Kenya and in the rough roads where the rally was to take place that I thought we would never make it home again.

At the same time, Faruk came back from Ethiopia. He came looking for me and found me with the help of my friends. When I saw him, I noticed that nothing had changed about my feelings for him. I loved him, and nothing could change that. So, I was lying to myself thinking that I could be happy with someone else. With the quarrel with my boyfriend, it was easy therefore to break up the relationship and start afresh with Faruk. After a month of his return, I discovered that I was pregnant. Faruk was very happy and warned me about any abortion. After seeing the doctor, I was not sure anymore who among the two men was the father, and I told him. He was disappointed, but we decided that we wait until the baby was born and it did not matter whether it was his or not. After all, he had children himself with other women.

My mother had started getting serious about me getting married and persisted that she did not like the idea of me living alone in such a big city. Despite the confusion in my life, I decided indeed to have my baby no matter who the father was. After all, I was afraid of yet another abortion. The previous one gave me a lot of bad consciences I could not dare do it again no matter what situation I found myself in. This was the biggest sin I think I ever committed to my Creator and I regret it very much.

"I will be happy to know that you are married, other than staying alone in this big city Cikũ. After all, I am getting old, and I would like to see your children before I die."

"Mama, don't talk about dying. You are not going to die. I am still too young to get married, and you are not too old, and you look strong and healthy enough." I did not dare tell her that her grandchild was already on the way yet. I did not know how to answer the questions which would have followed, so I decided to keep quiet. She came to know about it much later. Of course, she asked me who the father was, and I told her not to ask me such questions again, and that I would tell her at my own time. I loved my mother for the trust she always showed towards her children and especially me. I never saw her panic the way I do if my children do something wrong. She was always calm and never complained much like I do. Maybe the fact that she was much older and mature at my birth made a difference not to mention of her wisdom which God blessed her with generously. My elder sister and brother treated her very bad and never taught their children to love her. They all never come to visit her nor were they interested in her whatsoever. They came only when they needed something from my mother. I pity all her grandchildren who were not allowed to discover and value what a courageous, strong and wise grandmother they had.

I got a baby girl and named her after my mother according to the Kikuyu tradition. I refused to see both men while I was pregnant and Faruk did not even know when I got the baby. I had moved out of the place I was staying and got a better flat of my own somewhere else where they did not know. I warned all my friends not to tell them and changed my place of work as well.

When the baby was born, I knew immediately who the father was. She looked very much like me, but there were some features which were unmistakably from the former boyfriend. My girlfriend told him, and he came to the hospital immediately. He paid for the hospital bills, but I told him to forget about us since I was not ready to be a third wife. I was ready to bring my child up alone with his financial help, and he could see his daughter anytime he wanted. I discovered soon that he did not want to take any responsibility of his daughter as long as I did not want to continue with our relationship. My mother organized for an old woman to come to my house to show me how to look after my baby and show me the right kind of food to eat to make me strong quickly and have enough milk for the baby. I was fed with lots of food and soup mixed with some special roots called mteta, which is said to be good for the bones.

The black beans called "Njahi" in Kikuyu, mixed with green and sweet bananas made my breasts swell heavily and sometimes painfully with milk that my baby could not even finish half of each breast. I hated the stuff, but my mother had ordered that the lady should make sure that I ate it and drank the soup. She came once a week to see how we were getting on, and every time she brought more food stuff. I told her that I had a house girl who could cook for me and that we did not have to bother the old lady, but she refused.

"You must eat proper food and not this rubbish you eat here in town if you want to be strong again. You need your strength to look after your baby. So please follow her instruction Cikū, my child. We obviously know better than you as far as these things are concerned." Thanks be to God, we African learned at that time to honour, respect and value our parent's opinions and follow their advices. So, I never argued as far as these things were concerned because I knew deep inside that indeed she knew better, though I was not a serious rebellion type against parents anyway.

My mother loved farming very much and always said that soil was her life. The farm my brother bought with the help of my parents, step father and what he had got after selling the piece of land in the village, my father added money to buy 3 acres especially for my mother in addition to my brother's share. She, therefore, had a piece of land at Kiarie's farm which was near Ng'ong town about 50 kilometres from

Nairobi. She travelled there every now and then to work in her land.

She brought us (me and Mūmbi) all kinds of things from the farm, back to Nairobi. Mūmbi had also moved out of Karura forest and was also staying in the city of Nairobi. Njeri and Mūkiri lived with my mother still. Njeri also got a baby boy about three years before my daughter was born and later a baby girl who died, but she refused to tell us who the father was. My sister in law never liked the idea of my mother coming too often to look after her farm. She even refused my mother to stay in her house during her visits. She had to go and stay with a neighbour, who was also a relative of her first husband.

However, she never gave up or showed any hard feeling about her, except wondering why my brother was accepting what his wife demanded. However, as she said many times, she did not want to be the reason of their quarrel, so she accepted what she wanted.

She cried a lot about these attitudes of her children, that they had no affection over her, that they did not love her. I remember writing a letter to my brother regarding his attitude towards my mother when I was only 12. He kept this letter in his safe and reminded me about it when I grew up. I told him that it was correct to write him such to remind him, despite our different in age (he was over 20 years older than me) that, that lady was his mother no matter what he thought of her, and that he would never find another mother. I begged him in the letter to teach his wife and children to respect and honor his own mother. He was very angry with me after reading it as my mother told me but he did not mention it to me then until many years later.

My dearest mother was on one of those trips when she met that tragic accident that took her life away from us, three months after my daughter was born. On one Sunday afternoon, she prepared to go back to Nairobi and Kiarie escorted her with his car to Ng'ong town to catch a bus or a Matatu. (These are small buses which are packed with a lot of people than they are supposed to carry and have taken the lives of many Kenyans).

When they arrived at the bus stop, a Matatu had just taken off, and my mother insisted on running after it. My brother tried to tell her to wait for the next one, but she insisted on taking that Matatu as Kiarie related to us later. Kiarie, therefore, drove past the matatu which was stopping at almost a few yards to collect people, and stopped it for my mother to enter. She was squeezed in the front seat where there was a small space left and therefore was the last one to board the matatu, as it was overloaded already. The Matatu took off and after a few kilometres; it overturned at a roundabout in place called Dagoreti Corner. She was the only one who was badly injured. The others escaped with minor injuries.

They took her to Kenyatta Hospital where we came to learn later that she died at the casualty 3 hours after arrival. We got the news the next day, and we went to the police station where the matatu had been delivered and to get information about my mother. All the potatoes, green piece, beans, green maize, etc. were scattered all around in the accident car, and it was obvious to us that those were her things which she was bringing back for us to Nairobi.

I sat down in front of that Matatu and cried so much with a lot of bitterness throwing the maize here and there knowing how much the woman loved us and now she died all alone in an emergency room without any family member near her. I wished so much that I was with her. She must have died with a lot of pain and nobody to comfort her and probably through negligence of the staff in the hospital. On the other hand, I was happy that she did not suffer the pain for a long time. I do not want to imagine what would have happened if she survived with a such a severe injury where she would have needed a special care.

I never got over that tragedy till today. God knows how much I loved my mother and how much I wanted to do for her in future, to make it up for all the suffering she had gone through. I never got that chance. Instead, she died lonely, sad and very poor materially, although very rich at heart. I was glad at least that she had seen my daughter and had blessed her before she died. Although my mother knew for sure that I loved her very much, I still felt that she died before I could show it to her.

May the living God of Abraham, Isaac, and Jacob forgive all her sins even though she refused to know His Divine Son Jesus because of the condition of our country at that time and the culture background she was born in and grant her Eternal rest. I pray for her soul all these years and that of my father. May the Merciful Lord let perpetual light shine upon my dear parent's souls. May they rest in peace! I intercede in prayers for both of them very often, especially the whole month of November lighting candles for them and I trust in God, He is merciful!

The family of her first husband insisted that my mother should be buried in the part of family farm which was initially inherited by her and her first husband. The land was blessed in her name and that of her first husband by her parent-in-laws before they died. Although we were all in favour of her being buried in her farm at Ng'ong hills, where she had three acres, the family elders refused completely. So, we buried her in her first husband's farm. The husband through the influence of his second wife was against it, but the rest of the family insisted. The second wife was very furious about it and tried to fight hard against it through her husband, but his brothers threatened that if my mother was refused the privilege of being buried in her first husband's piece of land, which was also hers by right, the land of the parents-in-law was big enough and the other brothers would bury her in their own land. Of course, this would have been scandalous for him and a kind of curse on him; therefore, he gave in to the tradition and customs. He came to the funeral alright, but he was very embarrassed by all what had gone on, since the whole village knew about it.

The funeral was attended by many friends, relatives and people from our village even the Christians who tried to convert my mother into Christianity before and unfortunately failed. She was buried near a school, and the school children were all given free hour to attend the funeral. Despite her not being a Christian, a pastor was called, and we buried her like a Christian. He gave a fantastic speech about my mother which surprised me after knowing these people's attitude towards my mother's rejection to Christianity. It was a good feeling to know that they all loved her dearly, although it was the most difficult experience for me. I was sure and even today that my mother has her place in heaven. She did not know anything about Christianity, and I know that if it was brought to her in the right way and at the right time, she would have accepted Christ as her Savior. I know but for sure that she loved and feared the true and Living God. Her moral values were very high, and she hated anything to do with oppressing others in any kind of form. All in all, she feared the Living God of Kĩrĩnyaga whom she was brought up worshiping, and I heard her several times praying loud to Him when I was young.

I could not eat, speak or even attend to my baby. She was taken care of by one of the family member and the house girl. It was like I was walking in a bad dream and I waited so much to wake up and find it over. The whole family was kind of sorry for me knowing my situation that I had just got a child on the wedlock and now my mother has gone living me also alone without a father. I never asked my mother for financial help all the time after I left home.

I was earning so little money despite having a child, and I could not even contribute enough money for my mother's funeral as I would have wished. The father of my daughter contributed a little money on the funeral, and he attended the funeral. Kĩarie my elder brother insisted on paying for her clothes for the funeral.

"My mother always complained that I have never bought her anything, and now she is dead, and I did not fulfil this wish, so please let me buy her burial clothes alone."

"No!" I screamed with anger, knowing that he had a chance to make my mother happy and he did not use it. He was the stingiest of all my mother's children. No one said anything.

"We will all contribute to everything. If you did not care to buy her a dress or make her happy when she was alive, now it will not change anything." I told him in tears and in front of other family members. All kept quiet! My sister Mūmbi eventually spoke and agreed with my suggestion, followed by the others.

I sent my father a telegram to India and informed him about my mother's death, and he responded immediately. He sent a letter using express mail telling me about the property which included our house, worker's quarters and the lorry he had left in Kenya. He had made a Power of Attorney in my mother's favour before he left, he explained in his letter and now that she was dead his property was left alone. This was my first time to hear about a Power of Attorney. He told me that he was preparing new documents in my name for all the property he had in Kenya since I was now over 21.

The documents came, and this made my brothers and my sister Mūmbi very angry. A new war between us was declared. They started planning the fight against me by digging out all that my parents possessed, behind my back. They hid all the documents found in my parents' house. I was not allowed to know anything. They agreed on each other how to share all without me since I had taken what belonged to my father. I was not informed of anything. Immediately, the war began where my brother demanded to exchange the land in Karura forest with a land near his farm in Ng'ong. I said if he thought that was possible, I would agree on condition that the exchanged farm should be in my name. That was not his plan, so he refused.

"The property belongs to all of us and not you alone. Your so-called father left the property to our mother, and now that she is dead, it belongs to all of us." Mūmbi said.

"My father did not give my mother the property, but he gave her a Power of Attorney as long as he was not here in Kenya. Now that my mother has died the property went back automatically to the original owner, that is my father, and now he has made me another Power of Attorney, I found out what this means that now I have the full authority on these things and nobody else." I tried to explain, but they were not ready to hear any of these facts.

My brother Mūkiri (quiet Mūkiri who was injected to hate me) threatened to beat me up if I showed myself near those houses again. I called a family meeting, and they were warned about all those threats they were making against me. They were made to understand that the houses belonged to me and I could share with them only if I wanted. Since I was not staying there and no business was going on anymore, I rented the houses letting Mūkiri and Njeri with her child to stay in our main house. Despite all the hatred I still supported them with most of the money I collected from the rent, since they had no other source of income. Now Mūkiri wanted to cash the rent for himself. Slowly I came to understand my father, why he left without leaving money for me at any bank. He knew for sure that, such could even cause me my life. He knew how material greed my brothers and sister were because I heard him say those things many times.

Life became difficult for me with all the responsibilities at the age of twenty-one. I had a child out of wedlock, no parents, and two-family members who were looking upon me. I was earning about two thousand shillings which was very little money at that time with the inflation going up rapidly. I had to find an alternative to get out of the country to pursue further studies. One could hardly live on the salary alone. Many people did either illegal business 'Magendo" or young single mothers like me looked for older men "Sugar dadies" to support them.

The number of young women getting pregnant increased rapidly. Most of responsible fathers were those so-called „sugar daddies" who were less interested on the children born by their young mistresses. I had fallen into the same track though I had no idea what I was doing and my daughter was the result. I found the whole thing disgusting especially when I discovered the trick I was played on by the father of my daughter who was much older, and

I was terrified of doing any "Magendo." The father of my daughter refused to help me if I did not want to do what he wanted. It is obvious to me today that he never loved me as such but just wanted to have a young woman in bed from time to time. The government did nothing to help the victims like me whatsoever. He insisted that I should marry him, which he knew I would not, if I wanted him to help his daughter. I told him to go to hell. I never saw him showing any affection and interest towards his daughter at all, as a father should do.

I applied to several International organizations for sponsorship without success.

The company which I worked for had a branch in India. Long before my daughter's birth and even before pregnancy, the manager in India visited us on business several times and one day I had a chance to talk to him. They all knew me by name since I worked at the switchboard and the fact that I appeared in a year's Calendar as a model for the vehicles we were selling.

"How come you have an Indian surname, Alice?" He asked me.

"My father is an Indian, but he went back to India."

"Oh really, which part of India does he stay?"

"In Punjab. Is it very far from Bombay?" I asked excitedly.

"Oh yes, Punjab is very far from Bombay, but not as far as Nairobi," he joked.

"I see, so if you can travel to come here now and then I could send you to my father then," I said almost to myself, but he heard me.

"What do you want to tell him," he asked looking at me seriously.

"I need money to continue with my studies. I have sent him many letters asking him to help me, but I have a feeling he does not receive them. I have no idea how to raise so much money because I want to go to Europe," I said.

"Oh! You have big plans huh!! Not bad for a young person to be so ambitious. Anyway, give me his address, and I will try to contact him. I usually travel all over India on business, but it might take time before I go towards that direction."

I gave him all the details of my plans and my father's address. He advised me to try and get a passport by the time he comes back. He came back after one year, and he had not managed to contact my father. I had tried again to write to my father, but I think somebody there did not want any communication between us.

Some of them were answered, but they sounded very strange which started putting me off. I did not dare tell him about my daughter all the time in fear of how he would take it. In one of the last letters, he wrote that I should not think of continuing with my studies but look for a man and get married. That was not my father's ideas, or could it be? I was not sure, so

I stopped writing him. I thought that if indeed it was his idea, then he wanted to push me away to a husband so that he had no more responsibility over me.

Though I left the previous company I was working in and now worked in different one, the Indian man contacted me when he came for the next trip in Nairobi again. I told him that I was giving up on my ideas though I had already a passport, but the man decided to help me himself by buying a ticket for me.

He noticed how disappointed I was after he informed me that he had not managed to contact my father. I had counted so much on his help that I had made all the arrangements. I was supposed to join a frind of mine Lillian Njoki whom I had contact with in Belgium. She had been there for one year and had promised to find a school for me.

Lillian was the sister of the Nelly, my best friend in the School days, and after she left her husband who worked and lived in Mombasa, she asked me to help her by giving her a place to stay until she finalized about her trip to Europe which she had been planning for a long time. She stayed with me for almost half a year. When she arrived in Belgium, she wrote me and told me that she had registered me in a language course and had already paid for the first term and that I should try to join her as soon as possible. She encouraged me so much to leave Kenya and go to Europe so much that I eventually wanted to give it a try. Apart from Lillian, there was some force within my soul also which pushed me to continue with this plan. I believe it as my destiny. However, the Indian man's help helped me to make my final decision.

I asked my sister Mūmbi to stay with Victoria (my daughter's baptise name, which we shortened to Vicky, though I preferred my mother's name "Njoki" most) for a short time but she refused. I could not take her with me immediately not knowing where I was going for sure. But I knew I would come back for her as soon as I could.

I endorsed her in my passport to avoid problems later, but before I could get her endorsed in my passport, I had discovered that her father had registered in hospital after her birth that I was his wife, and so he was the father of my daughter. I had approached him and heard his opinion that he would never sign any document to allow me to take her "daughter" out of the country. We had a big quarrel, and I called him all kinds of names and left his office. I had no other option except to sign an affidavit with a lawyer that he had lied that we were married and that he was not the father of my daughter.

This enabled me to get her endorsed in my passport without his permission. Tit for tat! Fortunately, such documents are not so strict to achieve in Kenya, so I could do it without much proof. We had contacts with Faruk again, but I was convinced we had no future together. He often came to see us, and I told him about my plans.

He loved Vicky also very much and treated her like his daughter. He was very much against me leaving her with my family, though I thought this was most probably only for his own interest to make me cancel my plans and stay in Kenya. He kept on asking me to marry him but I refused. Whatever the case, I was determined to see my plans through if I had to improve my life and that of my child and the only chance I thought I had, was to leave Kenya. I asked my cousin who had six children of his own whether he could stay with my daughter and he agreed.

My cousin knew about my problems with my sisters and brothers, and he was the one who talked to them to stop harassing me. I could not ask my brother to take my daughter because they were already looking after Njeri's son, even though I did not like our sister in law due to her hatred to my mother and my whole family. Njeri could not look after her son herself because of her sickness, and since my mother was no longer there, we all decided that our sister in law could take him and we contributed money for his upbringing.

"The child should not stand on your way to success Cikũ. We will look after her till you come back. I know you are a good child and you will come back for your child," my cousin Peter said. His wife also agreed. When my sister Mũmbi heard about it, I think she felt ashamed, therefore she came to me.

"I had refused to stay with Vicky because I did not want you to go away, I admit now.

But now that I have seen that you are serious and nobody can stop you, I will obviously take her," she continued.

"No Mūmbi, thank you very much, but I have found another person to look after my child while I am away," I replied.

"But you cannot leave Vicky with our cousin Peter and his family. Think of what people will say about me refusing to stay with her. All my children want Vicky to come to us."

"But I asked you first, and you refused!" I reminded her.

They all convinced me and promised to look after her while I was away. Mūmbi's children loved me a lot at that time, and I knew they loved my daughter. Although Mūmbi could not really love me, I knew that she too had nothing against my child. So, in the end, I decided to leave her with Mūmbi. I regretted this bitterly later in life. Faruk promised to be visiting her as often as he could. I did not believe him, but I heard later that he fulfilled his promises. Her father never visited her even once though he knew I was away and his daughter was living with my sister.

In the mean time, Mūmbi had bought a social house with the help of her rich ex-husbands family's influence and were living there with her children. She had built some more rooms in her compound and was renting them. Mūmbi, as we agreed, was supposed to collect the rent from Karura houses, and she was supposed to help Mūkiri and Njeri with the money, take some for my daughter's expenses, and deposit at least three hundred shillings in my account every month. The whole rent amounted to about 2,000 shillings per month. This was not very little money at that time in Kenya. For example, my two-room apartment rent was 500 Shillings at that time. Everything was set, and I was ready to leave for Europe. I was somehow scared, and several times I had made up my mind to cancel the whole thing, but it was too late, and those feelings I had to go on with my plans, became even stronger.

Despite the feelings, pushing me so hard to continue with my plans, I had resigned from my job, given up my flat, sold all the furniture, etc, so I simply could not change my plans. I prayed that if God did not want me to take up that step, then He must show me some signs. There were none, and everything ran smoothly, except the following small incident.

I got a tourist visa for three months to go to Belgium according to my friend Lillian. I wanted to pass through England, therefore, I applied for a visa as well. The British Embassy asked for my passport which was to remain at the Embassy. I filled a form and gave the address of my girlfriend whom I was supposed to visit in London on transit.

When I came back for the visa which was about three days before my departure, they told me that the visa was rejected and if I wanted I had to wait further four weeks. I told her I was leaving in three days' time, therefore, I had to cancel my visit to England. I asked them to give me my passport back and was shocked to see a stamp in it which indicated that I had applied for a visa and was rejected. God! I was mad! How dare the British Embassy stamp such a terrible stamp in my new passport as if I was a criminal? I think this was not new to them. They had done this to many people I came to understand later. I had booked a flight to Belgium with a stopover in England, therefore I changed the flight and booked a direct one to Belgium, but still, I had to connect flights in Heathrow Airport. I flew with Kenya Airways to London, and I was supposed to change to Belgium Airlines in London. Faruk drove me himself to the Airport, and most of my family members accompanied me too. I promised to write to him and give him my address when I arrive.

I boarded Kenya Airways going to a place I did not know, opening a new chapter in my life. It was such a terrible feeling waving goodbye to my 3-year-old little girl, who looked at me with a face full of fear and many questions and for sure did not understand why her mother was going away. That last blink on my daughter's face and her waving with her small hand kept on haunting me for a long time. I prayed sincerely that God would be with me all the way, and with my child, whom I had no idea when I would see her again. My prayer went like this:

"God my Creator, lead me in this journey and be my advisor in every matter. I have left my origin country where you planted me because life has become unbearable. I have no one to depend on except You Lord. I go to look for a better pasture to bring my child up and myself too since I am an orphan now. Please help me not to do things which displease you especially and take Your Son back to the cross. All that I will do in a foreign country Father, may it be to bring you praise and glory. I have faith that it is your will too that I leave, and you have blessed this journey already then; I have seen your great Hand in all the preparation which I accomplished till now.

If not so, I would not be sitting in this plane now. Father, lead me to the place you have arranged to re-plant me to live, that I may live there in peace, and give me the task or the job you have chosen for me to do. I promise to do it best to my capability, and by Your grace, I should never leave Your powerful hand. I pray for Your protection not to perish in the world's evilness, and I pray for Your grace, endurance, and strength to fight all temptations and trials knowing for sure that You are with me always" -Amen!

(The prayer of St Michel; Our Father and Hail Mary.)

I repeated these prayers desperately after settling in the plain for several times until I dosed off and slept.

CHAPTER SIX

I was very furious with the British Consulate in Nairobi. I wished there was another way to avoid going via London. I hated the name England itself, but my flight was already booked, and I had to go through London. Unfortunately, there was a strike at Heathrow Airport, and we landed in Greenwich Airport, where we were supposed to be transported by a bus to Heathrow. When the control officer saw my passport with the stamp in it, he told me to stand aside and let the others pass. When he finished, he came back to me.

"Why do you have this stamp in your passport?" He asked me. That is when I knew the true meaning of that stamp.

"That sir, you may ask your good offices in Nairobi," I answered and snatched my passport from his hand. "I hope you are not going to add another ugly British stamp like that one in my passport. I want to get the hell out of your country as fast as I can," He was angry at my reaction!

"But we cannot let you leave the airport without a visa," he said, looking at me as if I was mad. I do not think he saw such an action in his carrier.

"Call the police and let them escort me to Heathrow. Did I ask to be landed here?" I think he saw the anger and bitterness on my face.

"Would you please follow me to the office?" He asked me. I followed him, and after he offered me a seat, he asked me what had happened.

"I wanted to visit a relative here in London for two weeks, so I only applied for visa, but they told me to wait for four weeks, which I could not since my flight was already booked. When I withdrew my application, they gave me back my passport with that nonsense stamp, as if I were a criminal! How would you have reacted in my situation?" I shouted at him. He asked politely for my passport again studying it carefully. The first stamp was the three months visa for Belgium, the second was British stamp, and the third was the departure stamp from Nairobi Airport. I think he understood my anger.

Everybody was waiting in the bus, but it could not leave without me. So, I related the whole story now in tears adding that I would not let them mess my passport anymore. He called the Airport manager who agreed that I should be given the visa I wanted.

"I do not need it now because I have told my relatives I won't be going to them anymore. I am being expected in Belgium. So, your visa is of no more value to me." I answered stubbornly stretching my hand for my passport. He gave it to me.

"But we must put something in your passport to enable you to travel through England to Heathrow," he begged.

"That is your problem to get me to Heathrow. I will not let you touch my passport anymore. Stamp the visa on a piece of paper if you must." They talked to me for more than half an hour even called Nairobi in my presence accusing them of what they did to my passport. He apologised sincerely before I allowed him to put twenty-four hours visa next to the stamp from Nairobi. We left Greenwich Airport for Heathrow to take my flight to Belgium.

God Almighty! I could not believe this. These Wazungu's match in and out of our country and nobody ever stops them. They had colonised us for over 70 years, stealing everything we had, and they had no shame to do a thing like that to me. I did not even want to see their country anymore. I wanted to get out of it immediately and never come back. How right my mother was about them! I have been in Europe for more than 40 years now, and I've never wished to go to England again. I have visited most of the other European countries, but somehow, I've never brought myself to go to England although most of East Africans believe that, if you have not been to London, you have not been to Europe. Well maybe in future, who knows.

By the time I reached Belgium, I had almost 10 hours delay. My dear friend Lillian was nowhere to be seen. I arrived in Belgium at three o'clock in the morning and asked for a hotel at the airport, and of course, I got the most expensive one. I had no idea about the exchange rate. I sent a telegram to the address Lillian had given me and told her where I was. Some Belgium friends of hers came to pick me up from the hotel in the afternoon informing me that Lillian was no longer in Belgium and I had to follow her to Germany where she had moved to. She got involved in some problems with the immigration office because they refused to extend her stay permit after it expired, and they asked her to leave the country. That is how she landed in Germany. As she came to narrate the story later, she left Belgium after her visa expired by crossing the border on foot to avoid any police control. She was not coming back to Belgium, and so I had no choice but to follow her.

I had to take a train to Germany the following day. My visa for Belgium was still valid, and I could travel through to Germany since Kenyans did not need a visa to enter Germany, except in a case of expiry of the stay permit in previous country like it was in Lillian's case. We sent another telegram to her in Cologne and told her about my arrival. We were supposed to meet at Cologne main station. I went through the border without a problem. I came to a huge station Kölner Bahnhof where I could not understand anything written nor a word of what was announced in German through the loudspeakers now and then.

I looked around the platform but could not see Lillian. Oh God, what would I do now? I went down the steps and stood next to the staircase in a big hall with my suitcase on my side. I watched everybody who passed looking for Lillian. She was not among all those white people who looked all the same to me. There were also black people who passed every now and then. I waited for almost one hour and eventually I decided to ask somebody for help. The next black person who came, I smiled at him, and he came up to me. I spoke to him in English, and thanks God he could speak English.

"Could you please help me? I was supposed to meet somebody here, but she did not come, and I have no idea what to do," I told him.

"Do you have the address of the person you were supposed to meet?" He spoke with a funny accent, most probably West African but I was sure he was not an East African. I showed him the address without knowing that the address could take me to the house. I thought it was a post box address like at home.

"I could take you there if you want, but first I have to meet somebody upstairs. I live near this address. If you could wait for a while, I will be back," he said and left. I thought he was nuts to imagine I could go with him, not understanding what he meant. I decided to go and look for a hotel again and send Lillian another telegram telling her where I was. As I picked up my suitcase to go, I heard my name being called and my heart skipped a beat. Turning around, I saw Lillian running towards me. I left the suitcase and ran to meet her. God, was I happy and relieved to see her! Everybody was staring at us.

"I am so sorry. I know I must have scared you. I went to our Embassy in Bonn and missed my train back," she said holding me to her. Tears of happiness were flowing down my face. "Hey, hey, hey, I am here now, don't worry."

Lillian lived with a German student, who had gone to Kenya for a student exchange program. According to Lillian, she had gone to stay with her family for three months in Kenya, and she had left the flat together with her two cats to her care. The flat was a small one in the cellar and very dark during the day. She had no money at all when I came, and we had to spend the money which I had brought with me. I had about D.M 3,000 which started dwindling very fast. I paid for a language school for both of us, food for us and the cats, and I had to buy some clothes because I did not carry any clothes from home. She had started a cleaning job somewhere, but apparently, she was not getting much from it.

I could not stay there, and Lillian could not understand why. I wanted to make something out of my life now that I was in Europe and I had no time to waste. Lillian had very different ideas which did not fit me. Her ideas were to get a rich German man and get married to him. She even tried to organize some dates with German men, but I refused even to meet them. That was surely not the reason which brought me all the way to Germany. She was always aggressive to black people who tried to date me or give us advises on how to organise our stay etc. Therefore, within no time we went separate ways.

I met a Nigerian student who also had a German girlfriend as I came to find out later. His girlfriend was a prostitute somewhere in another town, and she supported him financially during his studies. It was a very funny relationship, which I, coming from Kenya, could not understand at that time. He said he could not work and study at the same time, and that he let that German woman take care of him financially, but he never intended to take her back home, though that is what he made her believe.

I thought he was only trying to get me, but that is what he did to her in the end. He asked me to marry him and go back to Nigeria with him, but I told him that he was crazy to imagine that I have just come to Europe from Africa and would go back so easily. He helped me a lot though, by showing me how to go about the paperwork and such. I was lucky because Nigerians are known to be very smart in dodging the

German bureaucratic rules. They know all tricks to survive. Though most of them are known to be very tricky or even criminals. That one was a genuine and a responsible student and seemed to know exactly what he wanted or, so I thought. I had first to get a health insurance, which he told me was very important in case I got sick.

He took me there with his car, and I got an insurance policy for students, since I had a letter from the language school. With that, I had to go to the foreign office to get a stay permit for students. I got six months stay permit with the help of my school papers and the insurance. It was as easy as that during that period. I would never have known all those procedures on my own, especially due to the language barrier. He also took me around the Catholic churches and told me what to say to get some financial help. Sure, enough I collected about 2,000 D.M. in a week.

I told the church secretaries or the priests themselves that I have just arrived in Germany and did not have money to eat, as he told me to say. Although it was all true what I said, it was very difficult for me to beg for money like that, something I have never done in my life, and in a house of God. When I complained to him saying that I did not want to do such a thing, he insisted that the white people have stolen everything from Africa, and it was our right to get some of it back, typical Nigerian arguments. He drove me to those churches and insisted that it was a golden chance because my passport showed that I have indeed arrived in the country a few weeks ago. He did not take even one D.M. from the money. When I think of it today, I feel he really cared for me as he repeated all the time and wanted to leave me behind knowing I was on the right path. God bless him wherever he is!

I was always asking people for advises and help. I met somebody else who told me that he knew a lady from Zimbabwe who was working as a nurse and she had a child. She was looking for somebody to stay with who could look after her child when she had night duties. This was fantastic though it sounded like she wanted a house girl. My money was running out, and I could not find a job, and so with this kind of a thing, I didn't need to pay for anything except school fees and my fair. I accepted immediately.

The school was also a waste of money and time. The class I was put into was full of people who could already speak German but did not know any grammar. The lessons were conducted only in German, and the teacher refused to speak any other language although I later found out that he could speak English.

"Is it not possible to explain to me some things in English?" I asked him one day.

"I do not understand anything of what you say the entire day. By the time I check for a word in the dictionary, you are already ahead."

"I cannot speak English in the classroom. All those people there speak different languages, and I cannot speak all their languages. So, I must teach only in German. I am sorry." I continued though I did not learn much during the whole term and I could not trust myself to say anything, except a few things like , Guten Tag, ein Bier bitte, geradeaus, (which at first I pronounced es gade-ous) links, rechts and Aufwiedersehen and above all "scheiße" (shit!) which I could pronounce very well since it was said almost every second in the classroom and outside.

I started looking for sponsors at the churches, and I found one Catholic priest with the help of my Nigerian boyfriend, who promised to get me a school for a course in hotel management and that they would sponsor me. While he was looking for the school, we started talking about my life, and I mentioned about my child.

"You mean you have left a child in Kenya alone?" He asked me.

"Not alone, she is with my sister. I could not bring her with me, not knowing where I was going. I miss her very much though," I said.

"In that case, I cannot help you. I cannot support the fact that you have left your child behind."

"But that is not helping me either. If I can improve my education, I can look after my child even better!" I said.

"No, no I am sorry we cannot help you now! A church cannot support that." That was it. He refused to continue looking for school for me, and he even refused to see me again. I could not understand that logic whatsoever. I needed their help even more now that I had a child to support, but to them, I was a sinner who did not deserve any help from the church. I continued to respect my mother's attitude towards the white people still more. On the other hand, I thought that, it was the punishment of cheating in the church to get some money and I quarrelled so much with my Nigerian boyfriend calling him all names and that he was sent by the devil to tempt me to do such a terrible thing. He just laughed at me.

"You see where your stupid ideas bring me. That was the punishment of taking money from the church, and you are the one who literary forced me to do it." I said.

"Nonsense! Fact is you did not have money to pay for all your needs, so you did not cheat them! God does not mind if you get help from His house. Who punish them when they plunder our mother continent anyway?" He said laughing even more sarcastically.

When the time came for him to leave the country, he had a container full of all things one could think of taking back to Africa. He had managed to build a house in Nigeria, according to him and the poor woman worked so hard to buy everything needed for the house, including a car. Everything was shipped off, and he told the woman that he wanted to go first and finalise everything before she could follow him.

"You have worked so hard here in your country for my education and our transport back home, so it is my duty to finalise everything in my country and make you walk in your house comfortably and in style when everything is perfect. I cannot also marry without my parents. So, I will give you a big wedding in Nigeria."

The poor woman believed all that jazz. He had told me that he would not even give me his address because for sure I would be harassed by people who knew that we had an affair. He told me that he would not have any contact with anybody after he left the country. This is exactly what he did. As I heard from his friends, the woman wrote letters, but they kept on coming back with "Return to Sender-Address unknown." In a way, I was very sorry for the woman, and happy that I did not fall into his ideas. I liked him a lot, but I was not in love with him nor did I dare fall in love. He was indeed a good friend in his own ways, but I did not like any of his methods.

However, I believed later everything he had said like, "Alice you do not truly think that I would take a white woman back to my mother as my wife and a prostitute to make matters worse?"

"But you are not better than her. You are indeed prostituting yourself on her."

"Oh, shut up! You have no idea how Europe is. But I guarantee you that you will know one day. I do not blame you for your healthy African morals. After all, you are fresh from so-called "moral land." But let me warn you, it is difficult to keep that moral here if you want to live in style." He said.

"I do not need to live in style, but improve my education, go back home and earn money genuinely, and live in style through my sweat," I said.

"May God grant you just that my dear girl!" He said smiling, and I answered, Amen! Somehow, I believe he loved me a lot and did not want to see me drown in Europe like many African's did, and he kept on warning me until he left making me promise him that I would look after myself and keep my healthy African morals, obviously the morals of those many years ago.

I never heard from him again till today. But his words kept on ringing in my mind. In some ways, he was right especially the anger on white people and their oppression on the weak ones. Soon I began to experience in a hard way the new environment and its culture.

This is Europe which everybody back at home talks so great about. Going to Europe was a big deal for everybody in Africa. They think God must love you very much to have given you an opportunity like that in life. Oh, jay! Oh jay! I wish I had never seen it in my life. I wish I had never boarded that Kenya Airways flight. I wish . . . I wish . . . I wish . . . . was all I could think of hard times. I did not believe that I was blessed to have come to this continent anymore. I was not sure that it was the will of God.

Every morning when I got up, I had a funny feeling in my stomach, and it was indeed the fear. I tried to pray, but the fear in me could not let me concentrate in my prayers, so it did not help much. Outside there was quietness day or night which contributed to the fear, and the only noise which I could hear, and which made me feel worse was the sirens from the ambulances or the police. At first, I did not notice that no birds were singing in the morning like at home or a cork crowing, a dog barking, loud music from a neighbour's radio, or even the screams of the children as they ran up and down freely playing all day long. I just wondered why it was so quiet especially in the mornings, but later in springtime, I discovered what was missing; all those noises! I could never have imagined before that those noises could mean so much in my life.

I had taken so many things for granted back home before I came to Europe. Suddenly, I became conscious of my identity, appreciating daily my African heritage and I began to feel very proud about it. There were all kinds of new things and food which I had never seen before, but still, I began to miss a lot of things especially food like ugali with matumbo, sukuma wiki, nyama choma with ugali, mutton pilau, kachumbari, samosa, etc. I began to miss all my friends whom we had lots of fun together and mostly I missed their sense of humour, although they claimed that I had the most sense of humour.

People in Germany were totally different, even most of the Africans who had lived long in Europe had lost all their charm and sense of humour and had become as aloof as the Germans. Laughing seemed to be out of place for the Germans, and it looked like they just had no time for laughing. I was used to letting it out loud as it is usually a normal thing to hear in Africa kwa; kwa! kwa! kwa! But I came to realise that this kind of laughing was completely out of place in Germany. The only time I came to hear them laughing aloud was during Karnival which is a celebration that happens especially at the Rhein area, a week before the Christian fasting time. I thought it as a crazy time for all of them in this area, and they do all sorts of unusual things. I compared it to circumcision ceremonies in Kikuyu tradition before. They dress up in funny costumes, masks, etc., which I was told was to chase away the evil winter spirits or so. Many carnival lovers remain drunk all five days of the ceremony, singing dirty songs including exchanging partners. They say that most children are born nine months after these celebrations than any other time in those parts of Germany, and most children born at that time could most probably not originate from assumed fathers. I wondered if this was true!

I attended one Karneval party which is called "Karneval Sitzung," but I could not understand the jokes in German at that time which was told by different comedians who came on the stage, but I was completely amused and amazed by the way they were all laughing. They all started to laugh at the same time and finished at the same time quite abruptly with the drums and trumpet conclusion dadaaa- dadaaa-dadaaa, which made it so artificial.

After these drums, everybody is quiet waiting for the next joke. I could not help it but laugh at their way of laughing, and my laughter was always left hanging because I could not switch myself off so abruptly. Everybody turned to look at that kind of disorganized laugh, only to see an African with her kwa! kwa! kwa! Many seemed to be quite happy to imagine that I had understood their jokes and laughed so heartily. I laughed until tears came running down my face. I think if they knew why I was laughing, I might have been thrown out. This Karneval period is therefore the jolliest time for the Germans. Everybody seems to be happy, friendly even to the foreigners and very generous. When we went to join the Karnivalists in the pubs where indeed the real action usually is, we ended up drinking a lot and for free. The whole thing lasts from Thursday which is called "Weiberfastnacht" and finishes on Monday known as – "Rosenmontag". So, on Tuesday, before the Ash Wednesday, everybody is back to their old moods again and those who greeted you so heartily on Saturday, they do not even look at you. Many people remain drunk from Thursday to Monday night, young or old. A lot of immorality and evil actions are found all over on this occasion, with adults as well as children. You would think the world is coming to an end, so one must take all in life before Tuesday. I mean the whole thing is so artificial and crazy that I came to hate it as the years went on. I enjoyed the long weekends of this occasions inside of my house.

The winter was another issue. I had no idea what kind of clothes one needed. I came to learn later the kind of clothes one wears which are so heavy that they almost make you unable to walk due to the weight. For someone who was used to light clothes like me all my life, in our beautiful Kenyan tropical weather in our City in the Sun as we call it, was very difficult to adapt. I never experienced such an extreme cold in my life. It was rare to have less than 20 degrees in Kenya even in the cold season like July and August.

On my first Christmas in Germany, I received a card from the post office to go and collect a parcel which had been sent to me for Christmas by a friend from Berlin whom I knew from back home and had informed him that I was now in Germany. I went to the post office where I had to take a tram (street tram). It was bitterly cold that day in the sense that the cold seemed to be cutting through the skin like sharp blades. I was wearing a cheap leather jacket, over a cotton blouse, jeans, and ordinary shoes with nylon stockings and hands without gloves.

By the time I collected the parcel after queuing for some minutes, it had started snowing. It was my first time to see snow. The flakes were pouring down forming white layers on the streets, on the roofs of the houses and on the leafless trees. I had also witnessed the leaves from all the trees changing color from green to gold brown, orange etc. and eventually falling from all the trees in autumn leaving the trees completely bare and all the leaves lying on the streets. The trees looked dead by the time this terrible cold came. I never experienced this kind of nature changes on the plants in our country probably because there was no such an extreme change at ago. I stood in front of the post office watching the flakes with awe. I tried to catch some flakes but as soon as they fell on my palm, they changed into water. People were coming in and out of the post office as if nothing was happening. I decided not to wait for the flakes to stop falling and walk to the tram stop as well.

The trams were delayed due to the sudden heavy snowing, and I stood there for almost twenty minutes. My whole body almost froze, and I started feeling numbness in some parts of my body. I felt so miserable and homesick that I started crying. As the hot tears rolled down my face, they were forming into vapor as they met the chilly air. I had to laugh again when I saw two lines of smoke like vapor on either side of my chicks as the tears rolled down, crying at the same time. What kind of a place was this?

Eventually, the tram came, and I got inside. I could not feel my nose as I tried to clean it; neither could I feel my fingers and toes. It was warm inside the tram, but not warm enough for me. Once I reached home, I went straight to the bathroom and had a very long hot bath. I still had a return ticket to Kenya, and as I sat in the bath, I wondered if I should pack and go back home and forget about Europe. I wondered how the white people could stand that cold. Everything looked so dull, and people walked like they were dragging themselves. Oh God, what a country! "No wonder these people are so unfriendly, this cold can definitely paralyze one's brain and make one very aggressive!" I said to myself. I missed my mother terribly at this moment, thinking that if she were alive, she would never have let me come here and neither would I have had the guts to travel so far and leave my mum behind. Why did she die so early? She had same more years to live if it were not for that tragic accident.

A few days later, I got up early to go to school. Rose from Zimbabwe had gone to work, and her son had gone to the nursery school, which was just in front of our building. I had already moved in with Rose and her son. It was the best solution for my problems at that time. As soon as I came out of the house, I slipped and fell flat on my back. Luckily, I did not break any bones. I tried to get up but anywhere I tried to touch was slippery. I could not understand why it was so slippery. It reminded me of wet floor full of Omo washing soap I used to pour on the wet floor to practice James Brown numbers when I was a teenager.

That is how slippery it was. I went on my knees and crawled back to the main door and went to the house and forgot about the school. When Rose came in the evening, I told her about it. She explained to me about the slippery ice which is caused by the rain if the temperature is very low and therefore the rain water freezes and the streets become very icy and slippery that many people end up in hospital with broken limbs, legs, arms or backbone. Sure, enough it was all over the TV that night reporting how many people ended in hospital.

"God, how many strange things do I have to learn about this country?" I thought to myself.

"You have to wear special shoes for winter Alice," Rose said.

"What you wear is not right for winter. You do not have warm clothes either as far as I can see. We have no tropical weather here my dear girl!"

We were living in a very high building on the twelfth floor. On our floor, there were seven apartments, but

I had no idea how the people who lived there looked like. I was used to having contact with the neighbours back home and knowing them all. Here no one paid any attention to you. I always greeted people in the lift with a smile, but sometimes they just stared at me or each other without answering like I was crazy to greet them.

"Don't you have contact with your neighbours Rose?" I asked Rose one day.

"Oh Alice, this is Europe. People don't care about each other. Each mind his/her own business. It is not like in Africa where all the neighbours know one another, and family stay together," Rose said laughing at my question.

"But how can people live in these houses without contact with the neighbours. It is too lonely. What about if one gets some problems, who would help?" I asked

"They have telephones, one would call for help, and they have televisions to keep them busy!"

"You do not even borrow each other things like if you run out of salt and the shops are closed etc.?" Rose continued laughing at my stupid questions.

"You make sure you do not run out of salt. And if you do, then you must eat your food without salt until the shops open. Wake up, girl! You are living in another world."

"Are they like that among themselves, or do they behave like that to the foreigners only?"

"That is how they live even among themselves. You cannot just knock on somebody's door because you are a neighbour before informing them in advance, to borrow salt!" She said throwing her hands up and twisting her lips. Rose as far as I could value her, was very much Europeanized, or brainwashed and loved all about white people. She did not want to be identified with "primitive Africans." She never allowed me to cook my African dishes claiming that her flat stunk afterwards.

At the weekends when she was not working, we always ate boring dishes of boiled vegetables without spices except salt and rice or meat. She usually cooked typical European food. She usually ate in the hospital and her son in Kindergarten, so evening the child was to be fed with bread like Germans. I am the only one who needed to cook at home during the weekdays, and she made a lot of trouble when she found out that I had cooked my food. She became mean, bossy and stingier every day. I ignored her meanness and tried to do what she wanted, by eating out. Since I could not afford to eat in restaurants, I tried to do with junk food during the week.

Our immediate neighbour as Rose told me was an alcoholic and she never had any visitors. Rose said she had seen her once in a lift (yet Rose had lived in the same flat for more than four years) very drunk and helped her into her flat. One day a friend of hers came and knocked on our door. I opened the door, and Rose stood behind me.

"Have you seen your neighbour lately?" She asked us. She was drunk and was stinking of alcohol.

"No, we never see her," Rose answered in German as she translated to me later.

"We drink together every day, and for the last three days, we did not see her in our usual "Kneipe" (Pub). I've rang her bell, but she does not seem to be in, and I tried to telephone, but there's no answer. That is very unusual," the drunkard woman said. We tried to ring again, but there was no answer.

"Could you please let me use your telephone to call the police? I am afraid something must have happened to her." So, we called the police, and they forced the door open. The drunkard woman was right. Our neighbour had been dead for several days, and nobody had known about it. She had taken some sleeping tablets or something. I was so scared to imagine we had lived just next door to a dead neighbour unknowingly. I later learnt that those were normal cases in Germany. Some people were discovered dead in their flats after some months. She had only one daughter whom she did not have good contact with for whatever reason if not her drinking habit, but after she was dead, the daughter came to take whatever valuable was left behind. We helped her to clear the flat, and there was no sign of sadness in her at all that her mother was dead.

She behaved completely normal like nothing had happened. She gave a few funny comments which Rose told me I better not even want to know what she was saying about her dead mother. Rose just shook her head at hearing the things she was saying. That was also very strange to me, and I had to think of myself when my mother died, how terribly empty sad, and scared I felt that I could not keep my eyes dry for months every time she came into my mind, and that was often. This feeling did not stop for many years, and I still feel sad sometimes when I think of her.

Christmas time was like madness all over. People were shopping. All the streets were wonderfully decorated. I thought people must be very religious in this country to spend all that money to celebrate the birth of Christ. Of course, I learned later that it was all a big business and, had nothing to do with faith or the birth of our Lord. I was invited by a German family to celebrate Christmas with them. Most of the public places are closed, probably to obligate the families to be together on that day. In Kenya, the celebrations start from Christmas Eve till boxing day or as Germans call it 2nd Christmas day where the families usually meet on the Christmas Eve. For Germans, Christmas Eve is the most important day, and they celebrate and exchange presents on that evening. Christmas day is very quiet with nothing much going on, eating the remains of cakes and cookies, and all delicious goodies of the previous day. In any case that short event on Christmas eve is a very expensive one with expensive presents placed under an expensively decorated Christmas tree, most delicious dishes, drinks of all kinds, all cookies and sweet things of the highest quality, etc.

An ordinarily decorated Christmas tree costed well over a hundred German Marks then. The papers to wrap the presents costed also another big amount, not mentioning the presents themselves, and the children just tear those papers with excitement and which later end up all in the garbage. What a waste! The amount of money wasted on Christmas present wrapping papers in each Christmas could surely feed many of the starving people in poor countries for months.

I could not speak German, so I could hardly communicate with the Germans. I was always curious to learn many things. The German language was so difficult to learn. The grammar itself is so illogical to understand. I decided to watch children programs and cartoons every day with Tebo (Rose's son), including "Sesam Straße," "Sendung mit der Maus" etc. where I noticed I could understand a lot of things. I slowly improved and could understand more and more each day.

I noticed that most Germans were very proud and to some extend arrogant when it came to their language.

The German tourists in Kenya expect everybody to speak German. When in Germany, they expect you to speak German fluently, and most of them don't care if you do not know the language. Most of them do not even try to speak English which they all learn in school, especially the younger generation. In fact, I have been insulted many times when I said I did not understand the language.

"You should speak German if you are in Germany! "Scheiße Ausländer!" These *shit foreigners!* They would say angrily in German.

I made contacts with many African people in Cologne, and they all knew that I was looking for either a sponsor for my further studies or a job. One day after staying with Rose for about six months I got a call from Abdul a Tanzanian Somali who lived in Cologne and whom I was very close to. He was the only African who had maintained the African sense of humour, and he made me laugh all the time with his endless jokes.

Of course, I had some jokes to tell him too, and I remember I told him a joke about Indians in Kenya imitating their funny accent, and he laughed so much that all who were around were surprised to see me making Abdul laugh like that. He still laughs today when he remembers that joke. The Indian accent I learned in school became better and better, and I could imitate Indian way of speaking English almost perfectly, and this makes the joke even more funny.

We, therefore, enjoyed each other's company very much.

"Alice, there is a job for you!" Abdul told me excitedly.

"Oh, really? What job and where Abdul?" I asked.

"Teaching Swahili!"

"What? Teaching Swahili? Are you crazy? I cannot teach Swahili," I said sadly.

"Of course, you can! The job is good, and they pay very well, and you don't need any work permit," Abdul said.

"You are joking."

"No, I am not! Listen, I was supposed to do the job myself, but now I am fully occupied with my work so I thought about you because you are looking for a job and called you to do the job on my behalf. I can show you how to go about it. All I know is that if there is anybody who can do that job, you can," he said confidently.

"Where is that?" I asked.

"It is in a small town called Bad Honnef. It is about fifty kilometres from Cologne, and they pay your transport as well. It is a very good job for you, who is looking for a decent job, so come right over here, and I will give you all the details," Abdul said. I had told him how I hated those small jobs in bars, restaurants or cleaning peoples home and that I was looking for a decent job or study opportunity. I went to him immediately.

We telephoned there together, and I gave them my name. They asked me if I had ever taught before, and Abdul told me to say "Yes." They asked me to report at eight-thirty the next morning. I got the job. I was to teach Swahili to the experts who go to East Africa to work in development Government projects. Fortunately, I had only one student, in his middle age and seemed to be very kind and helpful to me. I told him the truth.

"Listen, sir; I have never taught Swahili nor any other language before. In fact, I hate teachers. But I need this job desperately to finance my child back in Kenya. My Swahili is perfect, and I was not bad in school either. So, we can both try to make ends meet. I do not speak German either," I told my student.

"Oh, that is alright, I speak fluent English, and I hated teachers too." He said sympathetically. Luckily, he was a very nice and kind man. In Germany, there are unfortunately not so many of his kind. However, thanks to our heavenly Father! He always made my ways quite easy though sometimes very challenging. I requested my student not to say anything to my boss about my confession.

So far, I had never faced such a heavy challenge in my life. I was studying Swahili in the evening more than my student. I wanted to be as good in my explanations as possible so as not to raise any doubts or confusion. He was a very intelligent man and could speak many languages, therefore, he helped me a lot to untangle most of the grammatical problems.

We worked hand in hand, and he said he found me very interesting being so young, and ambitious and so courageous. I also told him a lot about Kenya, political, cultural, and economical and many advices which he found very useful. I remember our first president Mzee Jomo Kenyatta died during the time I had lessons with my first student. At the end of the three months seminar, I knew almost half of Swahili grammar structure by heart, and the best part of it was that I began to enjoy teaching my national language in a foreign country!

"You are definitely going to be one of the best teachers here. I am sure of that. I wish you the best from the bottom of my heart, Alice!" he told me before he left.

"Thank you very much, sir. I'll need it," I said.

My first salary in Germany was an amount I could not imagine. It was too much money for me I thought at that time. I was still calculating in Kenya shillings. We were getting about 70 D.M per double hour (1½ hours) and we had three double hours per day. That means earning two hundred and ten Deutsch Mark per day, which amounted to over D.M. 4,000 in a month untaxed. My God, even a minister in Kenya, did not earn so much money I thought to myself! It was like a dream!

When I received my first salary, I went to Abdul and invited him out.

"Tell me where you want to go tonight. We cannot finish this money at all," I said proudly.

"You feel like Rockefeller, don't you? That is not much money here. You better save it for a rainy day. But I will come for a glass of beer," Abdul said. Abdul reminded me all the time about Thĩnĩ. They were almost the same age. Among the African people that I have come to know in Germany, Abdul is the best among them till today 40 years later. He helped me a lot during those days and gave me a lot of advice in teaching Swahili and moral support. So far, I was very lucky to meet such people, and I did not have anything against good moral advice in a complete strange country. Those kinds of advices I thought, would help me to organize myself. Many Africans in Europe I came to find out are very jealous of each other and are not able to help one another. If this was possible, it would have saved many people problems due to the language barrier. The authority workers make use of that advantage in the foreign offices by making people sign papers which convict them later. I went through that experience myself once. I will tell you about it later! In any case, I adapted the habit of helping any African, especially East Africans I came across with any problem I was able to help. Many took advantage of it misusing my generosity.

One should not feel that getting a job in Germany is easy. Oh, my God that is the last impression I would like to create to anybody especially people back home. I would say I was very lucky and God was really paving my ways Himself to get such an opportunity to find a job and a decent one at that.

Many people must do a lot of dirty work or immoral things to survive in Germany, like cleaning houses for people, serving in bars, or in discos, and even some girls prostituting themselves, get involved in drug dealers or getting themselves married to Germans without love for financial gains and stay permits. Some of the cases I came across were so disgusting that I really prayed to our Heavenly Father to help me not to go through such. I can only say that God heard my prayers and as He tells us in His word, " If you ask anything of Me in My Name, I will do it. (John 14: 14). One thing I know about myself is that I am not materialistic or greedy; obviously, I inherited this from my mother. I was always satisfied with the little that I had, and I was patient and never depended on anybody, being careful of my next step. I felt God was also with me all the time. Otherwise, I may never have found that job. What I did not know then was that I had reached my destiny!! This job was indeed where God wanted me to be. But the devil was also busy placing stones on my way.

I was to continue teaching the next group which started immediately after my first one. Ten students were divided into two groups since the courses were very intensive, we were only allowed, 4-5 participants. They looked for another teacher for the other group and got a Tanzanian student. She was studying at the University of Köln, and she wanted the job only during holidays, or so she told me. She, like me, before I came there, had never taught Swahili before. Therefore, she was a complete beginner, and she did not know where to begin. I noticed that although her Swahili was fluent, like most Tanzanians are, she had no idea about the structure. I gave her a few tips I had learned and showed her the books I used in my first course. The advantage she had was that she could speak fluent German having stayed and studied in Germany for twelve years. In any case, we worked together until the end of the seminar. She told me that she had finished her studies and was expecting to go back home in six months' time. The German authorities had told her that her stay permit would not be extended again. If she went back to Tanzania, she was expected to go to the youth service before she began to work, and she did not want all that. The job was good, but as I said before, we were working without papers. She asked me if there was any possibility of getting a permanent job in the Institute. I told her that as far as I knew all the teachers were working under the same terms and conditions.

"But one can try. It is really an excellent job, and it can take care of our stay permit problems. Working illegally is not good at all. I also believe there is nothing impossible." She said.

She started being very friendly with the head of the language department, making sure to sit with him at lunch time. Maybe I am very naive sometimes because things started happening without my knowledge. Although we were working illegally, there was a rule among the teachers of following the seniority list. That means the one who came first, always got the job first. It was not allowed to jump a teacher and favour the other. At the end of a seminar, I heard that there was another student and I took it for granted that I would teach the student being the senior teacher at that time. I was shocked when I checked the lessons plan list on Friday before going home for the next lessons and found the Tanzanian woman's name instead of mine. I went to enquire, and the head of the language department did not even want to talk to me. He said he had made up his mind to take her since she spoke German, and, he had heard that Kenyans speak very poor Swahili. Obviously, he got this false information from my fellow African lady.

We did not need to speak German to teach Swahili at all. All the so-called experts who go to East Africa were obligated to speak English. So, this was not an excuse, but I did not know what to do. We normally travelled together back to Cologne where she also lived, and on that day, she avoided me and sat alone in another compartment. I could not believe it. It was clear to me that she had maneuvered her way through, behind my back. If she had to have a contract, or a permanent job, then, of course, I was on the way, and so they got rid of me, as simple as that. I was promised to teach the next group, but they got a new teacher for that one too, who was to fall in the second place in the seniority list. As I was working illegally, I thought there was nothing I could do.

Before I lost my job, I had started plans for my daughter to join me. All the time since I had come to Europe, I had never written to Faruk, but one-day Faruk met somebody in Nairobi who lived in Düsseldorf and whom I had also met at the Independence celebrations in Bonn. The man went on holiday to Kenya, and Faruk met him. They started talking about Germany.

"Are there many people from Kenya in Düsseldorf?" Faruk asked the man.

"Yes, there are quite a few, but mostly men. There are only two Kenyan ladies that I know who live in Cologne," he answered

"Which part of Kenya do they come from?"

"They are both Kikuyus from Nairobi, except Alice looks like she is from the coast."

"What . . .? Alice who?" Faruk asked.

"Alice Mangat. I think she is half Indian and half Kikuyu," the man told Faruk.

"Damn it that is my girlfriend! But what the hell is she doing in Germany? I thought she was in Belgium."

I had asked my family not to give him my address or any information about me. I had no idea that he was seeing Victoria and visiting my sister's office every time to enquire whether I had written. My sister lied to him that I was not settled yet and that I had just called her on the telephone and promised to write, although I was writing home almost every week.

"Do you have her address?" Faruk asked the man.

"Yes of course, but if you call her your girlfriend and she never informed you where she is, that means she does not want you to know. So, I am sorry I cannot give you her address, but maybe I can deliver a letter for you."

"Oh, come on, do me a favour, she has not told anybody where she is. Even her family have no idea, and they will be happy to have her new address.

"Oh no, but as I said, I will be glad to take a letter to her." Therefore, I received a letter saying that Faruk was planning to come to Germany to join some Kenyan musicians who were having a band in Stuttgart and begged me in the letter to reply to him. He begged the man to talk to me and make sure that I replied his letter. I replied and asked him if there was a possibility of bringing Victoria with him. Oh! He called me immediately and told me that he, together with my sister were in the process of getting her a new travelling document. Before the immigration office could issue her with a passport to travel with Faruk, they wanted to know how I was going to support her in Germany. I could not prove that since I was working illegally and now in the process of trying to get a solution to that problem, I lost the job. I had also managed to remain in a one bedroom flat from Rose after she moved to a bigger flat on the same building. It was big enough for my child and me in case she came. I did not know how I was going to manage to pay the rent if nothing happened soon. I had saved enough money to keep me going for some time but not for long.

We had not separated with Rose in good faith because she tricked me to take over her flat and did not renovate it. She made me sign the papers accepting that I have indeed agreed to take over the flat without renovation, things I was not aware of. She was translating for me in the office, so I trusted her in her translation not knowing that she did it for her own benefit. When I came to find out the trick, it was too late. I took the matter to a lawyer, but the case ended up that I had signed the contract with its obligations and that was it.

I had to renovate the flat myself, which cost me a lot of money. I started learning hard the real meaning of "survival for the fittest." But I was so hurt and disgusted by these two African sisters, that I prayed never to be in such a desperation to plan ever to achieve anything at the cost of others in my life. I swore never to walk on people's corpse as my stepping stones to achieve anything. If there was no other way, I was ready to pack my things and go back home. Such ideas were not in my nature anyway, and I could never forget that my mother hated such things so very much, and repeatedly reminded us. I have seen the result of such evil methods in greed for material things, that they end up in more miseries than before.

I looked desperately for another alternative, forgetting the Institute. I was lucky again because I got a job at the Radio German (Deutsche Welle) as a freelance broadcaster in the Swahili department. Oh God, another challenge! I had never faced a microphone in my life before. Of course, I lied there as well that I had worked with the Voice of Kenya before. It looked like I had to lie every time to get a job. But I was sure that God forgave me knowing that they were harmless lies through desperation.

I was to moderate and broadcast the „Barua na Salamu" (letters and greetings) programmes, and the person who was checking my manuscript was a German who did not know a word of Swahili. This program was one of the simplest ones which involved just listener's greetings, and some of the listener's political or cultural questions which we answered as well. I played some requested music in between as well. It was a pre-recorded program. Therefore, I asked my boss if it was possible for me to visit the studios for at least a week before I started, to see how the other colleagues did their programmes.

"But we will not be able to pay you for those hours," the head of the department told me.

"Oh no problem, I want to be good at my job that's all," I replied.

I attended all the programmes for that week before I started, and I took home all the files where similar programmes were filed to study how it was done. However, I was scared and shaking the first day seeing a microphone in front of me and knowing how many millions of people would be listening to me. Fortunately, it was not a live program, as I said and I could repeat as many times as I wanted until I was satisfied that I had read correctly. The technicians were so angry with me because I kept them in the studio very long on that first day.

"You must study your manuscript before coming to the studio," one of them told me angrily.

"I did, and I am sorry, but I was very nervous being my first day. I will try my best next time." They complained to the manager as well.

"But I cannot let them send a program with so many mistakes. I was a bit nervous the first day, but I promise to improve myself," I admitted to my boss.

"It is perfectly OK, what you are doing Alice. Just don't leave the studio until you are satisfied that your program is to your satisfaction! Don't mind about these people. That is what they are paid for, even if they have to stay the entire day" he told me.

I did not want to have problems with anybody. The salary here was even better, and I was not working illegally anymore. I was paying my social security funds which meant I could extend my stay permit through the job, which was getting difficult to renew. The foreign office wanted to know how I was financing myself and why I was still in Germany if I was not attending any school. Therefore, I had registered in a language school before I joined Deutsche Welle, which sometimes I did not attend if I had to work. I only had to attend the lessons twice a week.

The next week I wrote my manuscript and practised at home with my cassette recorder until I was satisfied. This time it took us much shorter time, and their long faces which greeted me when I came in had brightened up by the time I finished. I was working with many people from Tanzania especially from Zanzibar. There was a lot of competition among the colleagues, especially the Tanzanians from Zanzibar and from the mainland. We were only two Kenyans by then, and none of the colleagues was willing to help me except the Kenyan colleague Juma, who gave me a few tips here and there. He also warned me about the other colleagues and told me to concentrate on my work and ignore their silly comments like "Kenyan's don't speak good Swahili," which might put me down.

"Your Swahili is perfect with a different accent and that is normal way we speak in Kenya." I took his advice and decided to stay out of their way as much as possible. Many of them tried to date me, but I refused.

While working for the Radio German, I met a former colleague from the Institute where I worked before in Bad Honnef. She saw me waiting for a tram in the underground station and come to talk to me. She was teaching English in the Institute.

"Hallo Alice? How are you?" Sissy greeted me happily.

"Hallo Sissy, Oh, I am glad to see you again!" I said happily to see her too.

"What happened? Why aren't you working anymore for the Institute?" Sissy asked me.

"Oh, they did not want me anymore."

Then I told her the whole story of how I lost my job.

"The head of the department added that I could not speak German well, so they preferred to take my colleague." She listened to me carefully and then she said.

"Is that the reason you think they have for not calling you again? No, no Alice, there is another reason you do not seem to know about you poor girl! Your colleague is indeed the one who spoiled everything for you in case you did not know. She is in the process of getting a contract with the Institute. Something which has puzzled us all since we have been fighting for such a thing for so long. Did you know that?" She asked me.

"Oh no I didn't know, but if it is so then she must be very lucky," I said.

"But you can't give up just like that. We all wanted to get in touch with you to ask you why you were not being called, but none of us know your telephone number. Your address seems to have disappeared from the teacher's list. That woman seems to be very clever, malicious and dangerous. Some of us have been working for the Foundation for many years, and we have never seen such a contract being given to any one of us," Sissy said.

"Oh! How wonderful for her! But how did she manage that? However, she used to say that nothing is impossible. Fortunately for me too, I got another job, so it's alright," I said.

"Oh, but it is not alright especially for us who are still working there. If they can manage to kick us out and get away with it like that, we shall all be jobless soon. Didn't you know about the seniority list?" She asked me.

"I heard about it, but it seems they do not follow it. At least not in my case."

"That is exactly the point. We want to insist that they follow that system. And you can help us show them that we cannot accept such things like it happened to you despite us working illegally."

"What do you mean, help you? How can I help you when I am not working there anymore?"

"But we are working there still, and some of us would not be as lucky as you are to get another job so easily. Please, Alice, you must follow it up for our sakes. I am sure the director has no idea what is happening in the language department. Your case might open his eyes. There have been other groups, and all the time they call a new teacher for Swahili. We all suspected that you were kicked out after we heard about the contract since you were the first Swahili teacher. Obviously, they had to get rid of you first since you would have complained and ruin their plan," Sissy said. It was very true, that much I suspected as well.

"What do you want me to do?

"I will discuss it with the other colleagues tomorrow, so call me tomorrow night and I will tell you what we have decided. I am sure they will all be very happy to know that I got hold of you since we have really been wondering how to get you. We are all behind you and remember you will be doing a big favour to all of us, even if you are not interested in working there anymore." We exchanged our addresses, and I called her up the next evening. She was so excited, and she wanted me to go to her house immediately in a taxi. She was ready to pay my taxi bill. God has mysterious ways to achieve His plans, and no demons can stand on the way.

"You cannot imagine how happy everybody is that we found you, Alice. We all knew somehow what had happened to you. We held a meeting at break time today, and they all asked me to tell you to write a letter to the Institute, language department, demanding the reason for not being called again, and why you were withdrawn from the seniority list and if they do not reply, send another letter to the director with the copy of the first one."

"Are you sure I will not put myself into problems? You know I worked or still you work there without papers," I protested.

"Which problems? If we get problems with the authorities, they too will. We do not employ ourselves," Sissy said.

A big struggle was on. I don't have anything against fighting for my rights, especially fighting against those who pick on the weak ones. The Tanzania lady was much older than me, an African who could have taken the responsibility of helping me like a big sister who had a longer experience in Germany. I had told her all about my child most of the time in tears, how I was missing her and suffering knowing that I left her in Kenya and how I was looking forward to our re-union. All these did not affect her, and she kicked me out mercilessly.

"OK my African sister, God surely knows his work, and He never sleeps. May the Lord be on my side while I fight for my right and that of the others who could be in the same boat," I said to myself.

We wrote a letter with Sissy's help. She helped me translate it in German, and as she predicted, the language department ignored my letter. We wrote another letter to the director telling him all that had happened, and I sent a copy of the first letter as well. Of course, we got a response immediately, claiming that, I did not know how to teach Swahili, and my Swahili as a Kenyan was very bad, including my German. They claimed that there were students who walked out of my class in protest, which were all lies. Luckily, one of the students from the last group had cancelled his trip to Tanzania and was still in Germany, and I still had contacts with him and his wife. I called them and told them the whole story. I sent them the copies of the correspondence between the Foundation and myself.

They were very angry about all the lies which were written about me, and they wrote a letter to the director clearing me off. According to his letter, he said I was more experienced than my other colleague, and my group could cope with the language much better than the other group. He expressed his sincere sadness to discover such things being allowed in an International

Institution like that one. The letter had a lot of weight. My former colleagues advised me to demand a meeting with all the teachers to clear all the misunderstandings. The Director did not reply to that one, but I guess he discovered how serious the matter was.

I sent another reminder which also went unanswered, in anticipation that I would give up. My former colleagues advised me to make copies of all the correspondence and they paid for it. I got a list of teacher's names from Sissy, and at break time, I went to the Institute and distributed the copies to them and later disappeared following their instruction. The colleagues took over. The teachers held a meeting and insisted that I should be given a chance to defend myself.

The Director had no choice. It turned out to be a very interesting case, and I was so excited to see the outcome. On the meeting day, Sissy told me to stop at the station bar before attending the meeting and take a short of cognac to help me speak without fear after I expressed to her my fears. She kept on insisting that I should keep in mind that they were all behind me and that they would help me. Sissy was good in such things, that I even imagined her being a good politician in her country. I found myself getting really excited about the whole thing. In any case, I followed all her instructions except the cognac part. Instead, I asked God to guide my tongue to speak without fear, and He truly did. I spoke in English and Sissy translated into German to those who could not understand English.

In the end, I won the case, and the director ordered that I should be called when the next group came. Sissy gave me a sign to keep quiet. The people concerned in the language department felt insulted from the letter which was written by my former student, and the director asked me to apologise for it. I refused.

"How can I apologise for a letter I did not write? He wrote down his opinion and the truth, against the lies which were told about me here. I am the one who needs an apology for the lies and humiliation I went through."

"Then you should apologise for distributing all the correspondence to your colleagues," one of them said.

"Not even for that! I am glad I did it. Otherwise, this meeting would not have taken place," I said. All my former colleagues were thrilled with my attitude and were all laughing and clapping.

"It will only be good and easier for you when you start working here again!" the director said smiling.

"Thank you very much, sir, but I am not interested in working here anymore. I have got another job already!" I told him

"What? And what was all this about?" He asked puzzled.

"I wanted to clear my name. That's all," I said lifting my shoulders. All of them still laughing clapped for me except my Tanzanian sister, the director, and her supporters.

"Your name? For what?" He asked, looking at me like I was nuts, or like he wanted to ask; "what name?" but changed his mind.

"For my records sir, I think it is important to clear such lies. They might affect my future. Who knows what destiny God has for me?" I said.

"Oh my God! The whole thing was just to clear "your name" huh? You wasted all that time just to clear your name?" The director said shaking his head.

"I am sorry sir, to me it was not a waste of time, I achieved what I wanted namely, I cleared myself from the false accusations. I also thank you very much for your time and fairness in this matter and hope that, you will stop such games played on to the other colleagues in future," I said and left. I had a better job anyway, and I did not have to work every day, therefore it was a very good opportunity to allow me to do some studies and the fact that my daughter was on the way, I would have enough time for her as well.

I had not heard from Faruk for some time. One evening though, I received a telephone call from him.

"I am calling from Dubai," he said.

"Dubai? What the hell are you doing there? I thought you were coming here to Germany with Vicky?" I asked.

"I got an urgent and unexpected contract to work here in Dubai for eight months. In any case, I could not get a travelling document for Vicky. They wanted a proof how you were going to support her financially in Germany. It was not possible to get her travel document since she is endorsed in your passport. I tried everything even telling lies that she was my biological daughter. It would be much easier if you went to collect her yourself. I took her for all the vaccinations needed therefore she is ready to travel anytime," he explained.

"Oh! Faruk, I was expecting her this month. I cannot leave now I just got a new job."

"Oh, it's OK. You can go for her later; she is actually alright. Your sister looks after her well. When I finish my contract, I will come to Germany, and we shall arrange together for her to come over. Don't worry now."

"Hey wait a minute. You said you were on the way to Stuttgart. You are not planning to come to me, are you?" I asked with surprise.

"Well, why not? I could come and see you and then proceed to Stuttgart, couldn't I? You mean you do not want to see me anymore? Alice, you know I love you, and you will never get away from me. Germany is not far for me. We belong together, learn to accept that."

"No Faruk! We do not belong together anymore, and you are not coming to me. I have my life to lead now, and I do not want you to come and distract me again. If you are coming to Germany, I cannot stop you, but all I wanted was for you to bring my child with you and if that is not possible, then you can go straight to Stuttgart, you do not need to come through here. Fact is, I am engaged to someone else, so forget about me," I said trying to sound convincing. It was not true that I was engaged, but I had a steady boyfriend, and we were very serious with each other. I had no intention of starting all over again with Faruk. As far as I was concerned, it was over between us.

"Tell that donkey to clear off before I come. You are my wife. I will never let you go." Then the phone went dead on my ears. I was so mad at him. I had told my boyfriend a Ugandan man, about Faruk and Vicky's plan to come to Germany, and he was also very jealous, although I had assured him that it was over between Faruk and me. He knew very well that Faruk was my first love and it is always difficult to get over such.

"If you know each other for such a long time, you are his wife, and he can claim you anytime," he said.

"What do you mean? You think I am a piece of an object and not a human being who has a right to decide for herself? We are not married, and he has no right to claim that I am his wife," I said angrily.

"Have you told him that we are together?" He asked me.

"Yes, of course, I told him! I even lied to him that we are engaged." I shouted.

"And you want to tell me that he accepted that? Come on Alice; you don't expect me to believe that, do you? The man is coming to Germany for the first time, and his long-time love is also in Germany. You want to tell me that he has no plans for both of you?" He said sarcastically.

"Oh, leave me alone. I don't want to urge with you."

Faruk renewed his contract and called me to tell me that he would be coming later to Germany. I prayed that he would stay right where he was and never come to Germany. I continued working for the Radio German and saved as much money as I could. Since I could not get anybody to sponsor me in my studies, there was no way I could finance my studies alone and work at the same time.

Therefore, I decided to save as much money as possible then leave Germany and go back home. I worked for almost one year, and then DW started reducing my programmes, limiting them to only four programmes a week. They wanted to have more female voices in the Radio as they claimed, and at that time we were only two females. In any case, when Faruk arrived in Germany, I had managed to save almost fifteen thousand marks.

When I saw him, I realised bitterly that, it was true what he had said on the telephone. I would never get away from him. His love possessed me, and nothing could change that. I was again cheating myself thinking that I could be happy with someone else. I also knew I could never be happy with him, but that did not change my feelings towards him either. I broke the affair with my boyfriend immediately, which hurt him a lot.

I felt guilty, but it was better than pretending to love him, which became even more difficult as soon as Faruk came back to my life. There were no plans to go to Stuttgart. It was just an excuse to get to me he confessed later. He knew that even in Nairobi I used to hide from him and so he came out with this story to make me stay where I was and where he knew.

Before coming to Germany, he had called me again and told me that the whole band wanted to come to Germany as well to try to get Work he asked me if I could look for a hotel for them to stay. My Ugandan boyfriend lived in Köln city Centre with his sister. I spend most of my time there and hardly went to my flat which was far out of Köln City. I had given my key to a Kenya young man whom I met in Köln, and he had no money and no place to stay.

He begged me so much to let him stay there for a while as he was looking for a place of his own, so I let him stay free at my place. My boyfriend and his sister had asked me to give up my flat and live with them, but I wanted to have my own flat where I could always go if things did not work well with us. I did not want to depend on any man. We got along very well all three of us, and we had a lot of fun together, but as it is always expected, we still had our problems here and there especially because my boyfriend was a very jealous man. We quarrelled many times, and he even became aggressive and started hitting me.

However, I told Faruk to come, and they could stay in my flat and told the young man to look for another alternative. The day they arrived with three other members of his band, they were so tired because the flight to Germany with a stopover in London had taken them almost 24 hours. When he saw me, he hugged me and kissed me as if we were together again. I could not resist his kisses. I picked them at the airport and took them to my flat. We spend a lot of time talking while the others slept. I explained to him that our relationship did not work in Kenya and that I had a boyfriend whom I intended to marry and please he should understand and respect that. He did not urge much except saying with a lot of anger.

"Then why did you respond to my kisses and even allowed me to kiss you? You can lie to somebody else, not me. I know you still love me and you know it and should accept that reality. I love you too, and I will allow nobody to take over my place. I am here now, and I will see how you will marry that bloody Ugandan bastard."

It was on a Friday, so in the evening we went to our usual disco, a club which was called "Dakar" and there we were supposed to meet my Ugandan boyfriend. At the beginning, they were quite friendly to each other and then suddenly, I noticed that my Ugandan boyfriend bought beers only for all the others but not Faruk. Faruk asked him if he could dance with me and he said no in a very aggressive way pulling me roughly to him. Faruk equally pulled my hand to the floor, and there they started a cold war. We went to another disco the same night, and they both insisted to sit one on either side of me. By the time the evening was over they were complete enemies. The Ugandan man claiming that I was his fiancée Faruk claiming that I was his wife. I got angry with them and decided to go home alone to avoid scandal. Home where? I went outside to take a taxi, and they both followed me one sitting again on either side of where I was sitting at the back of the taxi. I told the taxi driver to take me to my flat, something I did always when I quarrelled with my boyfriend, but he insisted that we drive to his flat. The taxi driver refused claiming that I was the first one to get into the taxi and he would drive where I asked him to. It was also to his advantage since I lived far. We ended up in my flat all of us the others following us in another taxi and they insulted each other so much especially my boyfriend to Faruk telling him that he was only a cheap useless, uneducated musician.

He further said that he was a journalist and could afford to give me a better and a decent future. I got mad at his boasting knowing that he was only a student then and I warned him to stop insulting my guest, but he continued even more aggressively, so I ordered him to leave my flat. It was almost 4 a.m. That was the end of that relationship. A week later we started afresh with Faruk, though I must say he behaved like my brother for almost a week avoiding hurrying me, but we could not hold it any longer.

He arrived in Germany with only three thousand German Marks. It was in autumn, and since he had come from a very warm country, he had no clothes for Winter. We, therefore, used most of his money to buy winter clothes for him. I asked him what he did with all the money he had earned in Dubai, and he gave me a story that he had been sending some to his children in Kenya. I had no reason not to believe him at that time, but I came to learn later that he never sent any money at home.

He had three months tourist visa, so by then, we did not have to bother with the papers. At the end of the second month, we decided to register him and get his visa renewed. Oh, the problems started then. The foreign office refused completely even to give him three more months to stay in Germany. We tried everything, but they refused. In fact, we met a very bad immigration officer who just hated him. We suspected the reason was because of his profession which stated in his passport as "Artist." He ordered him to leave the country latest on the day his visa was expiring in the middle of December. He put Faruk in the computer, which meant he had to leave and report at the border, or at the airport that he had left the country, otherwise the control police would come after him.

We had only about three weeks to find a solution. I also wanted him to stay. I do not know why, but that was the best time I ever had with Faruk since we knew each other. I did not have to share him with his fans, and he was so sweet that he kind of managed to convince me that he really cared for me too and had matured. He was a different man altogether from the one I knew in Kenya. He became devoted, loving, and showed some responsibility which I had never seen in him before. I also in my own way poured all my love that he had no doubt that I deeply loved him. He said that he was growing up and was no longer childish like he was in Kenya those days. We talked a lot which we never did in Kenya, and I thought I found out a lot about him that I did not know. Later I discovered that most of the things he told me about himself were lies and made up stories.

We got a tip from somebody that he could go to a neighbouring country for some weeks and come back later with a new tourist visa which would give him time to organise his stay. The nearest neighbouring country where a Kenyan did not need a visa was Denmark. We celebrated the Kenyan Independence party in Bonn together before he left. He had no more money left, so I started digging on my savings. I paid for the ticket and gave him some money for a hotel in Copenhagen. He arrived there well, and that was one week before Christmas. Two days later he called me, and he was crying on the telephone.

"Please, darling come over. I can't bear it alone during Christmas and in a country where I do not know a single soul. The cold is also killing me," he said in tears.

"But Faruk, it will be too expensive for us. Just be strong and wait for another week. I do not want to be alone either."

"Please Alice, I beg you, come over!" He begged me so much till I agreed. I left with the next train for Copenhagen through Hamburg and crossed with the ferry to Denmark. In the ferry, I realised something was very wrong with me. I felt sick, almost to a fainting point, and vomited several times. I thought it was seasickness and withdrew it from my head. Faruk was waiting for me at the railway station, and it was snowing. I felt so sorry for him seeing him standing there shivering, looking desperately at the windows of the train for me. He had forgotten to wear his gloves and his woolen cap which I always forced him to wear. When he saw me, he ran to me and held me so tightly, and I could feel him shiver either from the cold or like he was scared.

"God! I have never been so happy to see somebody in my life! Thanks for coming honey! I was afraid you would not come," he said still holding me.

„Where are your gloves and your cap honey? I told you, you must always wear them. You cannot afford to be sick now!"

"I forgot them as usual," he said like a small child.

On Christmas day, we were invited by a Tanzanian family in another town in Denmark called Aarhus, and that is where I confirmed that I was pregnant, remembering the sickness on the ferry.

"What are we going to do?" I asked Faruk in tears.

"Why are you crying? You should be happy! Sometimes I believe you don't love me, Alice. How can you be sad because you are expecting my child? Maybe this is our luck. God wants us to be together, otherwise, I would not have known where you were to follow you, and soon after you conceive," he said holding me also in tears.

"But we have not yet settled, and all these problems with our stay permit in Germany. How are we going to manage with a baby? We also want to bring Victoria to Germany. How are we going to manage all that?" I asked still crying.

"God will show us the way. Please don't cry. I am very happy. In fact, I already have a name for our baby. He will be called Faiz if it is a boy and if it is a girl we shall call her Faiza! That is the name of my favourite sister." He said giving me one of his best smiles and wiping his eyes. He was so happy that I almost forgot our problems. Why was I so careless in these things? Why did I not take care and kept on forgetting to take my pill? Why must I always get pregnant with this man every time he touches me without a plan? I made a promise to myself though not to think of abortion no matter how difficult it looked. I did not want to go through such an experience again in my life never! Despite all the problems, I saw it as a blessing and a solution to our problems. The baby would make us stick together no matter what problems we might face in this different culture we found ourselves in.

We left Denmark after a week to return to Germany and fortunately, we did not have problems at the border. One could leave Germany and come back immediately, entitled to a new tourist visa those days, but the trick was soon discovered by the German authorities. All these changed in the course of years and soon after our return to Germany, the law was changed that, if you came with a tourist visa and left Germany, you were required to stay out of the country for six months before you were entitled to a new tourist visa, unless you renewed it through the Embassy and with a genuine reason which was still very difficult.

CHAPTER SEVEN

We came back to Germany and started struggling with the authorities to find a way for Faruk to stay. One possibility was to get him a paper marriage and believe it or not; I was not against it. We found a lady who was ready to marry him for papers. He registered in her place, and we had to get the impediment of no marriage papers for him from Kenya. He called his relatives in Kenya and asked them to help him get all the documents needed by the German authority, to marry a German woman. At this point, I was almost sure that Faruk loved me the way I loved him, and I wanted to help him to organize himself in Germany. I knew that even if I married him legally, he was not going to get a work permit. I had already enquired from a lawyer who advised us on all the legal regulations at that time. What was a piece of paper anyway? Main thing was, I was in his heart, or so I believed. Africans do worse things in Europe to achieve residential permits.

I was also getting desperate about Vicky because I knew if things got worse, I was not going to manage to bring her, and I did not want my second child to be born without Vicky being with us. So, we decided that I should fly to Kenya to bring her, which was the easiest way since she was already endorsed in my passport, and all I needed was a ticket for her.

I, therefore, managed to fly in February 1980. I did not have enough money anymore, and the banks were very reluctant to give somebody like me credit, who did not have a permanent job. I begged one of my colleagues to sign a guarantee for me in the bank and God being so great he agreed, and I could take 3,000 D.M. I prepared myself quickly to fly to Kenya to pick my daughter while carrying the other one under my heart in my 3rd month. I knew God would not let me lose my baby through flying, so I did not even consult any doctor but send my prayers directly to God through my faith in His Son Jesus.

My daughter had already started school in Kenya. I told my family in a letter that I was coming on a weekend, though I was arriving on a Friday morning. I intended to go straight to school and enter Vicky's classroom and see if she could remember me. I was so nervous and afraid that my child had forgotten me. Many times, I had these nightmares that she would not even come near me (well the dream came true much later in life). I had been away for two and a half years, and that was a long time for a small child of her age to forget her mother. I took a taxi from the airport and went straight to her school. I was terribly disappointed and so angry when I discovered that the children had mid-term holidays, and nobody was in school. I, therefore, went straight to my sister's house. They were all busy preparing for my arrival the next day like cleaning the house, cooking and they had taken my daughter to a hairdresser to get a new hairstyle, etc. My sister wanted to send someone to get them come back quickly, but I stopped her telling her that I wanted to see if she could recognize me. When she came back and saw me, she jumped to me with a lot of joy calling me Mami, Mami! I was so thrilled, and I started crying joy tears of holding my child once again in my arms. Oh, how I longed for this moment all those two and a half years!

My daughter was somehow shocked to see me a day earlier like all the others. Most of the family members from the village came to my sister's house on that day too to go and receive me at the airport the next day.

"I am very happy I didn't tell you the real date of my arrival. How can you people take so much trouble? I need one or two people to help me with my luggage at the airport, but not the whole delegation. I am glad I learned a lesson. Next time I will also come unexpectedly," I said.

"But we all wanted to have a chance to see the new airport," my cousin said disappointedly. The new Jomo Kenyatta Airport was opened during my absence.

"You can go and see the new airport anytime. You didn't have to wait till I come back."

I was very happy to be home and to see everybody again. People at home are so different, so full of life, full of humour and loving at least at that time. The whole weekend we were busy entertaining all the family members who came to greet me. They brought me food, chicken (living), fresh milk from the farms, eggs, etc. They were equally happy to see me as I was to see them again. For the first time in my life, I felt the warmth of my sister Mūmbi towards me as well. She seemed to be so happy to see me too. I did not tell them about taking Vicky back with me yet. Maybe some seventh sense or Holy Spirit was advising me against taking my child to Europe. In any case, I found it difficult to break the news; I always have a funny feeling when I am about to do something which is not right. I was not yet settled in Europe, and another child was on the way, and those facts could also have contributed to my fear. At the same time, I could not have imagined leaving my child back in Kenya once again. Whatever was going to be I was taking my child back to Europe with me. We belonged together, and we had to struggle together. As my mother used to say often the Kikuyu proverb to my sister, which says, "Njogu ndīremagwo nī mīguongo yayo." (An elephant will always be able to carry its own tasks), I knew I had to take my tasks no matter how heavy they were. After about two weeks, the chance created itself.

"Mama, are you taking me with you to Germany?" Vicky asked after some time. My child had thought that I had come back for good. But when she heard that I was going back, the question came up.

"Would you like to come with me?"

"Oh yes, mama, I would love that. I would also like to see uncle Ezo again. He wanted to take me with him, and then he left without me." Vicky nicknamed Faruk "uncle Ezo." She said so excitedly. While she was a baby, she could not pronounce "Faruk," and she nicknamed him "Ezo" which made us all laugh every time she called him that. My sister told me that during his visits to them he tried to teach her to call him „daddy," but she continued calling him "uncle Ezo." Men are so daring that he did not ever think that I would have something against my daughter calling him "daddy."

"Uncle Ezo could not take you with him at that time. He had to go somewhere to work before coming to Germany. But now he is looking forward to seeing you too," I said.

"So, you are taking me with you?" She asked excitedly.

"Yes, darling, I have a ticket for you too." Mũmbi was shocked to hear this.

"You are taking Vicky with you?" She asked

"Yes, I have already bought a ticket for her." Vicky ran outside with excitement to tell her friends the good news.

"I am expecting another child and Vicky must come with me," I told my sister when we were alone. I was going to tell Vicky about the baby when we get to Germany I thought.

"Why don't you leave Vicky here with us?" She asked.

"No, I need my child near me. You don't know what I have gone through all this time without her," I said

"Yes, I know, one could hear and feel it in your letters. But we are afraid you may never come back here if you take her. She is our only guarantee that you would come back," she said. Blood is surely thicker than water. My sister was indeed worried about me.

"Oh, don't worry, I will come back home alright. Europe is not for me at all. I am not happy there, but I know the situation here is worse. I will work for some time and try to save as much money as I can, then I will come back for good and do my own business, even if it's a small one. I am lucky to have found such a wonderful job though it is not permanent." They had all been listening to me in the radio almost every morning. My daughter was also very proud of her mummy speaking in the radio.

I took my child with me to Germany, not knowing that I was doing her an extensive damage by bringing her into this strange society. I thought I was going to give her a good chance to get a better education, not knowing the price I may have to pay in future. To bring up a child in Germany was going to be another hardest challenge I couldn't have imagined. I thought it was my duty to remind my children their identity and to make them proud of it, but it turned out to be a very painful task.

African way of loving children and bringing them up is completely different from the Germans. It was a fight, an unfair one and to make matters worse I was one against many as far as children upbringing were concerned. German way of upbringing was to bring them up free without any directions. Children should do and say what they want. Parents are like their slaves, working, cleaning after them cooking for them and accepting or admitting their repeated humiliation and insults. I was not going to follow their way no matter what, I made up my mind. I would bring my children up with discipline of the African way giving them all the love they needed but make sure they knew what is wrong and right.

When I came back to Germany, Faruk came to pick us up from Frankfurt airport and greeted me with the news that the woman he was to marry had changed her mind and did not want to marry him anymore. She had met somebody else whom she wanted to marry for real.

"What are we going to do now?" He was so sad and desperate, that I felt sorry for him.

"We have to do something immediately. If the foreign office hears about this they will give you a notice to leave the country again," I said.

I went to see my lawyer and told her that my daughter was in Germany with us and that I was expecting another child from Faruk and we did not know what to do. Faruk managed to convince me that Vicky should grow thinking that Faruk was her father. We would tell her the truth when she grew up. So, we decided for the sake of everybody, that it could only be positive if we did that. I agreed without thinking much about it. I had managed to get her birth certificate without father's name; it just stated, "father unknown." But this was another situation now, and I never like to live in such guilt of telling lies. It would, however, be cleared out when my daughter was old enough to understand all. At this moment it was the only thing we were obliged to do.

"I am sure he will get the same visa that you get if you register that you two want to get married. Let the foreign office know that he has cancelled the wedding with the German woman himself because of the new situation of being pregnant and your daughter being here," she advised us.

We did the same and Faruk got the same visa that I had, in his passport. We had to get married immediately according to the foreign office. I had come to learn about the law in Germany, and I was afraid of getting any legal ties with Faruk. Deep inside, I knew that we could never live together. I was satisfied living with him the way we were, but I did not want any permanent bonds which would bring legal problems later. I knew the problems involved in separation and divorce especially where children are concerned. In any case, I had no choice because they warned that if we did not get married, he was not to get his stay permit extended anymore. We had to get some documents also for me from Kenya. The papers did not come on time, and Faruk began to drink a lot maybe through desperation of not working, and he began to beat me up when we quarrelled.

He slept the entire day, and in the evening, he drank a lot.

"Go around and look for work, just any work. There are a lot of black jobs around, and people do all kinds of odd jobs here in Germany Faruk. You do not have to wait till you get a job to stand in front of audience and sing. We have a lot of responsibilities now, therefore, you should not be choosy. Take what you can find," I told him

"You expect me to wash dishes or cleaning jobs? You must be joking. I would rather go back home. I am an artist, and that is all I can do," he said.

"Then start doing something about it. You must identify yourself as a Kenyan musician here and not copy other people. Germans want to hear African music from an African and not Michael Jackson copied music by an African. You will never get anywhere with that kind of a thing here. If you can play African music, you might get some people to sponsor you. You are a good entertainer; you can play congas very well including singing and dansing." I said

"Just shut up! What do you know about music you woman?" He said rudely.

I had spent the rest of my savings to finance Faruk and bring Vicky to Germany, and I had a credit of over 3.000 D.M. to pay back and to make the matter worse, Deutsche Welle started reducing my programmes even more. Faruk got a lot of contacts with many Kenyan's most of who were very jealous of us being together. We were a beautiful couple who most of his friends envied. I never learned how to cook German food all that time. I loved African food and cooked all the dishes which most of the people could not because they did not know where to buy the ingredients. I had discovered all the shops which sold our food. I learned to cook things like ugali with the grease flour instead of maize flour which was not available then, and spinach or kale instead of sukuma wiki and things like pilau, biriani, samosa, chapatis, maandazi for Vicky, etc. People ate dishes in my house which they had never tasted in Germany before. Faruk's friends began to come between us, by telling him to leave me and marry a German woman. They advised him that life would be much easier for him, than if he married me legally. Those who were sincere told him to stick with his children and me, and that the German authorities would not make problems with him if there are children involved. My lawyer and I told him the same too. At the same time, I also told him it was his own decision to know what was best for him. I was not so keen in getting any legal ties with him anymore anyway. My blood of Punjabi also played a great role in my life that I did not know how to beg anyone.

As soon as Vicky arrived, I organised for her to go to a German lady the entire day who did not speak English and who had small children, for her to learn German language. After a while, she got an admission in a Kindergarten. She was attending the afternoon nursery also in the afternoon to improve her German language, before she began school in August. She arrived in Germany in February therefore, she had only about six months to speak German. A week before she started school at the beginning of August, Faruk was picked by one of those friends who were against us being together and they told me that there was a meeting for all the artists in Münich, and he wanted to attend it with his friend to see if he could get into contact with the other musicians. He was to stay for one week. I was happy to hear that he could get such a chance and I happily agreed to let him go. I was expecting my baby at early September. Vicky had to be taken to school every morning, and somebody had to pick her up from school to take her to the afternoon nursery school where she spent the entire day till around five in the evening. We had to pick her up also from the nursery to bring her home. All these duties including shopping, cooking and the house cleaning, I had to manage alone despite me being far advanced in pregnancy. We had no car, so I did all the walking, since it was all in the same area. We lived on the twelfth floor, and most of the time the lifts were out of order. I sometimes thought I would deliver on those steps. Faruk was calling me every day sometimes even several times. I thought he felt guilty of leaving me alone with all burden heaped upon me. But if something would come out of that trip, then I would be happy for him I thought.

"Please hurry and come back. It is too much for me with Vicky in school. I cannot manage anymore," I begged him every time on the telephone.

"I will come back after a week or so," he said. "I can't leave now. I have to stay till the end of it."

"Could you give me a telephone number in case anything happens?" I asked him

"No, no, we have no telephone where we are staying. I will be calling you instead." But one day he called me at three o'clock in the morning.

"We just came back from a nightclub, and I could not sleep without talking to you. Honey are you alright?" He asked, and I could make out from his voice that he was drunk.

"I thought you said you do not have a telephone where you are staying!" I said

"Oh yes yes, we don't have a telephone, but today we came to visit another friend of Khalid (his Friend), and I asked him if I could use his telephone shortly," he said nervously.

"Then give me his number. I could call him during an emergency, and he could look for you," I insisted.

"I will be coming back the day after tomorrow, so don't worry. How is Vicky?" He asked trying to change the subject.

"She is fine and misses you," I said. I told him everything about the lifts.

"O.K. honey, I will call you tomorrow. I love you. Good night now," he said quickly.

"Good night!" I said and hang up. I had a feeling something was going on, but I was too tired to think further about it, so I slept.

He came back as he promised and told me that he did not get much success, but many people promised to look around for something for him. In the last week of August, I went to hospital in emergency because the uterus opened up. I had still 2 weeks left according to the doctors. First, they send me home, and the next day I came back again with labour pains. Faruk stayed for a while in hospital with me but I send him home because of Vicky, so I delivered all alone with my doctor and the nurses. I had a lot of pain, but my baby did not want to come out until Friday morning at 0.45.

Those days the doctors were not so quick with caesarean birth like today but still believed in natural birth. Eventually, the doctor decided that he either must do something, or I must go for the operation. When the final push came, the doctor climbed on the bed next to me with a knee under my chest and pressed to help me since my strength was failing me. First, I did not know what he wanted to do and when I realised it, it was too late to stop him.

My God, it was so painful I thought I would die and I could not push that huge man away from me even though I tried. I wished I could get even his arm to bite him and make him stop, but all in vain. He disappeared immediately after the baby was born because I think he could read the hatred in my eyes. You can imagine how his action busted me up. True enough my son's head was so huge that if the doctor did not help me, I would not have got him out naturally but still, I hated his method.

I was stitched so much, and I had a lot of problems later to sit down and breastfeed my baby. I told the nurses almost in tears that I do not want to see that cruel doctor anymore. They told me that his method was well known in the hospital. He preferred that than caesarean, but I told them that one day somebody would kill him for it. The next day when he came around the nurses had warned him that I was so mad at him, so he stopped at the door and looked at me smiling, asking if he could come in.

"At your own risk! If I get hold of your hand, I will show you the pains you caused me." I said still angry.

"OK I will not come near you, but I can talk to you from far, do you allow it?" He said still smiling. I had to smile too.

Faiz, as we called him through his father's wish right from the time we discovered I was expecting, came two weeks earlier than expected date probably due to all the stress, but he was healthy and weighed 4,100 grams and 57 cm long. He was from birth a duplicate copy of Faruk, except one could see that he was probably going to be much taller than his father and had his grandfathers (my father) hair and complexion. Vicky, on the other hand, looked very much like me but got typical African hair. That made me always mad because my son does not need that beautiful hair while my daughter needs it as a girl. That night when Faiz was born, after stitching me, cleaning and dressing my baby, they brought him to me, and I sat up holding my baby as he slept in my warm arms. Sitting up in bed alone in a big labour word after the nurses finished their work, I held my baby facing a big window which had no curtains. The room was in darkness, but I could see a huge cloudless sky in front of me. The sky was so clear but I could see only one star in the sky.

At first, I thought it was an airplane, but it kept on blinking without moving until I noticed that it was indeed a star. I watched that star for a long time thinking about my life and the life of my children. My son lay in my arms quietly not aware of which world he has come in. I wished he could have stayed a little bit longer in my womb where he was protected, instead of being in such a hurry to come into this cruel and merciless world. I had not even finished dusting everything and preparing a clean room for him. How were we going to support two children? I thought to myself.

Faruk seemed too irresponsible. I had still not achieved the right stay permit, no permanent job, no money. The star was still blinking at me, and this time I was sure it was not an airplane. There was no moon to be seen anywhere, but the sky was lit somehow.

"Faiz my darling baby," I told my son holding him up and showing him the star like Kunta Kinte did in the film "roots."

"What does that beautiful bright star want to tell us? Does it want to tell us that a star is born today? Oh, honey, I do pray for such a thing to happen to you. You look like a star anyway, and mummy through the mercy of God will take diligent care of you, that I promise you." I kissed him on the cheek, and I made a sign of cross on his face and holding him next to my heart, I said a long prayer to the Almighty God to protect my child and pour all the blessings guiding him in all his ways in life. I also thought I heard a whisper like from my mother or Holy Spirit telling me "Don't worry God will provide for you and your children Cikũ." When the transporter came to roll me into the room they had prepared for me; the star was still blinking at me.

Faruk was so thrilled that he forgot all his problems and concentrated on the little boy. He said he was so happy that he was born on a Friday, that as a Muslim he believed, it was a great blessing for a child to be born on a prayers day. Dreaming, I could allow him to dream, but I knew I would never let my child be a Moslem. Although Faruk was a father to many children in Kenya as I came to know later, none of them was born while he was around. He saw his children very rarely and hardly spend time with them when they were babies. So, he was kind of thrilled to see his son immediately after birth and see the infant grow into a beautiful baby boy. He was trying to be a good father to both my children at least at that early stage of our baby. Faiz brought a lot of happiness in the house, and we almost forgot our sorrows. He was such a beautiful baby that I had trouble going shopping with him. Everybody would want to look at him closely, and he would smile at everybody who talked to him. He is still like that till today. He was such a big baby that his first beautiful baby shoes I bought him while still in my womb fitted his foot halfway.

The first shoes Faiz wore with eight months when he started walking, was size 25. He had a big foot exactly like that of my father I always wondered over his huge shoes. My son's foot, therefore, could hold on the ground quite firmly, and he walked at the age of 8 months. On that first walking experience day, he tried to stand up with the help of the sofa, and we watched him struggling and falling several times, but he did not give up until he stood up. He looked at us and found us all watching him breathlessly. He gave us his best smile and tried to make his first step. He fell again, but we did not touch him because we saw that he wanted to do it all by himself.

He was getting more and more excited, so he got up again breathing heavily, with the help of the chair and this time he made several steps before he lost his balance again. I gave a sign to his father to keep quiet, and we were all quiet watching him. This time when he got up again, he walked towards me almost four of his small steps and fell on my laps. We were so excited and shouted laughing and hugging him, but he wanted me to put him down to continue his practice, so I put him down.

Oh, how I prayed for my baby to follow that habit of never giving up on all he did in life. All the falls he will do in life, he should always get up and move on! I was so proud of that picture, and it lingers in my mind always.

He had stories to tell us in his baby language he had formed at the age of five months, and he would talk and talk while we were sleeping. I taped him talking this language. If we showed him that we were listening to him, he would be so excited and speak with such urgency and even laugh at his language as if it was a wonderful joke he just cracked. I thought it genius at his age.

I could see that my daughter was a bit jealous of his little brother, but I never took it seriously thinking that it was quite normal considering their age difference and the fact that we were paying far too much attention to him than to her sometimes. I tried very hard to show her that she should be happy to have a baby brother in the house whom she could play with, assuring her that we loved her equally, but that we were just excited over a new baby. It looked like the case of my sister and myself. What goes around comes around as the saying goes.

The first Christmas for Vicky in Germany and after Faiz's birth, we were invited by a Kenyan woman named Florence, who lived in Freiburg and was a friend of Khalid, Faruk's limbo dancer friend. First, I did not want us to travel away with a small child with a train in winter and that being our first Christmas for all of us together, but we did not have enough money to make a decent Christmas for the children anyway so in the end I agreed.

We were all supposed to meet in Florence's house with Khalid and two German women who I came to understand that one was Khalid's girlfriend and they lived together. We travelled by train with the children to Freiburg. Faiz was about four months old. When we arrived there, Faruk changed his attitude towards me for no reason at all. He was drinking so much and not helping me with the children. He would not talk to me and behaved like we had quarreled, which was not the case. I can sometimes be quite proud in some cases, so I ignored him as well. Florence was surprised at his reaction, and she asked me what was going on.

"Ask him; I do not know. He started behaving like that as soon as we arrived here. I do not know why" I told Florence.

Florence had a party on Christmas day, so we all stayed at home. On the second Christmas (Boxing Day) evening, they all decided to go to a disco. Faruk had ignored me all the time.

"Well, you all go ahead. I have to stay with my children," I said.

"No, no Alice. You have not been here in Freiburg before, but your husband has been here, you should also have a chance to see Freiburg by night." They all looked at one another somehow shocked.

"When was Faruk here?" I asked.

"We came through here from Munich the other time, and we all went out," Khalid said quickly. So, I found out that the Munich trip was a lie and Khalid invented it.

"Oh, I see, he never told me," I said.

"I do not want to stay here with the children. She can stay with her children." Faruk said.

"Of course, I will stay with "my" children. Just go and enjoy yourself." I shouted and went to the bedroom. Florence had given us her bedroom since it was the biggest because of the children. She refused to go out as well and decided to stay with me at home. I insisted that she should not ruin her evening because of my children, but she refused and stayed with me. Faruk without shame prepared himself and left with the others.

"Florence, when was Faruk here?" I asked her after they had left and the children were sleeping. She kept quiet for a while.

"I should not have said that he was here in the first place. They are all very angry with me," she said.

"But you said it, and I heard it, so out with it. When was he here?" I insisted.

"Faruk was not in Munich at all. He was here all the time," she said.

"Here? What was he doing here? And why did he lie that he was in Munich?" I looked at her suspiciously.

"No, no, not the way you think, I had nothing to do with him. But I am very surprised at his behaviour towards you. He told me several times while he was here that he loves you and the children too, so why is he behaving like he does not care about you or the kids at all?" She asked.

"Now tell me what he was doing here," I demanded.

"He wanted to marry a German woman whom Khalid organised for him through the newspaper."

"Say what? Faruk wanted to marry a German woman here?"

"Oh! It was only paper marriage and not a real marriage," she said.

I was so shocked. I could not believe it. Florence showed me the newspaper cutting where Faruk had advertised himself for marriage. She told me then the whole story that Khalid advised him to marry a German woman because of his residential permit. They got a reply, and the candidate wanted to see Faruk immediately. That is why Khalid came to pick him up from Cologne in a hurry, and they gave me that story of Munich. When the woman saw Faruk, she wanted to marry him for real and go back with him to Kenya where she wanted to settle. She was a rich old woman with a daughter almost my age.

Faruk felt guilty of doing all that behind my back knowing that I had nothing against such a thing. But according to Florence his friend Khalid advised him not to tell me claiming that he should not disturb me with such things during my pregnancy. He cancelled everything though the last minute and came back to me, probably after the telephone call in the night when I was insisting on having the telephone number. I was so sad to see people causing all these problems between me and Faruk, and fellow Kenyans to make the matter worse.

Khalid was a snake in the grass because he was jealous of Faruk having a young beautiful Kenyan woman. I was sure about that. He had told Faruk many times that he should not marry a Kenyan but a German if he wanted to succeed in Germany. Faruk came back and told me what he was telling him and my response to all that was always the same. "You will have to make up your mind what you want. To struggle with the children and me or follow your stupid brainless limbo dancer and former beach boy friend's (Khalid was a limbo dancer in Germany) advice and go for the success he promises you. One thing I must tell you, those idiots are all losers and they want you to be a loser too. He is a snake in the grass like he coils himself to do his limbo dancing. I have seen those Africans married to Germans, and I have not seen any of those successes he promises you. If there is any success to anyone, we all know that it lasts only for a very limited time." I told him similar words many times.

"No wonder Faruk was behaving so funny the moment we arrived here. I am sure it was guilty conscience which was disturbing him," I told Florence.

"But please Alice, I beg you do not ask him here. Wait until you get home. I do not want problems here because I have other guests as well," Florence said.

"Don't worry I will not say a word." I kept my promise, but all the time I was boiling inside like hell. I did not even want to see his face anymore. How could he do things like that behind my back? Surely, he knew how much his stay permit was important to me as well. I felt so humiliated that all those people there knew all the time about those things and I did not. We left the following day, and I did not say one word to him all the way. He tried to talk to me in the train, but I did not open my mouth at all. I could see that he was suspecting that something terrible was wrong but could not trust himself to ask me so he slept all the way instead. When we arrived in Cologne, I prepared the children for bed, and after they had slept, I called Faruk where he was sleeping on the sofa. If there was anything that man loved, it was to sleep. He never had enough of it.

"I want to talk to you!" I said. I saw alarm in his eyes.

"What about? I am tired, and I guess you also are after such a long trip, so go and sleep we can talk tomorrow," he replied.

"I must talk to you now! I don't care how tired you are. Remember I made the same trip as you and when we arrived I am the one who cooked and prepared the children for bed while you relaxed on the couch? But don't worry, you know I am a machine." I said.

He sat down rubbing his eyes with his hand.

"I want you to tell me with your own mouth, where you were four months ago when you told me that you were in Munich," I said.

"What do you mean where I was? I was in Munich like I said," he replied looking down.

"No, you were not, I happen to know where you were and what you were doing. But I do not want to believe it till you tell me yourself. And if you do not tell me, then I will tell you where you were and with a proof, and if I do so, that will be the end of our relationship. So, if you value our relationship you better tell me the truth yourself," I said.

"I don't know what you are talking about," he said still trying to lie.

"Oh yes, you know very well what I am talking about," I said. I gave him another chance to confess to me, but he refused completely to tell me the truth, so I told him all that Florence told me.

"Do you still claim that you do not know what I am talking about?" He kept quiet. "I am going to sleep. Tomorrow morning you start looking for a place to go. I do not want you near me anymore. Khalid can have you now. Go and marry your German woman or one of the prostitute friends of his girlfriend. Apart from what you did, it is obvious that you do not value this relationship at all." That is when he realised things were bad and that I was dead serious.

"I did it for you and the children. I was afraid to hurt you during your pregnancy. I broke the whole thing because of you. Why did that woman Florence not tell you all that? Are you blind or what? Don't you see that Florence wants to break us up?" He tried to defend himself.

"Florence is breaking us up or Khalid, your dear friend? But why Faruk? We were arranging something like that together before, and I was pregnant still. You cannot give me that as an excuse. How were you going to keep it a secret?" I asked.

"I would have told you as soon as the baby was born."

"Yes, I heard that this was an advice from your Khalid. Of course, he did not want me to know who was breaking us up. And why didn't you tell me about it when I got the baby?" I asked

"I cancelled everything anyway, so I thought I should forget about it as well," he said.

"O.K. somebody was kind enough to tell me about it, whatever her intentions were. You also tried to full me now when I asked you to confess." I said.

"Please Alice, try to understand. I love you, and I need you. We should stick together and not let people like Florence or Khalid come between us. We came from far away together."

"Tell that to your stupid limbo dancer pimp. Get out of my life and this time for good Faruk." I said and went to bed. The next day, he packed his things and left to go to his friend Khalid. He kept on calling me and every time I heard his voice I just banged the phone. After a few days, I heard from Florence that he had left Germany and had gone back to the Arabian Gulf. I did not care. As far as I was concerned he could go to straight to hell. He kept on trying to call me from there as well, but I always put the telephone down. He wrote me many letters and sent me pictures of the children which he had taken before he left Germany. I never replied to neither one of them.

I changed my telephone number so that he could not reach me. I was not going to allow him near me in my life again, that I was sure of. Soon after that Deutsche Welle cut me off completely from the program list. When I enquired, they told me that they did not need my services anymore. I started to contact the workers union for help, but nothing could be done.

Deutsche Welle did not want me anymore. After about half a year, I discovered the reason why they cut me off so suddenly. I had worked for too long with the Deutsche Welle as a freelancer, earning far too much money, and there is a law in Germany that you cannot engage anybody as a freelancer for so long without engaging them permanently. The court would have forced Deutsche Welle to employ me permanently. The Personnel office discovered this after they received a letter from the foreign office, enquiring about my position in Deutsche Welle so that they could renew my stay permit. The Personnel office decided to cut me off from my work without telling me the reason until six months were over. The person I contacted from the workers union either knew what was happening or she did not bother to consider my case properly. After six months, I could not do anything anymore. DW promised to give me only 2 programs in a week, which was very little money. However, it was a door closed to get more doors open which would lead me to my destiny.

Two months after Faruk left, I received a telephone call from a Kenyan girlfriend. She knew the whole story about Faruk and me.

"Hey, your husband just called me.!" Akinyi said. Although I felt proud before when people called me his wife this time I detested the name "husband."

"Who Faruk? He called you from Bahrain?" I asked her.

"No, my dear, from Frankfurt. He is back in Germany." My heart skipped a beat.

"Oh my God, since when?" These nightmares will never end!

"I do not know, and he said he has your new telephone number, but was afraid to call you because you always bang the phone on him. He wants to know how the children are."

"Tell him to go to hell and that my children are not his business anymore. Are you sure you did not give him the number?" I asked her.

"No, I would not do that. But you are unfair. You don't have to be enemies. He is the father of your children, so talk to him at least," she begged.

"Forget it Akinyi. I do not want to see him, at least not yet."

After she put the phone down, the doorbell rang, and a postman came with money send to me by Faruk with a telegram. I wanted to send the money back, but luckily a German lady who was looking after my children when I worked was with me.

"You cannot send the money back. Are you stupid or what," she asked me in shock.

"But I know this is only to soften me up, and the next-door bell will be Faruk himself. I will not allow him to buy his way back to us." I said.

"Never mind, just take the money. You need it for the children, and they are his children."

So, I took the 3000 Deutsche mark he had sent us. Two hours later, the doorbell rang and when I asked who it was there was no reply, and there was nobody to be seen through the spy hole at my door. The doorbell rang again, and I opened the door to look outside. Faruk had hidden on the side of the door waiting for me to open and he put his foot at the door quickly before I could bang it on his face. How I knew this bastard's mind!

"I just want to talk to you, and see the children, please Alice." That was all. I was mad to see him and happy at the same time. I allowed him back into our lives again. I could not believe how weak one could be, but surely as far as this man was concerned, I was completely helpless and probably very stupid. He somehow knew also that although I was very proud, my love for him was stronger.

The workers union managed to get me some more programmes again in Deutsche Welle, but I was not supposed to earn more than 800 D.M. a month. We could not live on such little money, and I could not go to the social welfare because my lawyer advised me that the moment I did that, they would send us back to Kenya. They would prefer that than to pay the Social money to provide for all of us for God knows how long. She warned me that they would not renew my stay permit again if I went for the social welfare.

I managed to get few jobs here and there, like working in trade fairs through our Embassy, teaching Swahili privately, and I started braiding African hair for many ladies I knew. I managed to get African hair products and cosmetics from England and sold them to my fellow African people in Germany. Such things were not available in the shops. This business was illegal, but I risked anyway.

Faruk continued to drink even more. He never helped or encouraged me in all those things I was doing to support the family. He would beat me up for every small thing through the influence of alcohol which I had to buy it as well. He was a different person all together when he did not drink, although very moody and miserable, he never hit me. I tried to be patient with him, taking into consideration that I was probably the only one he could take his frustrations out on, but slowly I was getting fed up of his behaviour and irresponsibility.

He did not know how the rent was paid, nor how I was supporting the family and I sometimes thought that he did not care. I had many sleepless nights thinking of how we would solve our problems, while he slept soundly next to me. He never even bothered to ask me if the rent had been paid or not.

Although I hardly made it to church at all, I believed still to be a good Catholic, and I prayed as often as I could. I tried to teach the children about God by reading them the children bible stories, but their father was against it. He refused me completely to take them to church and wanted his children to be Muslims. I was not very much against another confession at all at that time since I did not know the bible as I know it today and I thought the aim was always one, to worship God, although I did not agree with some religion rituals. I also did not know anything about the Muslim faith as I came to know later. Therefore, like my parents did not come between me and my faith, I was also not against my children's choice in worshiping God in any faith, so long as they grew to honour and fear their Creator, the Living God of Abraham Isaac and Jacob. However, he never tried to teach them about his faith, neither was he himself behaving like a God-fearing person. I do not think he had seen the inside of a Koran except holding on to those general regulations of Islam.

For example, I was not supposed to buy any pork in our house, but he was doing worse things than those which are forbidden to Muslims than eating pork. He was drinking and smoking, and I never saw him pray even once, but he would quarrel with me if I prayed with the children the way I knew. Muslims are supposed to pray five times a day. I also noticed that he only quarrelled with me on religion if he was drunk. Vicky was already baptised in Kenya as a baby before I left, but he refused me to take Faiz to church for baptism.

As far as I am concerned Faruk was a Muslim because he was born in that culture, but he never practised nor did he know anything about his religion and I did not want my children to grow up without knowing God. I told him this, but nothing I said or did was of any value to him anymore. I was simply a stupid woman who did not know anything. This is a general opinion of African men about women especially Muslims, so it did not matter to me. I came to learn that Koran does not respect woman's rights and they should submit themselves to their men. I told him to cut that out of his head and that I believed I am also a human being to be considered and he cannot change my mind and neither my faith. My parents were not against it who did he think he was to do so? After all, I was the one supporting him and his children, and he should be ashamed to imagine that I could coil myself in a corned whenever he sneezed.

Faruk had no appreciation of what I was doing, and if a small argument came up, he would hit me without a second thought. Most of the evenings he was drunk. Twice the neighbours had to call the police because Vicky screamed aloud begging him not to hit me again and calling for help. Both these times I sent the police away lying that it was a minor domestic quarrel and it was over, and all was well. I did not want him to get involved with the police. He had not managed to finalise his papers, neither had we registered his return to Germany. While in Bahrain, he had managed to get a six months visa to England and that was the visa he was using,

England being a member of European Community. One day before Vicky's seventh birthday, we were invited by a Kenyan friend who also had a birthday

"But I cannot stay long because Vicky has a birthday tomorrow," I told our friend.

"OK. But just come for a while," she insisted

So, we went with Faruk leaving the children under the care of my German neighbour. He drank so much and did not want to go home. I kept on reminding him that we had a birthday party for Vicky the following day and I had invited all the afternoon nursery children in her group. Therefore, we had to leave in order to manage the preparation in the morning. After midnight, I got fed up with him. He had drunk almost a whole bottle of whisky and was very drunk.

"If you don't come, then I am going home alone," I said.

"Then go!" he shouted.

I left to look for a taxi because my girlfriend did not have a telephone. She had just moved into the flat. Before I could reach the taxi stand, Faruk caught up with me and just started beating me up on the street.

"How dare you leave me behind? Is that how a wife should behave in front of people?" He said hitting me hard with his fists knocking me down and continued kicking me with his feet when the Taxi came. The man stopped and saw him beating me and kicking me.

"Stop beating her or I will call the police," the taxi driver said in German. He stopped immediately and walked away staggering. I got up and got into the taxi. I was nose bleeding, and the taxi driver wanted to drive me to the hospital, but I refused. Faruk had no money with him, but I did not care anymore how he would reach home.

I did not go to take the children from the babysitter lady since it was too late, so they slept there. Early in the morning, I went to wake them up. My face and my lips were swollen, and I had black marks on my hands and feet where he kicked on me. I had not slept at all, so my eyes were also red and swollen due to lack of sleep and from crying.

The German lady knew about the beatings, and she knew that he had beaten me again the moment she saw me. She told me that Faiz had cried the whole night with fever and she thought he was teething. She had given him an aspirin, and he fell asleep at around five in the morning. Before I could drink a cup of coffee she put in front of me, Faruk came and rang the bell at the German lady's door. It was about 7 a.m. He walked in, and it seemed like he was still drunk. I had no idea how he came, but he could have walked because otherwise, he would have been home earlier if he had taken up any transport.

"I want to see my children!" he said.

"Get out of my house, or I'll call the police," the woman said. "Faiz is not feeling well. He is teething, and he has just slept. You cannot wake him up,"

"Call the police I don't care! I want my children, that is all I want!" he repeated. He staggered and fell breaking a glass table. He got up and went to the children's room. Vicky was already up, getting ready to go to school. He went and picked Faiz from the bed where he was fast asleep and carried him with one hand and took Vicky by the other hand. She managed to tear herself from his grip and ran out of the room and hid behind me scared as hell. I thought he had run mad and the German lady and I followed him to my flat. Faiz was screaming at the top of his voice.

"Give me my child please Faruk. He is sick and has fever," I said crying. He threw a hand like he wanted to hit me, but I managed to dodge it and take the baby away from him. Faiz's screams seemed to have irritated him. I gave the German lady the baby, and she ran back to her flat with him. A few minutes later the police arrived. The German lady called them after she went back to her flat.

"Get out of my house. I do not care whether you are the police or not. This is my wife, and I can do what I want with her," he told the policemen in broken German.

"Oh no, you can't. You can do that where you come from, but not here. You are also drunk!" I asked them to help me bring him to bed because he was drunk and that was the reason of his behaviour.

"If you do not go and sleep, we will have to take you with us," the policeman told him.

"Shit! Go to hell you bloody Germans." He shouted in English which they understood, so they took him with them. I was not bothered where they took him. I was so scared of him, and all I wanted was for the police to get him away from us. I was busy the entire day with Vicky's birthday party, which we set at my German neighbour's house, though I felt awful.

I was convinced he had run completely mad. My poor child was looking at me with such sad, scared eyes like she wanted to tell me something. I tried to show her that everything was alright, but I knew that these things were affecting her as well. I had to tell lies about my face to the nursery school teachers that I fell on the steps. I could see that they did not believe a word I said and I suspected that Vicky had told them what happened. Faruk came at around four o'clock with a camera. The German lady did not want to let him in, but I was afraid that he would make problems in front of the school teachers again, so I told her to let him in. He did not seem to be drunk anymore, so at least I knew he would behave. He came and took pictures of the children, talked a bit to the nursery teachers as if nothing had happened. I felt like bursting inside when he applied his charm and smile to them like a very devoted father. Later he went to sleep in our flat because he had not slept at all except for a few hours at the police station. When the party was over, I went with the German lady to my flat. Faruk was sleeping on the sofa, with the television on. When we came in, he got up and could not look at me in the eyes.

"I am not going to stay with you under the same roof Faruk, not anymore. You have to leave, or I will leave with the children, and you can have the flat," I said flatly.

"You cannot move from here. This is your flat anyway. Alice, I don't know what happened to me, and I do not know what to say. All I know is that I am terribly sorry," he said.

"I cannot accept your apology anymore. If you know it is my flat, then please go. We cannot stay together at all," I said.

He told us what had happened to him that the police had taken him to the police station and made him sleep for a while. Then they had woken him up and checked his papers only to find out that he did not have a stay permit for Germany. They checked all the stamps he had before and discovered that he was not even supposed to be in Germany, so they had taken him to the foreign office. The foreign office wanted to deport him immediately unless I went to them to confirm his story.

"Alice if you let me fall now, they will deport me, and you know what that means," he said.

"Do you think I care what happens to you now? You came here to mess my life up! It will be for my advantage and the children if they deported you, then I will be sure never to see you here again, and I will be able to re-organise my life again which you have messed. I cannot allow my children to grow in this domestic brutality." I said in anger.

"Please, you cannot do that to me. Help me I beg you. They said if you do not come with me tomorrow, they will deport me. They held my passport too." He held his hands together like in prayers in front of me in tears.

"I am not going with you anywhere! And now get out of my house," I shouted. I was not afraid of him now, and I also knew that he could never hit me if he was not drunk.

He started crying uncontrollably; the German lady shook her head because she saw that I was getting soft. I had never seen him like that before. She pulled my hand, and we left the house and went to my children. I followed her because I could not sit there and watch him cry. The German woman just shook her head saying "those are just crocodile tears, don't get soft about them."

I came later with the children, and I could see that Vicky was so scared of Faruk. He had stopped crying and was sitting in front of the television chewing on his lips thoughtfully. He tried to apologise to Vicky, but she just looked at him with scared eyes. Faiz would not let him touch him. When the children went to bed, he brought up the subject again.

"I know I have wronged you to the extent that I don't expect you to forgive me. I even feel ashamed of myself, but please do this one more favour for me. I promise to do as you wish, even go away from you if you clear me out of this mess," he said.

Despite my anger, I could not let him be deported. I thought of his parents, his other children in Kenya and him without a job in Kenya with the inflation as I read in the newspapers. Nobody would understand or forgive me if I let him be deported no matter how wrong he was. I would be blamed for it. So, the next day I went with him to the foreign office, and he got his passport back. They warned him that if anything like that happened again, they would surely deport him. The police wrote me a letter telling me that they were going to take him to court for beating me if I wanted, but I asked them to forget about the case and drop it. He swore and promised me in front of the foreign office that he would stop drinking.

He changed for a while and stopped drinking, telling me that he was looking for a place to stay. He became a loving man, taking care of the children and devoting himself to us again, and my anger started evaporating, and my feelings for him started changing. I decided to give him yet another chance. I registered him again in my house, and the immigration office said they would give him only six months stay permit to allow us to get married and if we did not get married in those six months they would not renew it. Knowing all that I knew about him, I agreed to marry him through the pressure the foreign office was giving us.

All the papers came, and we registered to get married in Cologne town hall in November 1991. He also signed an affidavit that he was the biological father of my daughter as the lawyer had advised us, so that we could all hold one name as a family. He had managed to get a job in a discotheque as a disc jockey, in a small town out of Cologne. He came in the mornings because we did not have a car, and public transport connection from there was very poor, especially late at night. I, therefore, managed to get a car from a friend, which we could pay in instalments. I paid the first instalment of 300 D.M, and he was supposed to pay the rest, as he worked.

He started drinking again in the club and made a mistake of beating me up once more. I had gone into his money purse while he was sleeping, and I took some money out to go and buy food. He did this himself, helping himself in my money purse anytime and I never complained. He did not find that to be alright if I did the same. He made a huge story out of it and was so angry eventually he hit me very hard that I fell hurting my head. This was the day Princess Diana got married, and maybe Diana's wedding made me feel very funny about our planned wedding. It looked too perfect to me, and somehow, I thought it all not right. I wondered whether they really loved each other, or it was just a royal obligation. I just did not know why but I changed my mind there and then, ever to get married to this man.

The next day I went and cancelled the wedding and threw him mercilessly out of my house taking my house keys away from him. He was now working, and he could look after himself, I thought. He called me every day, but I always put the phone down. He sent many people to come and talk to me, but I could not accept his apologies anymore. He did not even try to keep his words, so I refused to let him back again. He tried to hunt for me in the discos where we normally went during the weekends with a neighbouring Tanzanian girlfriend, but I refused even to talk to him. One day he met me in those places again with my girlfriend and begged her to ask me to agree to talk to him that he had something very important to talk about.

"There is nothing important between us anymore. I do not want to see him or talk to him anymore. I have had enough of his shit!" I shouted at my girlfriend.

"Give him a chance to talk to you Alice, he is the father of your children. You cannot just shut him up like that. Just listen to what he must say," she begged. I refused completely. He sat at a corner looking at me until we left.

He followed me outside and when I saw his car I wanted to break it into pieces.

"I wish I have an axe or something to break this damn car into pieces," I said aloud. He was standing right behind us.

"If I give you my shoe to break the car, will you talk to me?" I thought he was mad to think that I was joking. He just did not know how angry I was with him.

"Give me your shoe, then we shall see." I had taken quite a lot of alcohol as well, and when he gave me his shoes, I broke most of the windows. The shoe slipped and fell into the car, and the idiot gave me the other shoe. My girlfriends and a barefoot Faruk stood aside and watched me, but nobody dared to hold me. I broke some of the lights and the more windows and left to go home without talking to him. I felt very good somehow though I felt I should have broken his teeth or nose other than the car.

He followed me home, but I refused to open the door for him. On the way, back he was stopped by the police and lost his licence. He also had drunk alcohol and driving a damaged car. The next evening, he called my girlfriend and told her that he was in Denmark, and that was the reason why he had wanted to talk to me so desperately the previous night. He had only two reasons to be in Denmark. Either he had been unable to renew his visa without me, or he had gone to get married there. Many people were doing that to avoid the paperwork in Germany. In Denmark, you needed your passport and a birth certificate, and in a week's time, you could get married, and the marriage was legal in Germany. I did not care whatever the reasons were.

A few weeks later he came back and tried to call me several times. I always put the phone down. I was not interested in hearing his stories. He, therefore, called my girlfriend and told her that he had been trying to call me, but I had refused completely to talk to him, so he had to send her to me. He told her that he got married for papers in Denmark, to get the work permit to support the children and me. He said he had done his best and tried to talk to me about it first, but I had refused, so he had gone ahead and did it without discussing it with me. They did not have any affair, and the woman knew about the children and me, and she had wanted to meet us.

Oh God! I do not know how I could have come across somebody like Faruk. I thought he was the most shameless person I had ever seen. He got married for the children and me! What was happening to this world? A man who calls me his wife marries for my sake! Of course, he expected me to be happy about this and to accept the situation and the life would go on! I hated him so much at that time, and I did not want to see him again neither did I care to listen to his silly excuses. He was married, and I did not want to know why or how or to have anything to do with him anymore.

He never gave up. He was staying with some of his Kenyan friends who were trying to call me on his behalf, but as soon as he came on the phone, I just put it down. One day he came up to my flat and rang the bell. I did not open, and he was there the whole evening, trying again and again until I opened the door. I wanted to call the police, but I just could not bring myself to pick up the receiver. Whoever said love is blind was damn right!

"How can you be so hard on me? I thought you loved me?" He said

"Not anymore! And now that you are married, you don't expect me to go on loving a married man, do you?" I said sarcastically.

"Aach, you know what that marriage is all about. You are my wife, and that is only paper marriage to take care of my damn stay permit. You cancelled our wedding so what alternative did I have? I can work and support you and the children now! I cannot live without you and the children. I also know that you love me. Otherwise, you would have called the police and not open the door for me," he said applying his best smile and winking at me.

"You promised to go away from us if I helped you, remember?" I reminded him.

"My problem was these stupid papers. I was frustrated to the end, almost running mad. Could you not try to understand that? I have nothing to do with the woman I married; she agreed to marry me to help us," he said.

"And what do you have to do in return, sleep with her now and then?" I asked

"Nothing! She is just a kind woman and knows how much I was suffering. I have never slept with her. I swear in the name of God," he said.

"Which god? As if you know who God is! Do not misuse Gods Name knowing you are lying you shameless creature. This will be my first time to see a German woman sacrificing herself or rather her life for nothing. You must be very lucky. But, unfortunately, I am not interested in sharing your luck. You can tell your grandmother that kind of a story, maybe she will believe you. I am not as stupid as you think Faruk. Your swearing does not move me. You do not even know that God exists," I said getting mad.

"But it is true Alice I have nothing to do with the woman. You can meet her and talk to her if you don't believe me. My God honey, I want to be with you and the children. I am not interested in any other woman let alone a white woman!" I got real mad then and started abusing him calling him nasty names just to get the anger out of me. He was chain smoking all the time, letting me say all what I wanted, I felt so much frustrated, and suddenly I started crying. He did not touch me but just sat there watching me for some time, then he came to me slowly and lifted me from where I was sitting.

"I will never beat you again. I swear with my mother if you do not want to me to sear in Allah's name. I will try all my best not to hurt you. I know I have done so many sad things to you, and you should not forgive me, but honey I beg you try only this one more time. I suffered so much these past weeks when you refused even to talk to me. I know for sure that I love you and I need you more than ever. If you don't believe me, then ask yourself why I am here? I have my papers now, and I can stay in Germany and do what I want."

"This is your song every day, but you do not even know how to keep your word. I sometimes think you do not even know what you are saying. Why do you make me suffer so much Faruk? If you love me, then go away from me!" I said in tears.

"I cannot go away from you. I love you, and I love my children. Please help me to change myself. I want to share all my life with you, Alice. God knows that this is what I want. I have been running after you ever since I met you. You were only a teenager! You always find a way to dodge me, but I always follow you and find you. I have come all the way to Germany because of you. Do you think that any other woman would mean anything to me now? I tried many women after I broke with you, but it never worked. I cannot get over you, and the truth is I do not want to go away from you. We belong together honey otherwise I may never have traced you in this country."

I felt so helpless and disgusted with myself for even listening to his stupid sweet talk. I just could not believe the power this man had over me. I sometimes wondered whether this was love I had for him or sympathy or possession. Sometimes I found him so naive and thought I should stick to him and help him to organise his life. Somehow, I felt that he really loved me, only he did not know what to do with that love. Was this the devil's work then of destroying our love? Then if God planned that we should be together, why did He let him marry another woman no matter for what reason? Why did God let it happen? Why didn't he show him another way? Was it my fault for cancelling our marriage? Was it my fault that I refused to talk to him? This happened many times after a bad quarrel, but he worked me up with his sweet talk every time that I start blaming myself for all. What seemed to be clear was that my Creator surely did not want me to have a permanent unity with this man. He did not want us to get married. It was simply not His will.

None of those questions had any other answers, but I was scared, frustrated, angry and very confused. Somehow, I still managed to forgive him once again, took him back in my flat and lived with him knowing that he was married to another woman. I met the woman, and it seemed true they did not have anything to do with each other sexually at that time, but I could see that the woman would not mind if Faruk had other interests in her. I could not help to notice the way she looked at him, and I tried my best to be friendly to her, but I could never be able to hide my feelings so somehow, she knew we could never be friends and that I had seen through her intentions.

Faruk was to remain registered in her flat as her husband, but he lived with us. His official letters were posted to us by the woman, and Faruk called her now and then, to find out if there were any official letters for him. He continued to work in the Discotheque which was near where the woman lived. She also worked there as a waitress, and I believed they had some affairs which I was strictly not supposed to know. During the New Year eve, we all met there, and she was very friendly and offered me a Champagne bottle. *"Yes, you bitch we can share a bottle of Champagne like we share the man."* I thought to myself. I wanted to refuse, but Faruk insisted that I should accept it claiming that I was unfair to the lady for nothing. He became loving to me again and the children for a while, then the Discotheque closed, and he was jobless once again.

My stay permit had become a problem as well. Deutsche Welle refused to give me more work completely, and I was pressed by the foreign office to prove to them how I was living financially. I could not say that I was living with the father of my children who was married to another woman and working illegally in discothèques, neither could I tell them that I was selling cosmetics at home and making African hairstyles, which was also illegal. I had started ordering African cosmetics from England, and I could make the African hairstyles quite well. This is how we survived at the mercy of God, and it was illegal I started looking seriously for another job but where was I going to get another job?

Abdul called me again and told me that the lady who made me lose my job at the German Foundation for International Development (DSE) had returned home to Tanzania and the DSE were looking for another teacher. The man who was previously in charge of the language department was also no longer there. So, I called them, and they told me that they had students who were to begin in February 1982. I was overjoyed to get the offer.

The foreign office had taken my case to a conference, and they had decided to send me back to Kenya. My stay permits which was expiring in the middle of February was not to be extended under any circumstances. My God! How could I pack and take my children back to Kenya without any money? How would I start in Kenya with two children? Inflation in

Kenya was getting worse than when I left. And my child Vicky was just getting to speak German and getting used to the school. To make the matter worse, I had finished all my savings.

"But I got a job which will begin in February," I told the immigration officer. This was the beginning of January.

"We are not interested in that. The committee has decided that you should leave the country at the end of the stay permit in your passport. Nothing will change that, and your stay permit should not be extended," she said rudely. All the officers I had met there were rude, arrogant, and real mean. I sometimes thought that being unfriendly to foreigners was one of the qualifications needed to give those people that post. They all seemed to hate foreigners.

"How can you send me back home now? My daughter goes to school here. After all, the job I have got is not a job any German can do. I am not taking away any job from a German," I said.

"It does not matter. You go and teach your language in your country. We do not need you here. We shall pay for you and your children's ticket, including the transport for your luggage. That is generous enough and now don't waste my time anymore. Report to the social office near the place you stay and arrange with them for your transport back to your country." I left the office crying, not knowing what to do. Faruk was at home, and I told him everything. Our role had exchanged. Now I am the one who was worried of my stay permit. Marriage secured his.

"We should look for somebody to marry you and pay him. I hear some people do that and they charge around 3000 D.M," he suggested.

"No! I will not marry anybody for those damn papers. I have my home; if they send me back, then I will go back home. I would not put too much trust in those kinds of papers if I were you. One day you will believe my words. Germans never do anything for anybody for nothing. In fact, nobody does anything for anybody for nothing these days," I shouted. I called my lawyer and told her everything.

"Could the DSE give you a letter stating that you will start work there in the middle of February?" My lawyer asked me.

"I do not know, but I expect they should." At that time, the DSE had changed the system, and the teachers were no longer working illegally. They were still working temporarily but were now contributing to the tax and social security funds.

She called the D.S.E. and explained to them my situation. Luckily, they agreed to send a letter immediately to me by fax.

We went to the foreign office together with my lawyer the next day. When the lady saw the lawyer, she changed her voice.

"Mrs. Mangat should not stay in Germany any longer, and this has been decided upstairs in a conference room. I am sorry, but you did not have to waste your time coming here. I explained all that to her yesterday," she repeated.

"She also explained to me all what you told her. But I am not of the same opinion as you and your committee. I will have to take her case to court, and in the meantime, the social office will have to support her and her children, whereby the case might take several years. In the end, I guarantee you that she will win the case because you cannot push the children around like that. Here is a letter from the DSE that she can start work in February. She might lose this chance if you do not comply. You either give her a stay permit to allow her to get a work permit or you will have to compensate her later after she wins the case which I guarantee you she will, for making her loose the job at the DSE. Do you understand what I mean?" She asked. The woman looked up, her eyes wide open.

"I cannot change that. I am only doing my work, and I was told not to extend her stay permit anymore," she said.

"Then go back to the person who told you that and repeat exactly what I said. She is not going back to her country unless she wants it herself. I will not allow you to force her on it because I will fight for her rights.

Come on, let us go Mrs. Mangat," my lawyer, said to me. I was a bit scared but happy at the same time, at the way she spoke to the cruel woman and I thought she must have messed any chance I may still have had. I looked at her so desperately.

"Wait, wait a moment. I have to go upstairs and talk to my boss; please wait outside for a while." She took the letter, my file and left the office. My lawyer had to go to court so she also left telling me not to worry that I would get my permit alright. An hour later, I walked out of that office with some six months stay permit. I was to go to the labour office to get a work permit for the same period as my stay permit. The stamp I got stated that I was not supposed to work anywhere else in Germany, with an exception at the D.S.E., teaching Swahili. I got one year's work permit for this and went back to the foreign office to get further 6 months stay permit to match with the work permit. This time I was made to sign a paper which said that if there was no more work at the D.S.E. for me, I am obliged to return home to Kenya. The translator did not make it clear what that really meant, or I did not understand her well, so I signed without getting an advice from my lawyer, a very foolish action I regretted later.

We had not been able to pay our house rent for almost three months. Since cosmetic business was not operating anymore, I had practically no money at all, and we received letters asking us to pay or move out. So, I asked Faruk for the first time to find somewhere he could borrow the money, and we could refund it later.

The banks refused to give me any money knowing that I did not have a permanent job. A German friend of the family at that time, Markus Groß, agreed to give him the money which had accumulated to 2000 D.M. to pay the rent and we would pay him back slowly. The salary in the DSE was not as good as before, but I was happy that it was official and I was paying for my social security funds in Germany. It would be easier for me in future to renew my stay permits. I was glad that I had cleared my name in the DSE those past years; otherwise, they might never have taken me back. Jesus surely paves my ways miraculously.

After I had worked for almost three months, Faruk started his drinking again, and he changed his attitude towards me. He refused to take care of Faiz while I went to work. The German lady could not look after Faiz any longer because she had started work. So, I would take my poor baby with me all the way to the Foundation. There was a nursery school where we could leave the children till we finished work.

The journey from my flat to the D.S.E. took almost two hours, therefore I had to wake up at five o'clock in the morning to prepare Vicky's clothes for school and breakfast, then wake Faiz around five thirty and prepare and feed him to leave the house at 6.15. The train to Bad Honnef left Köln main station at 6.50, and I needed at least 30 minutes to get there with the street ban. I left an alarm clock next to Vicky's bed because Faruk would not wake her up to go to school, neither would he do anything for her, so she woke up by herself, prepared herself, ate her breakfast and went to school. She had to be quiet not to wake her "dear father" up.

When I returned home almost five in the evening, Faruk would be watching television, and the house would look exactly as I had left it in the morning. I would go shopping with Faiz in his pushchair, clean the flat or do the washing, cook, bathe the children and put them to bed. By the time I finished all that, I was dead tired that even eating was a problem. I did not beg him to help me at all. I thought those are things he should have seen himself as a human being, but unfortunately, he never even realised, how his baby was suffering travelling all that way early in the morning and sometimes in bitterly cold weather, while he was comfortable under warm blankets.

This was when my love for him started dying, and I grew very cold towards him. I hated even our intimate moments. I refused to discuss any issue with him and decided just to do my own things without him. I did not care anymore where he went and what he was doing during the day. Luckily, he never beat me again. I started appreciating his marriage which had saved me from becoming his legal wife.

God's ways are very strange because he has His own timing. As the time went by, my many why-s and how-s were answered one by one. Although I suffered a lot, everything that had happened was to my own advantage, or so it seemed. God was paving my future showing me the way other that the one I had taken which He had not planned for me.

CHAPTER EIGHT

I do not know how I managed everything and teach at the same time, but I did. Sometimes I would cry all the way in the train, prepare my lessons or sleep because I was always exhausted, but the moment I entered the classroom, God somehow gave me the strength and helped me to forget all my problems. I became very interested in teaching Swahili, and I thoroughly enjoyed it.

The people we taught usually were different than the Germans living in Germany. Most of them have lived outside in the so-called third world countries for many years, and they had diverse ways of seeing things. If I ever had problems with my students, it was mainly with those going out for the first time. They came in the classroom with a lot of arrogance, especially when they saw a woman (and black) they did not take the lessons seriously.

Most of them came in the classroom with the attitude that an African language must be very easy to learn, there was nothing much to learn, taking for granted that it should be like children language which you could learn in a week or so. There were also many of them who were sympathetic and wanted to learn as much as possible, language and culture knowing their success in our countries depended on the first contact namely we, the tutors. This was the attitude my first student was before I was kicked out before. So, these were very co-operative and hard working.

I came to know the Swahili grammar structure very well, knowing every explanation thoroughly. I learned this through the questions asked by the students. It is my opinion that teaching a German as an African is very difficult. Despite, always wanting to know why; how; how come, most of the time they tried to test if I knew what I was talking about.

If I did not explain anything to their satisfaction, they always gave a very dissatisfied reaction, giving me a blink that almost pronounced what is in their mind, like saying "you see these African have nothing in their heads!" and to avoid all that, I made a point of learning how to give a satisfactory answer to every question. I made a point to study all the Swahili grammar books in the market at that time I could get hold of. If they asked me about any vocabulary, most of them referred to the dictionary once more to confirm. My life was under pressure at home and at the work that I felt like exploding anytime.

We were not supposed to teach much grammar, or at least we were supposed to avoid giving much details of the grammar structure, but most of the students wanted the structured method. I also concluded that one could never teach a Bantu language through direct method due to the noun class arrangements which complicates everything and which is completely new and different to the European languages. Basic Grammar structure is necessary if one wants to learn Swahili language quickly or any other Bantu language for that matter. It is not possible to teach anybody any language within a month or even two months and expect this person to speak the language fluently.

At the same time, I wanted my students to achieve as much as possible in my class to help their further learning and I discovered and decided on some very important details of the grammar structure which I could cover within 1-2 weeks depending on their learning capability and motivation which enabled the students to build their own sentences in a standard way. Without that, one would need many years to learn how to speak it correctly.

You can easily see that with the Indians who live in East Africa for many years or even born there but never tried to learn Swahili the correct way. I could make a motivated student speak Swahili slowly but correctly in an intensive course of six weeks. I was sure then, that they needed about four to six months of practice in the country, to speak the language almost perfectly, if they stayed at a place where everybody around them spoke Swahili perfectly, like at the coasts of Kenya and Tanzania. The students who went to work in big towns like Nairobi, Dar-as-salaam, etc., were less fortunate to practice their Swahili because everybody speaks English.

It took me over ten years to convince my seniors that my method was helpful. Even though none of them could speak Swahili, they always claimed to know better. Of course, there are many things one can adapt pedagogic, methodical, etc. and from other languages, but it was not important to them to consider my argument since it was a language they did not speak, all I was expected was to do just what they wanted. I refused and followed the method which was satisfactory to those who were really motivated and interested in learning Swahili, and this was larger percentage than those who complained about my teaching. Most of those who complained were the ones who did not find it necessary to learn it, or did not find it important, etc. They were but a very small number.

I tried my best to explain why it was necessary to teach the short basic Swahili structure at the beginning, but it sometimes seemed like I was wasting my time. I had a feeling that they did not take me seriously since I was not a trained teacher. I was also faced with a lot of challenges from the other colleagues who wanted to take my place, because as I came back, I took over my position being first in the priority list. Many other teachers, Kenyans, and Tanzanians came to work with me when there was a second group of students or more. Swahili had most of the students among the vernacular languages taught in our Institute, being a language spoken in most countries of East Africa.

The Tanzanian colleagues all claimed to know Swahili better than Kenyans and brought this claim to the department, with the intention of getting rid of me again. It is true that some Kenyans really do not bother to learn Swahili the correct way because they are so involved in their tribal languages, but there are also people who speak and write Swahili perfectly in Kenya. Apart from that, Swahili is our National language. There are Kenyans, for example, Faruk born at the coast that have no other mother language except Swahili, therefore it made me really sad when they generalised it and used this to push me away again.

The first president of Tanzania, Mwalimu Julius Nyerere is indeed to be thanked more for encouraging Swahili in Tanzania during the times of socialism. Apart from that Tanzania has about 122 tribal languages, while in Kenya there are about 42. In each district in Kenya, they practised their tribal languages especially during the colonial time where the tribes were not mixing like today. In Tanzania on the other hand, almost every village has their tribal language, so Swahili is very useful for communication. I have also come to realise that many Africans especially in Kenya are ashamed of their tribal languages or Swahili and seem to value foreign languages more. I am so proud of my mother language Kikuyu, and I speak it fluently, including writing it perfectly, I simply cannot understand this attitude. I also came to discover that many Tanzanians education was very law and most of them did not know any grammar of their tribal language, Swahili or English, so their teaching was strictly based on direct method. How does a teacher tell of a noun if he/she does not know what a noun is?

In any case, nobody managed again to get rid of me because I was already very well established and organised in my work, and many of my students gave very good feedback reports about my lessons, saying that my teaching method was very good and affective. My students were interviewed now and then, by the head of language department to find out if really, I could teach the language, and fortunately, they all gave a very good report about me and my teaching. Every time I met a Tanzanian for the first time, she or he would ask me the same question when I said that I come from Kenya. This happens till today.

"Do you come from the coast?"

"No. I come from up country. Why?"

"Because you speak very good Swahili and Kenyans do not speak such good Swahili."

"Well, you have met one today who speaks Swahili well and does not come from the coast," I would reply irritated.

I was surprised to find out that many Tanzanians whom I met did not even know that Swahili is a National language in Kenya as it is in Tanzania. I have many Tanzanian friends here in Germany, but they simply do not accept that Swahili belongs to the whole of East Africa, and that we should join hands in developing it, instead of fighting one another. All languages in other countries are spoken in many dialects. I tried to work hand in hand with them, in spite of knowing their opinion, and the fact that there were some of my seniors who were totally against me and they used this as a weapon to make us fight against each other.

These are unfortunately Wazungu methods well known all over to make our heads knock. Many times, we had a lot of arguments with Tanzanians regarding Swahili structure, but in most cases, I managed to convince them that I was right. One day one of them from Zanzibar took over my student because I fell sick for one week, and when I came back, my student was behaving very funny towards me.

"Alice, you told me that the verb "kuwa" is written with "w"? The other teacher told me that it is written "kua"!"

"No, he must have confused it with "kukua" which means "to grow,"" I told him.

"We checked in the dictionary, but he claimed that the Zanzibar teacher said that the dictionary was also wrong, being written by Europeans," he said. I was shocked.

"No, the dictionaries are not wrong, though in some cases he could be right, some things are not correct, but that is normal in many books, this one I guarantee it is right," I said.

"He also said that the word "mtaa" means "road" and "street," that they never use the word "Barabara" in Tanzania. I am supposed to believe him more because he comes from Zanzibar, and he said that in Zanzibar they speak the purest Swahili. I have heard and read it many times too from other people." I felt so bad, and I decided to have a talk to my Zanzibar colleague. I always prefer to clear things openly.

So, I called him in my classroom at break time. I explained to him until he saw his mistakes and his confusion in grammar structure and he eventually apologised. I made him explain to my student that all that jazz he told him in my absent was indeed not true. He admitted to him that I indeed had more experience in grammar than him. It was very embarrassing, but it was the only way to continue teaching the man and retaining his confidence. Later I tried to talk to him for his own benefit in working with us in future. His aim like the other lady from Tanzania was to take over and become the main Swahili teacher instead of me.

"Even if you feel that I am wrong in any explanation, it would be better to come and discuss it with me. You see, now you have learned that the word "kuwa" which is irregular and very important verb in any language is written in Swahili with "w." Speaking a language fluently and melodically like you guys from Zanzibar do and with Arabic accent does not mean that you can teach it. There are many things to learn, and we could teach one another instead of fighting an embarrassing fight against each other.

These students normally come together in the evening and discuss about their learning. They discuss about us teachers as well. If you do not try to learn the structure of your own mother language, you will always get in trouble and probably lose this chance of working here," I told him. He also came to see that I knew what I was talking about as far as Swahili structure was concerned. We became good friends after that, and I tried to explain to him anything that he could not understand in the Swahili structures, because he was given another course parallel with mine.

I had the same experience with several other Tanzanians, and this made me feel very sorry for us Africans after realising the reason why our development is slowed down. As Nyerere wrote once that: „ The biggest crime committed during colonialism was to make us Africans believe that anything which we believed and possessed was primitive and did not have any value and we should feel ashamed of it" is very true.

Any white person would suggest anything, and no matter how silly and illogical it would be, it would be accepted by most of us, but if even a better suggestion comes from among us, it is always challenged by our own people trying to show how stupid the fellow African is. The brainwashing of our people which my mother was talking about was clear to me now even than before. My question was, why did we not realise these strategies of a white man to make our heads knock for their own benefit, and refuse to follow them?

We did not have sufficient books to teach with, so at the beginning, I formed a habit of preparing my own teaching material. The only free time I had was in the train if Faiz would sleep, or at lunchtime when he would be in the nursery school, and I could sit for an hour and prepare my lessons for the next day. I filled every paper I wrote, and so, as time went on, I had only to photocopy most of the lessons and exercises. We did not have computers then, so I wrote with hands most of the time. I have faith today to know that, it is God who provided me with the strength, otherwise I would never have managed.

My relationship with Faruk deteriorated. I did not feel like going home after work and see his face. He came in when he wanted and went out when he felt like. I did not ask him where he had been and I did not care. I started hating him, to the extent that I quarrelled with him if I found the house dirty, which I had not dared do before.

"You cannot even clean a plate after eating the food which you do not know where it comes from! What kind of a man are you?" I asked him one day.

"Have you seen men cleaning dishes at home?" He answered arrogantly.

"And have you seen women go and earn money to support their families, while their husbands sit on their fat asses at home doing nothing? Go and work and bring us money here, and when you come home in the evening with the money, you do not even have to remove your shoes, I will do it for you!"

"You have no respect for me these days. Is it because I am living on you?"

"When didn't you live on me ever since you came here?"

"Don't you know that I am a man and you should respect and submit to me?" He would accuse me. All Muslim man again.

"A Moslem or not and whatever you have learned not to value women, I would respect you if you respect yourself first. I don't know what I liked in you in the first place!"

"I will get out of your life one of these days, don't worry!"

"Why don't you do it right away? What are you waiting for? I don't love you anymore, and you know it," I told him. I was surprised at myself the moment I said this. It was very convincing that he looked so weak and helpless.

"Yes, I have surely felt it. You don't even want to sleep with me anymore. We were so much in love with each other, what happened Alice?" He asked me.

"Ask yourself that question. You do not even know what love is. Sit down and think about all what you have done to me and compare it to what I have done for you. Put yourself in my shoes and tell me how you would feel!" I said angrily. He did not say anything, so I continued.

"What kind of a partner are you? You only know how to take but never give. You don't even care about these children. I must take this small baby every day with me in this cold to work while you sleep warmly under the blankets, and you are not even sympathetic of the suffering he goes through. He is your own flesh and blood! I would never let my own child suffer like that!"

"I did not come to Europe to look after children! I must go around looking for a job. How can I do that with a child?"

"Yes, you came to make children but not to look after them you shit! Others must do the dirty work for you! You abandoned your other children in Kenya, and you don't even write to them. You don't care whether they live or die." I felt like bursting. If I had the strength, I would have beaten the shit out of him. "What kind of a human being are you really? You are blessed with such beautiful children, and you do not even know it. How could I have loved a stupid, cruel and irresponsible creature like you?" I shouted tears rolling down my face. He still did not say a word, so I went on.

"You got married for us you said, why don't you take those damn marriage papers and go and buy food with them in the supermarket?" I continued, and he kept quiet, looking absent-minded on the television and chewing on his mouth. He had a habit of biting the inner skin of his mouth under his lips when he was in stress. He knew he had made a terrible mistake of marrying that woman already. The woman was making some demands of some kind, which he never told me, but I knew something was going on.

The quarrels went on, and I pressed him very hard to leave us alone, until he agreed to go away. I was glad that he left and this time I packed his things and told him to please go for good.

"If you have any problem, I will help you if I can, but living under one roof is no longer possible, you must have seen that yourself. I have given you so many chances yet you do not respect my kindness and love I had for you. We have children together, so we cannot afford to be enemies, if that was not the case, I would not want to see you ever again."

He was so mad, and of another opinion claiming that I chased him away and for that reason, he swore revenge. Poor guy that is what his religion teaches him to revenge and never to forgive.

"I will show you that I am a man, you damn woman. I will make you suffer until you are sorry for chasing me away like a dog!" He said and left.

"Mummy, is papa going to come back and live with us again?" Vicky asked me after some weeks. I thought she was missing her father. I had noticed that Vicky had accepted Faruk as her father totally. Faruk was never bad to the children. He loved them in his own way, but he lacked any sense of responsibility even for himself.

"Do you want him to come back then?" I asked her.

"Oh no, if you let him come back, then mum please let me go back to my auntie in Kenya," she said.

"But why, I thought you loved your Dad?" I asked her.

"I do, but I am also scared of him especially when he drinks and beats you up."

That was it! Those words made me come to my senses and made a final decision. Faruk would not come back to us again. I realised how my poor child must have suffered in fear all this time, and I was so occupied with my troubles that I did not notice what damage I was doing to her. Faiz was still too young to realise anything, but it would not take time for him also to know what was going on. I did not want my children to go through such a life. So, I had to cut him off from our lives completely. With 29 I was left as a single mother with two children to care for, in a foreign country, no permanent job, no relative around, no reliable stay permit, etc. But I entrusted my life and that of my children entirely to my God.

The question of Faiz getting circumcised was also delayed, and I did not want to keep him so long. He was already 2 years old and had not been circumcised. I knew that the longer it delays, the more difficult it would be to heal. This is one tradition which is very strict in Kikuyu culture, and I knew I had to do it. The circumcision of boys in Kikuyu tradition is still taken very seriously. So, I looked for a doctor who could do it and found one. Germans do not usually circumcise their boys unless it was medically necessary, but many foreigners were living in Germany as well who have these traditions and so there were some doctors experienced in male circumcision. In the middle of all these worries, I managed to get my son circumcised. Kikuyu tradition in circumcision is celebrated very much by the whole family. I was alone to deal with it. He could already speak a little, and I tried to explain to him what was going to happen.

"Faiz my darling, the uncle doctor is going to repair your "pipi man" (in German "Pipi" is children language for urine and this word made my students always laugh in the classroom because "Pipi" means sweets in Swahili.) It will not be so painful, but only a little bit. This will change you to a man now and not a little boy. Papa is not there anymore, and you are now to be the man of the house. I hope you will not be scared!" I told him.

I did not know if he had any idea of what I was talking about, but he looked at me and nicked. After the operation which was done under (anastasis) we went home, and when he gained full consciousness, he looked at the bandage and looked at me in teas and said: "Mama uncle doctor has destroyed my "pipi man." You told me that he was going to repair it. Now it is *kaputt,*" he said. We had to laugh together with his sister. *"Kaputt"* means in German damaged/ destroyed.

"No, my darling he did not damage it. I would never let him do that. He repaired it, and in a few days' time, you will be alright. I know that you are a brave man now and not a little boy who will cry for such a small operation, are you? If you feel pain, tell mama, and I will give you something to stop the pain." He looked at me in the mist of tears and gave me a weak smile.

"No mama, I will not cry about it anymore, I am a man now." I thought he did not understand that entire "man" thing. Wow! My baby was growing up.

Faruk made so many problems for me later, like coming when he was drunk and ringing my bell very late at night just to scare us or so I thought. One day he came at home while Vicky was alone and he rang the bell. I had something to discuss with the same babysitter just 2 floors down in the same building. I took Faiz with me and left Vicky sleeping. I had told her never to open the door for anybody even her father if I was not at home. She took a chair and stood at the door to see through the spy hole and saw Faruk standing there. She did not put on the light but went slowly back to bed and did not answer the door.

"Papa was here mama," she told me when I came back. She did not sleep after that.

"What? I told you not to open the door!"

"I did not open the door mama," she said.

"Then how do you know that it was daddy?"

"I stood on the chair and saw him. He had red eyes like he was drunk. Please don't let him come back here mummy. He will only start beating you again."

"Don't worry darling, he will not live with us again," I assured her.

I called him the next day where he was staying to ask him what he wanted.

"I was not there. It was not me at the door. You must have mistaken me with somebody else," he lied and put the phone down on me. The German man whom he had borrowed money to pay the pending rent from, started coming after me demanding his money because he claimed that Faruk was not working so I should pay. I was told that they were always together.

"He is your friend, and surely you can wait till he gets a job. I am not going to pay his debt. You should appreciate that I tried to pay you part of the money while we were together. The rest he should pay you now that we are not together. After all, he was working when he borrowed your money, and when I work, I pay all the bills here. Now I am left with all the responsibility of providing for the children alone," I told him.

I knew that this was one way of Faruk's revenge. One day the man came to my flat demanding his money aggressively.

"If you do not pay the money, I will take the matter to court and Faruk will be my main witness that you are the one who took the money and in return, I will show him a way in which he will not pay for your children's ever. I was a policeman before, and I know all those tricks." I got so mad and slapped the man as hard as I could at the same time screaming. He wanted to hit me back, but I dodged it, and immediately it seemed to click in his head what I was up to, that the neighbours would come and witness or call the police because I started kicking and fighting him without fear.

He was only defending himself now and trying to get through me to the door and disappear. I blocked the door completely scratched his face, holding one side of his mantle tightly which made it tear in two pieces behind but was still held together by the collar. I do not know where I got all that strength, but I was really mad. I think the whole anger of Faruk came out then. The man tried to run for the door, but I kept on pulling him back screaming. Eventually, he managed to tear away from me and ran away his coat flying like a batman since it was in two pieces behind before I could call the police. After he left, I could not call the police because there was no evidence of our fight at all and I did not know what damage he had except his mantle which was torn.

Faruk did similar things to humiliate and terrorise us again and again until I decided to move out of that flat. Some German family friends offered to give me a room in their house until I could find something in Bad Honnef where I wanted to move to. It would be near my working place, I thought. I paid them 700 D.M. for a bedroom and food monthly, although I usually ate in the Institute, so I hardly ate there. They looked after Faiz, so I did not have to take him with me anymore.

Unfortunately, they turned out to be very bad people and socially very poor. None of my friends knew where I was staying, in fear that Faruk would find out, though it would have been easy for him if he wanted to know. He never even tried to call me at work, or visit Vicky in school, to ask her where we were staying. It was not easy to find a flat in Bad

Honnef; I tried everywhere without success. People told me that Faruk was seen several times with a German woman. Somehow, I was relieved that he had seen sense although it did hurt knowing how I was struggling with the children alone, while he was enjoying his life with yet another woman.

Two months went by, and the German family wanted me to leave when they saw that there was no hope of me getting a flat. I could not go back to my old flat because it was already taken and my furniture thrown away. So, I was stranded with my children and regretted leaving my flat in panic and in a hurry without finding another. Luckily, I still had my job. Later I came to understand this unprepared and wrong move was God grace's which He allowed, because soon after we moved out, the place became the biggest and known ghetto in Köln.

I am normally very strong and never give up easily, but this time I was completely defeated and did not know forward or backwards. The German family told me to go to a hotel and stay there, that they needed the room for themselves. It was a notice of one week. I decide to leave immediately, but where to? I did not know anything about the homes they call "Frauenhouse (women house)" where they keep women in trouble with their husbands, and I was scared to go for any Social help as my lawyer warned me.

I called another German girlfriend called Gabi, whom I met through another Kenyan friend. Gabi was in love with a Kenyan tour driver whom she met during her holiday in Kenya and wanted to meet Kenyan people. Apart from that, she was very kind and helpful in every way except she was an alcoholic. Gabi was also married to a 30 years older man than herself. She was in her middle 40's, but still, she was planning to divorce the old man and marry her Kenyan tour driver lover and leave Germany for good.

I was sitting with my children in a restaurant crying, after leaving the German family not knowing where to go or what to do. This was my first time to ever think of suicide, but I withdrew the thought as I saw the sad face of my daughter which stared at me full of questions which I think she was afraid to ask. I knew she was not happy in that house anyway and her school was very far and she travelled alone. Somehow, I was happy that we were no longer there. I did not feel good in that house even one day. However, I was responsible of these two children. I should never think of such things like suicide.

I loved them so much, and I was the only person they had. It was my fault that they were in this world and in this situation, so it was my duty to struggle with them till the end. I swore there and then, to prove to Faruk, that I could make it without him, and without any man for that matter but only with God's help. I was ashamed to call the African friends that I had because they all had warned me about Faruk and knew how miserable he made my children and me. That is when I remembered about Gabi and called her. I was in tears and could not even explain to her everything.

"O.K. tell me where you are, and I will come to you!" I gave her the address of the restaurant, and within an hour she was sitting with us listening to my sad story. I had been introduced to a protestant priest in Bad Honnef, and I had spoken to him on telephone asking him to help me find a flat. I had not told him all the details about my situation. Gabi suggested that we should call him and tell him that I was practically on the street with the children. He asked us to go to Bad Honnef immediately. Despite knowing that I was a Catholic, this man helped me without referring me to a Catholic priest. Many churches in Germany usually do not help people from other confessions. He asked me whether I was a Protestant and I told him the truth, that I was a Catholic Christian.

"I have no idea where I could put you all up. Could you not take them with you to your place Mrs. Becker until tomorrow? I might have a solution then," the priest said.

"No, I cannot. My husband will not allow them to sleep there," she said.

"I have no place at all. Maybe the children could share the rooms with my children, but for you Mrs. Mangat, it would be a problem."

"OK. I will take Alice with me, and she can sleep at my neighbour's place until tomorrow," Gabi said. Her husband knew about her being in love with a Kenyan, and he did not want to hear anything about Kenya leave alone having a Kenyan sleep in his house. He was seventy-five years old then. I slept at Gabi's neighbours, who were very kind to me. I didn't care where I slept; my mind was so occupied with my problems to even care whether I slept, at Gabi's or not. My children slept at the Pastor's place whom I met that day, though they looked very kind and Christian like. I was so scared for my children, and I missed them terribly that I had a lot of nightmares. It almost killed me to imagine how scared they were in a total strange place and with strangers.

I asked God in tears to look after my children and promised Him never to leave them again even for a day. The next day, I was supposed to renew my stay permit which was expiring in a few days' time. Gabi took me to the foreign office. The officer in charge asked me to sign a certain paper again which he read and translated himself. Either I did not understand again, or I was so occupied with my problems to notice what I had signed for. I discovered a few months later what conditions related to the one year's extension.

We went to Bad Honnef after that, and the pastor had found a place for us to stay temporarily. He organised that we get a room in an old people's home until we found a flat to stay. We were to eat with the old people, and I had to pay an amount of 300 D.M. per month, for the room and extra money for every meal until I got somewhere else to stay.

"Why don't you tell the head of the Institute your problems, maybe he would help you Mrs. Mangat?" the Pastor asked me.

"Oh no, I do not want them even to know that I have problems. They might decide not to give me work anymore. You see, we are not permanently employed," I said.

"But still you should try to get help from them at least to look for a place for you to stay. As a big Institute, they might have more influence than me. Surely that should not give them a reason to throw you out; they should help you." I did not want to tell him what happened to me once in the Institute and that I could not afford to take any risk.

"No, please I'd rather they did not know. That is the only thing I am holding on to. Without the job, I would be in a lot of mess than I am already," I told him

He was not convinced or rather he did not listen to me. So, the next day he called the head of the language department without my knowledge and told him the whole story. My boss promised to see what they could do for me. The Pastor asked him if it was alright if he would write a letter which I was to send my applications with, in case I found an advertisement in the newspapers, mentioning in the latter that I was working with the Institute. He believed that the letter could have some influence if he stated that. My boss had nothing against that then, even if I was on temporally basis, I had worked throughout for some months, and more students were expected.

We looked for a place for almost three months, and all the time we stayed in the small room at the old people's home. Vicky started school in the same town, and I continued taking Faiz with me to DSE Kindergarten. Gabi visited us often, taking us for meals though Eugene, her husband was against it. She liked my children a lot and kept on telling her husband about us, but he did not want to hear about any Kenyan people stories whatsoever.

"But you should not judge all the people the same. You have not even met Alice, and she has not done anything to you personally," Gabi insisted.

"I do not care; I don't want anything to do with those Niggers," he said.

"Alice is a very nice person, and the children are so sweet. You will like them. Please give them a chance," she insisted.

"What do you want me to do?" Gabi's husband asked.

"I want us to invite them for Easter. Can you imagine her spending Easter holidays with small kids in a home for old people?"

"No, I do not want them here. Forget it!" Eugene said.

"OK. At least let us invite them for lunch somewhere else in a restaurant on Easter Sunday," she begged until Eugene agreed. She called me and told me that they would pick us up on Easter Sunday to invite us for a meal. We were waiting for them at the gate when they came. I was always afraid of any visitor coming to visit us because we were supposed to be quiet. The children were not even allowed to play outside. I had to take them every day to the nearest park to play. They somehow understood our situation, especially Vicky who was a bit older and respected the orders which we were given.

Eugene fell in love with my children the very first time. Faiz who was almost three now sat on his lap the whole time even at the restaurant. My poor baby was really missing a father figure, or so it seemed. From then on, he allowed us to go to their house every weekend to avoid being in the home. He liked me also because I was talking to his wife a lot of sense trying to stop her from drinking and discouraging her from the idea of leaving her husband alone to marry somebody like a tour driver. I knew the kind of a person she was in love with because I read most of her letters which she received from her lover and wrote back the replies for her, since her English was not very good. The man in Kenya, a tour driver, was interested in her money. But Gabi's problem was that she was very unhappy in her own country and wanted to get out at any price.

"Alice these are terrible people. They are my people, but I tell you I am ashamed to be a German. I want to get out of here as soon as I can. I cannot live here anymore. I do not understand how people like you can leave your beautiful country to come and live in this misery." Gabi said to me many times. I would not have taken her seriously since she was an alcoholic, but I had heard similar things from most of my students.

"Kenya is a beautiful country, you are right Gabi, but without money, it can be very hard. The money you want to take to Kenya with you, if you are not careful, will run out within no time and then you will not find Kenya as good as you think. There are also bad people in my country, and they also make use of kind people like you Gabi! So just be careful. My people have also changed a lot due to poverty and the hard way of life in Kenya," I advised her again and again.

They had managed to save quite good amount of money, and her husband had agreed to the divorce and give her half of it, taking into consideration that he married her at a very old age and she had a right to enjoy her life now the way she wanted. Luckily, they had no children. He accepted that he was an old man and had no right to tie her down. Reluctantly he agreed to let her go to Kenya if that is what would make her happy. He talked many times through tears, and it was obvious that he was hurt. I felt so sorry for him and understood his reaction towards me at the beginning. At the same time, he knew he could not stop his wife from going no matter what he did or said. I was impressed the way he was fair to her as far as financial agreement was concerned. I also knew that her boyfriend in Kenya was only after that money.

The Pastor found a flat for me, where an old lady was staying and wanted to go to a home, therefore she wanted to give up her flat mediately. The pastor grabbed the chance and fought desperately for me to get the flat. The housing company was against it claiming that many people were in the waiting list.

"But those people have a roof over their heads while this lady is practically on the street, with two small children, so she should be given the priority." I waited for almost two weeks to get the result.

"They do not want to give you the flat. The neighbours are giving all kinds of reasons that you should not be given the house. They claim you have very small children who will make a lot of noise and there are old people living there. You are so young, a black woman and without a husband, they fear that men would come in and out of your house and therefore you will be a problem to them." At least he was honest to tell me the truth. I had gone through many similar things while looking for a flat, and I was sent away the moment they saw my face. Pastor Berger did not give up but continued fighting for me seriously until they agreed to give me the flat. God bless him!

The old lady was supposed to renovate the flat before going away, but we wanted to move in immediately. She agreed to pay one month's rent for me, and I should renovate it later. The flat was in a very bad condition, so I had to renovate it immediately. We moved in, but I did not even have a chair. I could not start buying furniture before I finished with the renovation. I used to spread one of my Kangas on the floor, and my children would eat there like many people usually do back home. We slept on mattresses which we spread in one room while I renovated the other rooms. It was a two-bedroomed flat of about 60qm. I did the renovation myself since I did not have money to pay for a professional to do it. One-day Pastor Berger come over to see how we were settling down and found Vicky doing her homework on the floor. This was a shock for him.

"Why didn't you tell me that you do not have a table and chairs? Where do you eat?"

„On the floor!" I replied comfortably, but I noticed his shock immediately.

"Heh! But you cannot do that. The children need a table and chairs," he said.

"Oh, that is alright Pastor Berger, they need many things, but I cannot afford everything at a go, and I have to finish the renovation first. We sit on the floor back home, that is absolutely no problem for me," I said.

"But you are not in your home country now. You are in another culture. What do you think Vicky's friends in school would say if they knew that she does her homework on the floor?" He asked.

"Oh, it will not be for long now, and I will get a table for her. I really do not think that is a problem," I insisted.

"But it is a big problem for Vicky Mrs. Mangat if the children start mobbing and insulting her. Children here can be very cruel on such things. I will bring you a table and chairs this afternoon."

"Oh no, I would not want to bother you anymore. You have already done a lot for me."

He ignored my protest again and brought me a table and three chairs, from the church hall which I was to return later.

Gabi finalised her trip to Kenya, and in the meantime, she helped me a lot in moving into the new flat and the renovation, but before she left she told me:

"Alice, after I go, my husband will be totally alone with nobody to care for him. I fully realise it, but I cannot help it because I must go. Promise me that you will take care of him and visit him often with the children. He loves your children very dearly, and of course, he likes you too now. You will be the only person he will be able to talk his problems with knowing my husband and my people here. They will kind of laugh at him because I left him, but I know you and the children will be able to cheer him up if only a little and when you find time. I have very bad feelings leaving him, but as I said. I must go."

"Don't worry Gabi; I would have done that even without any promise. We like him too, and I feel very sorry for him knowing I have not managed to convince you to stay here. I know also that you are making a very bad mistake and you will regret it. But if you feel better, then I promise you I will look after him the best way I can. You know my schedule is also very tight because of my work and children, and the fact that we do not stay very close to his place, but I will try to go as often as I can at the weekends.

The small town I moved to was very different from a big city like Cologne. Bad Honnef is located near the city of Bonn about 15 kilometres away. It is surrounded by seven hills which gave the area the name of "Siebengebirg" (Seven Hills). The river Rhein runs along the town of Bad Honnef, with two beautiful islands situated right in Bad Honnef. It has a population of about 24,000. I had a feeling that the air and the atmosphere was completely different from the big town where I had lived before. Compared also to the high building in which we were living before in Cologne, the new flat was one storey building, and it had only four family flats.

My neighbours did not approach me at first, and I hardly knew them, but I knew that they observed everything I did from their windows or watched me through the spy hole. I did not want to live like in Cologne where I did not know my neighbours, so I realised I had to do something to get to know them. I did not believe that all Germans were like Rose had described them. In any case, if they were all like that, then I had to try to change what I could with my neighbours, I decided. It was easy and different in a small town as I soon found out.

One day I gathered my guts and rang the bell at my immediate neighbour's door, I had already seen that she was watching me through the spy hole the moment she heard my door open.

"Good afternoon Mrs. Steinmann," I said.

"Good afternoon Mrs. Mangat, what can I do for you." She did not invite me in. I stood at the door. This is not normal in my country. You invite somebody in first, especially your neighbour and then ask him/her what he/she wants.

"Mrs. Steinmann, I wanted to ask you, if I could keep a set of my keys here in your house, because my daughter has a habit of losing her keys and I do not want her to sit outside in the cold when she comes back from school before me. That is, if you do not find it a bother when she rings your bell," I said nervously. Of course, my German was not so perfect at that time, but I managed to put my message through.

"Of course, I do not mind. You can give me your keys, and I will keep them safe for you," she said. So, I gave her one set of my keys. Another day, I rang the bell, and she opened still not inviting me in.

"Oh, Mrs. Steinmann sorry to bother you, but I wanted to ask you if you have onions in the house. I am short of onions. I will give you back tomorrow when I go shopping," I said. It was late in the evening. I was still trying to find my way through to her. I had onions myself in the house alright.

"Sure, sure I have onions!" she said and disappeared back into the house leaving the door open. She came back with a handful of onions, but I took only three small pieces. The next day I gave her onions back.

"Mrs. Mangat, you left the lights on this morning, and I opened the door and switched your lights off. I hope I did the right thing," she said.

"Oh yes, that was very kind of you, such things happen every time with me. Sometimes I am very forgetful due to the morning rush with the children. I am always in hectic. I never seem to wake up on time," I said smiling. She saw the onions alright, and she confirmed this much later.

"That is alright. Aren't you working today?" She asked me. I was home very early.

"Oh, my son is sick, and I had to take him to the doctor." We continued to talk about my son and my work still at the door, and I told her that it was very bad when the children were sick because if I did not work, I did not get paid. She wanted to know as much about me as possible, so most of the things I told her were through the questions she asked me.

"Oh dear, but you can leave him with us if he is not very seriously ill. That is bad if you do not get paid. I do not understand that," she said.

"Well, it is simple. I am only on temporary basis. We do not have permanent contracts." I explained.

"Oh, then go to work tomorrow my child and leave your son with us," she offered.

"That will be wonderful. I can pay you for that," I said.

"Oh no, we would not take any money from you for such a thing. We cannot also do it for long, but if it is a short illness, then we could help you." I was surprised at my luck.

The old couple fell in love with Faiz. He was so sweet and made them laugh the whole time that they used to come for him even when I was at home. The Steinmann family were very kind to me especially Mrs. Steinmann, and I wanted to be closer to her. On Mother's Day, I went to the supermarket and bought her a big basket full of all kinds of things which were already packed for such occasions. She was so happy that she broke into tears. I did not know why she was crying and I got a bit scared thinking that I did something wrong. She called many friends to tell them about it, including her son whom I had never seen before. I soon found out that he lived just three streets away from us. I wondered why he did not often come to see his parents. Or did he come when I was at work? Well, I had never seen him before, and I had even come to a conclusion that they did not have any children. This was not a strange thing in Germany, as I came to learn later through my own experience.

From then on, we became very good friends. She would invite me in when I rang the bell. I took many pictures of them and my children, and some of those pictures were still hanging in their sitting room when we moved out of there 13 years later. They both accepted my children and me fully. When I told my African friends, many of them told me that I must be very lucky, that such things are not common in Germany. I knew that she inspected my flat always when I was not there, but I did not care. Most of the time, my flat looked like a bomb had exploded inside, since I had no time to tidy up before going to work, but I did it when I came back, and it did not disturb me. Her flat, on the other hand, was always very tidy and everything on its right place. This seemed to be one habit the German housewives had. In any case, she had nothing else to do the entire day.

Mrs. Steinmann kept telling us how to do things like she did not trust that I knew anything or rather thought that I could not do anything on my own. She would come and show me how to preserve food in the fridge; she would show me how to use the washing machine, how to take care of limestone from the coffee machine, etc. I played naive just to make her feel appreciated and useful, even to the things I knew already myself, but my daughter was getting mad about it.

"Why don't you tell her that you know how to do all those things she tells you? She talks to you like you are a child or an idiot. It is like you have never seen a fridge before," Vicky said one day.

"It is alright with me. She just wants to help, that is all," I said.

I bought Vicky a bird on her birthday, but she never had any fun with it. Mrs. Steinmann told her never to let the bird come to the sitting room that the bird would die. She would not let Vicky take the bird from the cage. I had no idea about keeping a bird, and I trusted that in this issue she knew what she was talking about.

Eventually, the bird died, because the children kept the cage at the window one day and they forgot to shut the window, so the unfortunate thing froze. She did all that with love though sometimes she went too far, but I tried my best to understand her.

Vicky was admitted in one of the primary schools in Bad Honnef, and the director told me that she was the first African child to be in their school. She had to repeat one class because her German was still not very good and due to the problems, we had gone through, her schoolwork was not very satisfactory. I agreed that she should repeat the third class. She did not have any problems with her schoolmates like in Cologne where she was insulted many times, and she came home crying.

"Mummy, the children call me nigger. What is a nigger?" Vicky asked me one day after she started her class one in Cologne. She had never heard of that word before.

"Oh! Those are silly children who call you nigger. You should tell them not to call you that, and if they don't stop it, then tell the teacher," I said.

"But what does it mean?" She demanded.

"The Germans refer black people as niggers. They say it is the name for the colour of our skin," I tried to explain to her.

"But I do not like them calling me that! I am an African, can't they call me an African, a Kenyan, or just my name as I call them? I hate those children who insist on calling me, nigger!"

"Just tell the teacher darling or ignore them," I said.

"But she also hears the children calling me nigger, and she does not do anything!" she continued. I did not know how to deal with the situation at that time at all, and so I kept quiet hoping that the children would get used to having a black child in their class and stop insulting her. I hoped therefore that in small-town things might be better than in Köln. It turned out to be much different but not better.

In our new home, we had a big garden in front of our house which was attended by one of our neighbours. The old man did not want to see my children in that garden whatsoever.

"But why can't the children play here in the garden?" I asked him once after he had chased my children out of the garden.

"This is not a playground. There is a playground just around the corner, and your children can play there," he answered.

"But I do not want my children to go there. It is too far from the house, and I like to keep an eye on them while playing. Why should they not play in our garden? What is this garden for if the children cannot play on it?" I asked.

"This is not Africa. The children cannot play everywhere they choose," he said rudely.

"And how is Africa in your opinion? Have you ever been to Africa yourself?" I asked

"No! But still, your children should not step on this garden, and if they do, then I will report you to the housemaster," he said.

"I think that is a clever idea. I would like to have a written notice from the housemaster that my children are not allowed to play in this garden and the reason for it," I said.

"Good. You will get the letter alright but, in the meantime, make sure that the children do not step on this garden."

"Oh no! They will continue to play there alright, until I get the letter. In the meantime, I ask you kindly to leave my children in peace!" I said.

"You want to dictate us how to run our lives here? Who do you think you are?" He shouted at me. I was also angry now, so I shouted back.

"No, damn it! I have no right to dictate to you how to run your life, and neither do you have any right to dictate to me on how to run my life. If it is wrong for my children to play here, then I demand to know why! You cannot keep on chasing them away like that without telling them why they should not play here."

The next day I received a telephone call from the housemaster.

"Mrs. Mangat, your children should not play in the garden."

"And why not? I want a written explanation why they should not play there. If you do not write me that letter, then they will continue to play there."

"If you must have a written warning then we shall send you one, in the meantime make sure that they stay away from the garden."

"As I told my neighbour here yesterday, my children will continue to play in this garden, till I get this cleared from your head office. They are still very small to go far away just to have an open place to play. You know how children are sometimes murdered in those playgrounds, and I will not send my children to any kind of danger when I have an alternative. I can keep an eye on my children when they play here outside, but not if they go to the playground."

The letter never came, and the old man kept on nagging at the children, but only when I was not around. I told them to ignore him. The children learned how to deal with him on their own terms. One-day Faiz who was only four years old asked him in a very friendly way.

"Mr. Müller, why do you behave like a Nazi?" I don't even think my son knew what the word "Nazi" meant, but he must have heard it somewhere and knew it would hurt a German to hear it. My daughter related the incident to me later and told me that Faiz applied all his charm as he asked this question, which the guy just looked at Faiz without a word and turned and went back into his house. Probably he thought that I had told him to tell him that, but I had nothing to do with it. We had watched some films about the Nazi time together, and I suppose he could have got the word from there too.

One summer day the same neighbour's grandchildren came to visit him, and they went to join my children outside to play. I went outside and sat with them where my daughter had spread a blanket and were all sitting on it. The old man came out of the house then.

"Don't you think that this is a good picture? Aren't you happy to see your grandchildren playing here? Or should we send them all to the playground?"

He did not answer but turned away and went in the house.

It is strange, but as far as I remember, in Africa, old people enjoy very much to see young children jumping around and playing outside. The old people sit outside watching them play. No one disturbs the children while playing, but in Germany, it looks like the old generation is jealous of young ones and they make a lot of fuss. You can get a house to rent easily if you have a dog, but not if you have children. Though I left my children to play outside as much as they wanted, in the afternoon between one o'clock and three o'clock they were not allowed to make any noise because people take a nap at that time. I always had to call them inside, and they would watch television or play with their toys in their room. It was almost like the old people home all over again. In any case, whatever the reason, Mr. Müller did not bother the children anymore after that.

Just when we were settling down, I received a letter from Mr. Groß's lawyer in Köln, telling me to pay the money Faruk had borrowed from him within a time limit and if not, I was to be taken to court. I took it as a big joke but still decided to take a lawyer myself to reply the letter.

"So, you know about this money yourself Mrs. Mangat," the lawyer asked me,

"Yes, and I think Mr. Groß wants me to be his witness because they did not have any written document as to who took the money and why. I am not ready to be his witness, so we say that I do not know anything about the money at all. The father of my children took the money, and I will not give this man a chance of calling me in court to give evidence against the father of my children. Let them sort their matters alone without me. Fact is, they are friends."

Some weeks later my lawyer requested me to go and see him in his office.

"Mrs. Mangat, the person you were protecting, is indeed the one mentioned as the first witness against you that you are the one who took the money," I cannot explain in words how I felt. I knew Faruk was cruel, but I always had reasons for his behaviour, that he was irresponsible even to himself and being jobless, etc. But I never thought that he was so dirty minded and evil. Love is surely blind! God this was the last thing I had expected him to do. This surely took me completely by surprise. I thought he was ready to defend us and protect us even if he was away from us and not try to destroy the kids and me.

I discovered suddenly what kind of a man I had loved all the time and believe me I felt so sorry for myself than anybody else I related this story to. I still thought that this was his way of revenging with me by scaring me and to pay the money for him and that he would not be crazy enough to come to court and tell lies for that amount of money. I sincerely believed and hoped those were the reason for all that, but how wrong was I? He came to court, and we even met at the lift which brought us together and my daughter to the courtroom. Vicky was with me. He did not even greet us. This was my first time to see him after almost a year.

He was the last witness to be called in.

"Who took the Money Mr. Abdullah?" the Judge asked him.

"Mrs. Mangat took the money from Mr. Groß," he answered.

"What did she do with the money?"

"She paid the house rent which was three months overdue," he said.

"Who was staying in that house," the judge continued.

"Mrs. Mangat, her two children, and myself."

"Who is the father of those children?"

"I am the father of the son, but the daughter I have only adapted her."

"But I have court documents here that you have declared yourself as the biological father of both the children."

"As I said I only adapted her."

"This is not what these papers say here. They say you are her biological father! Your change of mind and your reasons do not interest us. The fact that you have declared yourself to be the father is all that counts. If you declare such a commitment, then you must know that you must bear all the consequences throughout your lifetime. Are you aware that if I give this information of your statement further to the youth ministry, they could sue you for it?" He kept quiet, but their lawyer apologised on his behalf.

"So, you were staying in that house with Mrs. Mangat and your two children, is that right?"

"Yes, sir."

"Don't you think that it was also your responsibility to try and get the house rent paid?"

"Yes, I tried to call Mr. Groß for help also, but I did not get him on the phone,"

"But Mrs. Mangat got hold of him, and he gave the money to her, am I right?"

"Yes, sir."

"Don't you then think that it is also your responsibility to pay the money back to Mr. Groß other than pushing everything to Mrs. Mangat and sitting in a courtroom and give evidence against the mother of your children, expecting her to pay the whole amount alone?" He kept quiet; I felt the embarrassment myself as well.

"Mrs. Mangat, does Mr. Abdullah pay for the maintenance of the children?"

"Not a penny sir."

"Then I will bring this matter to the youth department in your area and let them take care of it. Mrs. Mangat, I would have asked for more details about this case, but I know it will take much longer and for you, it is a pure mental stress. I would, therefore, advice you to pay this money back and forget about the whole thing. The amount of the money is not worth the pain you must be going through, I will arrange that you pay as comfortably as you can." I was crying throughout the questioning, and I think the judge sympathised a lot with me. The whole thing was so dirty that I could not imagine how somebody can bring such shame and evil to himself. There were other witnesses who all gave false information which was very contradicting. One was Mr. Groß's new girlfriend Faruk had introduced to him from Tanzania. God was showing me how our people were.

These women from our continent were worse than Germans. If it was a lot of money, I would have understood. But 2,000 D.M. could surely not make me go to court to lie against my fellow African woman struggling with her children and supporting the father who was not supporting in anything in regard to those children. I did not have any witness because there was simply nobody who was there when we took the money except Faruk, myself and Mr. Groß. This man Mr. Gross sat there with a fake smile like a jackal on his face but could not look at me.

Most of Faruk's so-called friends who came to give that false evidence were people who wanted to see our relationship buried, and this hurt me to an extent I cannot express in a book, especially to see Faruk listening to them to that extent. I understood the German witnesses because I know most Germans don't care or fear God. But Faruk and that African woman should have known that such a thing does not go unnoticed by God Almighty, or was Allah a different God than the Living God of Abraham Isaac and Jacob? They knew for sure that, that was a curse he had put on himself. It was my first time to be in a courtroom accused, and all was caused by somebody I thought I loved and that he loved me too. What a bloody fool I had been!

When we left the courtroom, I found them all standing downstairs in the hall, all looking at me to see how their evil work had affected me. I was all the time in tears. I stood holding Vicky's hand and looked at them each at a time tears running down my face, and none of them said anything. I cried all the way back to Bad Honnef. My daughter just stared at me and sometimes tried to talk to me, but I was in such a terrible condition.

"Mama please don't cry. Everybody is wondering what is wrong with you. Look Papa gave me DM 20 while you were in the courtroom." I had not told her what had happened in the courtroom, but while the witnesses were called one by one, Faruk went to talk to Vicky while we were all inside. He was the last witness to be called in. This showed clearly that this man did not know what he was doing.

"I thought he did not talk to you," I said wiping my eyes.

"Oh yes while you were inside he came and talked to me. He asked me how we, Faiz and myself were, and he said he loved us very much, that I should not forget that and I should tell Faiz that as well. Then he gave me this money." I wish she had told me while we were still there and I would have thrown the money on his face most probably accompanied by a lot of abuse, and maybe we would have fought there. I was even angrier now, but I did not want to show my daughter that it had affected me even more.

The next day I went to the youth office as the judge ordered and booked an appointment and when the appointment day came, I told them all the details of

Faruk, to claim the children maintenance from him. The judge had already called there and told them to give me as much support as I needed. They managed to find out where he was working and they attached his salary. I was to receive DM 600 per month for both the children. I also received at the same month the court order to pay Mr. Groß DM 50 per month until the whole amount of DM.1,400 was paid which was decided that I should pay. I do not know how this calculation came to this, but I was sure those were all God's miracles. So, in the long run, Faruk paid the money himself indirectly, and I was left with 550 DM for my children every month, which I did not have before. May God blessed that kind judge who understood my position and helped us. Sometimes I wonder how God performs his miracles to protect his weak and oppressed people. This was evidence that God stood on my side all the time I thought I was left all alone. It also brought a total separation with Faruk finally for the rest of my life.

I was very sure then that Faruk would not make it in Germany. One cannot expect success on other's pain and sorrow and especially if this person is your own blood. I was so disturbed to the extent of getting nervous breakdown, and for sure he knew how these things were affecting me. If I fell sick, the children would have suffered since I was the only person they had. How then could he do these things to me knowing that I had a son from him who needed a healthy mother to look after him? My only explanation was that he wanted to break the ties on me and the children completely.

The reason for this could have been, as I came to hear later that his German wife whom he married and told me that they had nothing sexually had got a baby girl from Faruk and he did not visit her or even wanted to see the baby. The woman filed for a divorce, and the foreign office wanted to send him back to Kenya. This I came to learn much later after the case. He had to look for another woman immediately, and he got one alright who promised to marry him. Faruk told her a lot of lies which he knew I might review to her and this was dangerous. Probably he thought that giving evidence against me in court would disgust me so much that I would not want to see him again. See my foolishness, as always; I tried to look for all kinds of reasons for his behaviour.

I was almost to fall into a depression through all that happened. I could not sleep; I had a lot of nightmares; I cried all the time even on the streets; I found myself talking to myself, that even prayers became a problem to remember. The devil almost got me in his power, and I got very sick. Through all these stress, I got a swelling in my ovaries which busted up on my way home from work on one Friday afternoon. I was taken to hospital and operated the next day. They told me that one of my ovaries was completely infected and they had to remove it. Without a permanent job, this was very serious case, because I did not know who would look after my children, and how long I would be sick.

Many worries also tortured me about how our financial situation would deteriorate the longer I stayed in hospital. These worries contributed to further illness. The neighbours looked after my children, and after 2 weeks in hospital, I insisted to go home. I had a lot of pain in my stomach where I was operated, and one of the doctors did not believe in me when I said I had pains. I was, therefore, send home. Two days later I could not walk due to terrible pains. I went to see my house doctor, and after looking into the scan, he sent me straight back to hospital. I was operated in emergency the same afternoon. All my womb and the right ovary were full of puss, that they could not figure out how this could have happened. I ended up losing my left ovary as well. It took a very long time to heal, and my doctors warned me that this all happened through the stress and I should avoid such worries and concentrate on my health. It was easy said than done! However, I turned to God again in desperation and begged for mercy for putting Him aside and trying to do things with my own strength which ended up to disaster. My children needed me and I should never leave them alone, I pleaded with God in tears.

This was indeed an experience I was sure never to forget so long as I live. I had no idea how I was going ever to accept to live with a man under one roof again, loving and respecting him as it should be. All I knew was that I hated men, and I was very sure that no man would ever cheat me or come near my heart again. So, I build a shell around me which I swore no man would ever penetrate through. I decided that my heart would never rule my life again and that I should have depended on my 7th sense which always told me the opposite of my feeling for Faruk. Was this the quiet voice of my guiding Angel? I can only thank my God for loving me so much and protecting me as I asked Him to on that Kenya Airways plane. He never left me even for one second all those years.

"Do not be afraid, for I am with you; do not be alarmed, for I am your God. I give you strength, truly I help you, truly I hold you firm with my saving right hand. Look, all those who rage against you will be put to shame and humiliated; those who picked quarrels with you will be reduced to nothing and will perish."

-Isaiah 41:10-11.

Other Books

1. Swahili Structure, 1990
1. Swahili for Foreigners, 2000.
2. Swahili for Foreigners Book II-2011.

Contact details

Author email: alicemangat.author@gmail.com

Amazon Author Central: https://www.amazon.co.uk/-/e/B001JO7Z7C

https://authorcentral.amazon.co.uk/gp/profile

Website: http://www.kiswahili-mangat.com/what-we-offer/african-recipes.html

Social Media: